P9-DNL-132

Also by Harry Dent
The Great Boom Ahead
Job Shock

THE

Roaring

2000s

*Building the Wealth
and Lifestyle
You Desire
in the Greatest Boom
in History*

Harry S. Dent, Jr.

Simon & Schuster

 SIMON & SCHUSTER
Rockefeller Center
1230 Avenue of the Americas
New York, NY 10020

Copyright © 1998 by Harry Dent
All rights reserved,
including the right of reproduction
in whole or in part in any form.
SIMON & SCHUSTER and colophon are
registered trademarks of Simon & Schuster Inc.
Designed by Edith Fowler
Manufactured in the United States of America

10   9   8

Library of Congress Cataloging-in-Publication Data

Dent, Harry S.
  The roaring 2000s : how to achieve personal
and financial success in the greatest boom
in history / Harry S. Dent.
      p.   cm.
  Includes index.
    1. Economic forecasting—United States.
  2. United States—Economic conditions—1981–
  3. United States—Social conditions—1980–
  4. Investments—United States.   I. Title.
HC106.82.D46   1998
332.024—dc21   98-9943   CIP
ISBN 0-684-83818-4

Acknowledgments

THANKS TO my literary agency, Susan Golomb, for helping me find the best publishers over the years. Thanks to my editor at Simon & Schuster, Dominick Anfuso, for helping to focus the theme of the book. Thanks to Shelley Nelson for editing and organizing the text. Thanks to Martie Sautter, Phil Plath, and Clifford Hunt for graphics and charts. Thanks to my marketing agent, Harry Cornelius, for helping to spread the word. And thanks to Donna Windell and Eva Sturm-Kehoe for administration.

This book is dedicated to:
>
> my wife, Cee
> our children, Abel, Iomi, and Nile
> my parents, Harry and Betty
> my nephews and nieces: Josh, Harrison,
>   Johnny, Blake, Clay, Graham, Elizabeth,
>   Sarah, and Harry, II.

Contents

Introduction:
The Secret to
Building Wealth . . .
and Lifestyle

IT IS COMMON WISDOM today that the key to building wealth is taking risks. People who take higher risks get the higher returns and wealth. There are risk/return graphs in investment and business that prove this. Most of us by now have heard that stocks have higher risk and volatility but higher returns over time than investments like bonds. New entrepreneurial ventures have higher risk and failure rates than established businesses and tend to create greater fortunes. And this is definitely true. But here is the paradox I have learned through many years of hands-on business experience with successful people:

The best entrepreneurs, executives, and investors I have worked with who actually achieve the highest returns and build the most wealth don't see it that way! Despite often being involved in unproven ventures and changing management or investments, they don't perceive that they are taking big risks at all. They are simply doing the obvious. They are very definite that what they are doing or investing in must and will succeed. They have a clear understanding of change and fundamental trends that seem all but inevitable to them. They appear risky and unclear only to people who don't understand such changes and naturally cling to familiar patterns that are more comfortable.

Was Lee Iacocca unclear about the changes that were necessary to save a dying Chrysler Corporation in the mid-1980s? It was obvious to anyone who didn't have a stake in the old ways of doing business. How long did it take Gerstner to figure out as an outside manager what it would take to turn around IBM in the mid-1990s? Haven't much of the public and outside analysts been clear that Apple needed radical changes before its near demise in the mid-1990s? Was Steve Jobs unclear about the potential of personal computers in the late 1970s? Or Bill Gates about the need for a software operating system standard in the mid-1980s? Or Gordon Moore about the doubling of semiconductor power every 18 months since the mid-1960s? Was Michael Milken unclear about the need to finance such new emerging companies through nontraditional means in the 1980s?

The many failures among the high-risk ventures come from naïve people who are hoping to make an easy killing, such as winning the lottery or getting instant salvation or overnight success in business. It is not that new directions or investments are proven or that it will be easy or that there won't be challenges. That's the hard part. These successful people have the clarity and conviction to push through such challenges. They foresee the need for a new product or service or the viability of a new technology or investment. Why? They have a unique history of experience that has already validated it for them. They have done their homework and know it is possible. They understand the fundamental trends driving the changes they are investing in. And their experience and homework has also taught them that it won't necessarily happen overnight or be easy. Therefore they usually don't expect it to be. But if it is much harder than they thought, it's their belief in the feasibility and inevitability of what they are doing that keeps them moving ahead until their vision becomes a reality. It's the strength and attraction of their vision that allows these people to overcome the obstacles that appear as risk, uncertainty, and volatility to others.

Clarity about long-term fundamental trends is the key to dealing with the random and uncertain short-term events that inevitably come in the path of any goal. A clear vision of future change and the discipline to stay the course are the keys to building wealth and success, whether in business or investments. Setbacks are only opportunities to learn, adapt, or invest more. It isn't a matter of chance to these successful people. In this incredible era of change and progress, the lion's share of wealth is going to the top half of 1 percent of the population — those with this understanding of change and a systematic approach to taking so-called risks. Eighty percent of today's millionaires are self-made, not through inheritances.

In *The Millionaire Next Door,* the authors' surveys of wealthy people have found that the typical millionaire achieved such status by systematically underspending and oversaving from modestly above-average incomes. The law of compounding interest and investment returns built wealth over time, not overnight successes or excessive risk-taking. And a high percentage was self-employed, from successful small business owners in mostly nonglamour industries to big-time entrepreneurs.

I watched one small business owner establish a simple business that sold a narrow line of shorts to Wal-Mart. He managed a $5 million business with two small factories in towns far away from his home office in Paradise Valley, Arizona. No management complexity, no bureaucracy! Roy focused on one simple concept that he could master and control without a bureaucracy while still maintaining quality. Though he had many opportunities, he adamantly refused to let his business grow beyond his ability to maintain his personal knowledge, control, and, most important, his beloved casual and family-devoted lifestyle. His profits were high, his business consistent, and his lifestyle almost perfect . . . without the stress of international competition and a workaholic lifestyle that would have eclipsed his family values. He achieved wealth and the ultimate lifestyle!

I worked with another entrepreneur and investor, a penniless immigrant, who consistently bought raw land around two of the fastest growing cities outside of L.A. Where was he buying? In a seemingly unattractive area compared to other booming suburbs closer to downtown. The results: he turned a $7,000 original investment into $50 million in less than a decade. This was worthless land in the desert that his analysis of the consistently expanding sprawl indicated would almost certainly be in demand within 5 to 10 years. He had documented exactly how this had happened in similarly unattractive areas within the same radius in other growth cities. It was a certainty for him. He bought in a circle around these two new growth cities and had the patience to wait for the development to approach in whatever direction it chose. And he had the conviction to convince other investors to leverage his investment and join in the inevitable profits with him.

Scott McNealy of Sun Microsystems started saying in 1986, "The network is the computer." This was something that almost no one in the highly innovative computer and software industries even remotely understood at the time. It wasn't until 1995 when the Internet suddenly emerged into the mainstream of this country that this vision became one of the greatest trends of all time. Sun is now positioned at the center of this revolution. The stock market and the press have rewarded him enormously. He had the staying power to stick with his conviction until it became the reality he foresaw. He didn't give up or change strategies simply because the industry didn't acknowledge it yet.

Anita Roddick built the Body Shop, a worldwide franchise of personal-care stores, out of a conviction that there were more natural and healthy ways of caring for ourselves. She also assumed that people would be moved by the impact of such natural consumption habits on the benefits to traditional industries of third world countries and the resultant preservation of rain forests versus clearing for cattle production and urban development. This message and cause allowed her to attract motivated employees and eliminate traditional advertising expenditures that many baby boomers considered offensive. She simply assumed that many other people shared her values. And many did indeed! Her personal experience and that of many people she associated with made this a near certainty for her. She understood and invested in one of the most fundamental trends of the new generation: environmental and health concerns.

Peter Lynch, one of the best investment managers of all time, had an intuitive sense of the new retail and business formats that could bring a better level of service at radically lower prices to the consumer. He was not only a great stock and technical analyst by training and experience, he was also an adamant and early consumer of such concepts. These were the very types of consumer trends he was drawn to through his own personal experience. He saw the value of long-term trends before most of us did. He could spot a Wal-Mart or Home Depot or PetSmart right from the beginning. It was a near certainty to him that such concepts would succeed. And he had the professional experience to evaluate whether such companies were financially sound and undervalued.

He helped lead the explosive trend in mutual funds by proving that a focused, professional investment manager who technically and intuitively understood a sector of change in our economy could create incredible wealth for everyday investors who didn't have such skills — all in an easy-to-track "packaged" investment program. Peter Lynch never pretended to be able to predict the economy or fortunes of such companies in the short term. He bet on the long-term fundamentals. He experienced many short-term setbacks and failures. But the 10 to 30 times returns he experienced over time on the best calls made him a legendary fund manager, more than making up for the bad calls.

Warren Buffet did the same thing for the incredible surge in successful brand names in mature industrialized countries like ours around the world. You know . . . companies like Coca-Cola, GE, Gillette, and McDonald's. He has been accumulating large positions in such companies since the early 1980s. He bought when most investors considered these to be relatively mature companies with slower growth ahead and high valuations from historical performance. He wasn't focusing on the past trends in countries like the United States but in the emerging third world countries where 5 billion new consumers were absolutely destined to follow the same buying trends we had already established and realized in the past century. Talk about long-term fundamental trends! And these emerging consumers didn't need to go through the brand wars that occurred in the United States. They already knew through international television and communications which brands were the top ones here. As long as such leading companies had sound management, financial structures, and clear strategies of investing heavily in these new markets with dominant market shares, he was patient enough to wait for the inevitable growth and profits.

He buys value waiting to happen on the basis of projectable long-term fundamental trends. He has patience. He buys when he sees such value and holds for the long term. He doesn't try to anticipate short-term trends in the economy or in such companies any more than Peter Lynch did. By 1997 he had stopped buying heavily in Coca-Cola while accumulating shares of McDonald's. Why? The stock markets had seen his vision of companies like Coca-Cola and driven valuations too high, at 46 times earnings in mid-1997. He didn't sell Coca-Cola as it was still likely to grow at its earnings rate of 18 percent a year with less than 2 percent volatility well into the future, which is still a great return with low risk. But he bought McDonald's because the short-term nature of the markets was overstressing the obvious maturing of the burger market in the United States versus the much greater long term potential overseas.

He is a long-term investor just like many of the very elite households in this country that are building wealth in this unprecedented boom. Meanwhile, most of us make more modest gains. And a significant minority is falling behind as the rapid pace of change makes obsolete our past businesses, jobs, and investment strategies.

Investment is actually very simple. It is just like diet and exercise. I don't know about you, but I don't need to hear many more statistics about diet and exercise. It is pretty straightforward. It comes down to broccoli and chocolate cake. We all know that broccoli is better for us but we tend to choose the chocolate cake when we actually sit down to eat. The chocolate cake is simply irresistible, it tastes better, and it even feels better in the moment. But it isn't the best for our long-term health, or even for our energy and mood later in the day.

A clear vision of fundamental change and a persistent and disciplined strategy of investment in time and money: those are the keys to building wealth, especially in a time of sweeping change that threatens old ways of thinking and doing business. But most investors think about timing the markets, picking the hottest stocks and funds, trying to beat the odds instead of the simpler, clearer long-term approach of a Warren Buffet. The purpose of this book is equally simple:

To help you understand the fundamental trends that can be reliably projected into the future to allow you to build the wealth and lifestyle you desire in the greatest boom in history.

I have spent 25 years analyzing such trends, beginning with an undergraduate education in economics, accounting and finance, followed by an M.B.A. at Harvard Business School in business management, marketing, and strategy. I have worked at the highest levels of business strategy with Fortune 100 companies at Bain & Company. I then worked in strategy and turnaround management with many entrepreneurial growth companies. I have been the CEO or CAO of several such companies, dealing with real human and business change at the extreme.

Unlike an academic or an armchair economist, I have been directly involved in the dramatic changes occurring in our largest multinational companies and, more important, our vibrant emerging companies that are creating almost all of the growth and jobs in our economy. I was paid for forecasting fundamental changes in old and new industries: changes that companies had to invest their entire assets and strategies in. I had to be right or suffer the consequences. I have been an entrepreneur, having conducted research that has spawned my own business, which is not only succeeding beyond my original vision but may allow me to prosper while living on a Caribbean island. I have achieved the lifestyle I wanted, not from daydreams but from vision, patience, and understanding long-term trends that I determined were inevitable.

Over my unique life and business experience, I learned how projectable such fundamental changes were. I simply adapted the proven tools in my profession of business and industry forecasting to the broader economy. I didn't consider this a risky proposition, although it took many years and much more struggle than I anticipated for such forecasting tools to be recognized. I also learned through entrepreneurial ventures, crisis management, and short-term investment trading how random and unpredictable short-term changes, events, and setbacks can be. How many experts have consistently predicted short-term events and market movements? Elaine Garzarelli was the last such expert timer to live and die by "the sword." And she was really good. Nobody has ever proven the ability to predict the short term over time.

Instead I developed an intuitive sense of the sweeping but simple trends that were changing our lives, businesses, and investments. And very simple quantitative measures to verify and project such trends. That is where the real payoff is, just as the greatest entrepreneurs, business managers, and investors have proven throughout history. I have conducted extensive research, in many cases going back hundreds of years and even thousands of years of history, to validate these changes and develop a clear and understandable vision of where we are headed in this incredible boom . . . and even the inevitable downturn that will follow.

This book is about bringing my proven tools of forecasting to people like you who may not have the time or interest to go through my experience in business, research, and forecasting. You can absolutely have a vision of the future because it is the predictable human and economic behavior of people like you and me that actually drives change in our society and economy. Therefore, you can understand these changes in very commonsense terms. Economists who have failed to forecast the most important changes of this era have missed the most fundamental insights, despite their obvious intelligence and meticulous analysis. They have missed the forest for the trees.

The predictable impacts of the birth and aging of new generations drive economic, technological, and social changes that influence our lives, jobs, businesses, and investments over time. The impacts range from innovation to spending to borrowing to saving and even to the purchase of everyday items like potato chips or motorcycles. Consumer marketers have used age, income, and lifestyle demographics very successfully as a "snapshot" to determine how to best exploit trends in consumer behavior today. This book is about seeing such demographic and generation shifts as a "moving picture" to see the changes that will inevitably occur in the future to change our lives, career, business, and investment opportunities. You can understand and invest in the future just as the most successful people have in the past. History is all about raising our standard of living through innovation and learning. It has also been about bringing a high standard of living to more and more people. The rich don't just get richer over time. Every day people move to higher standards of living and actually reduce the gap between the rich and the poor over time.

Yes, history proves that the gap between rich and poor has narrowed dramatically over the long term, despite volatile periods of change that temporarily tend to benefit the rich. The average person was a serf or slave for most of history versus very few nobles, knights, or information-elite. This also happened in the last economic revolution from the late 1800s into the Roaring Twenties. But that innovation cycle and the new emerging economy created an unprecedented new prospering middle class in the 1950s and 1960s. The innovation of such entrepreneurial people is necessary to create new revolutions that "trickle down" over many decades to more and more people. It doesn't just happen overnight, like the secrets to building wealth I have already described. The S-curve principle described in this book is one of the many simple tools that will make change more obvious to you. It will show how most new products, technologies, and social trends move into our economy and create change and opportunities predictably . . . but not in the straight line that most experts forecast.

I have been projecting the most fundamental changes in our economy, business, and investments since the mid-to-late 1980s with the simple tools I will present in this book. I am not someone who has become suddenly bullish with the incredible stock rises between 1995 and 1997. In 1988 I began speaking to business CEOs on my research predicting the greatest boom in history and unprecedented changes in business and management—despite the infamous 1987 crash. I published my first book *Our Power to Predict* in 1989, in which I forecast an incredible boom to around 2010, with a Dow of 10,000, falling inflation and interest rates, and the resurgence of America in world markets. In this book I have updated my forecasts to a Dow of at least 21,500 and likely higher by including the massive wave of immigrants into our country since then. In late 1992 I published my best-known book, *The Great Boom Ahead,* which reiterated and expanded on these forecasts just as depression and debt crisis books were all hitting the bestseller lists and negative views of the future were widespread. That book has become the bible of many financial advisors and investors over the past years because the forecasts have proven to be largely on the mark. It's not that I predicted everything right in the short term. I overforecast the severity of the recession of the early nineties after predicting it in 1989. I underforecast the stock boom to follow despite being wildly bullish at the time. I assumed that my prediction of the collapse of Japan's economic miracle and the fall in suburban real estate prices would have a greater impact on the fundamentals of growth of U.S. consumer trends in the short term. But consumers spent as the reliable statistics I will reveal in this book would have suggested despite these setbacks. That was part of my lesson in focusing too much on near-term trends. I wish I had had Warren Buffet or Peter Lynch as a mentor at that time.

The Roaring 2000s is about projecting the inevitable trends that have already been established by the massive baby boom generation that will impact our economy and our lives as it predictably ages. I will bring a much updated view of the Internet and information revolution and the massive changes that will result in the coming decade in our work and business structures as they are finally moving into the mainstream of our economy. This will create a surge in productivity, wealth, lifestyle opportunities, and conveniences in our lives—just as automobiles, electricity and motors, phones, and new consumer products such as Coca-Cola did dramatically beginning in the Roaring Twenties and expanding into the early 1970s. I will look at the predictable trends in the stock markets, business and entrepreneurial opportunities, jobs and careers, lifestyles, and real estate investing that can allow you to achieve your dreams in the greatest boom in history. And lifestyle is what it's all about, not merely achieving wealth. Although anyone who is wealthy would quickly agree that it is better than being poor. Surveys of happiness in this country have shown that wealth affects the sense of well-being by a factor of only 2 percent. Happiness is more about relationships, friends, family, and community . . . and a balanced life. It's more fundamentally about living, learning, experiencing, and growing as a human being. It's ultimately about evolution. It's what you do with your life that counts, and wealth can be a critical tool for achieving the freedom to maximize your experience and your impact on others.

Money or economic wealth is ultimately about giving yourself the freedom to choose the lifestyle that you want and to champion the causes you believe in. That is the new ethic in this era of prosperity when many of us have already achieved the fundamentals of survival, security, and living.

This book is more about how you can achieve the lifestyle you really want. Not just wealth . . . but the satisfying career, the opportunity to start your own business, the ability to innovate and establish your own business unit within your present corporation, the ability to live where you want to and still maintain or advance your standard of living, the ability to better manage change as an executive or professional within your company, the ability to manage your life to spend more time with the people you love rather than commuting and becoming a workaholic in today's stressful society of two-worker couples and downsizing of jobs.

The ability to greatly evolve and advance one's standard of living has not always been possible for many people throughout history. We are living in the greatest period of change and progress since the printing press revolution and the discovery of America and the rest of the world after the late 1400s. Such times create the greatest opportunities for advancement of people from all socioeconomic sectors. The greatest advances in such times have often come from the drive and motivation of lower-class people and penniless immigrants. As I stated earlier, 80 percent of the millionaires today were self-made through either systematic investment from above average, not extreme, incomes or from entrepreneurial businesses.

I will show how these revolutions are predictable and how they create changes in our economy and society. This will allow you, if you are open to change, to take advantage of these anticipated trends using your own unique experiences and insights. But it is up to you to apply these insights creatively to your own business and living circumstances to redesign how you work and where and how you live. We are in the midst of the greatest economic boom and technological revolution in history. And it hasn't occurred yet. It is about to emerge: just as cars, electricity, and phones did in the Roaring Twenties. The Roaring 2000s will come with the aging of the massive baby boom generation into its peak productivity, earning, and spending years and the emergence of their radical information revolution into the mainstream of our economy.

Tighten your seatbelts and prepare for the greatest boom in history: from 1998 to 2008!

I said this in late 1992 in *The Great Boom Ahead* and I will say it again: Stay invested and take any short-term setbacks in the stock market or in your career as an opportunity to invest more in change and growth. And when the next long-term downturn in the economy eventually occurs, I have advice for prospering in that stage as well.

Best of success to you in the Roaring 2000s!

PART 1

The Roaring 2000s

CHAPTER 1
The Greatest Boom
in History:
1998 to 2009

WITH THE DOW ROARING from under 4000 in late 1994 to near 9000 recently, most people can't imagine a brighter investment picture. However, this follows the rampant debt-and-depression psychology of the early 1990s. Is this just a market gone wild, with an equally harrowing crash to come, or the sign of a new era of prosperity? The brief crash in October 1987 caused many experts to wonder if this bull market was over as did the Asian meltdown in late 1997.

In 1997, Byron Wien of Morgan Stanley commented that he had studied trends back to Babylonian times, and things "have never been this good!" My long-term studies more than confirm this statement. I have been forecasting an unprecedented bull market in the economy and stocks since 1988. But, for now, let's just put this bull market in the perspective of the past two centuries.

There have never been two consecutive decades of high, sustained stock performance like the 1980s and 1990s. Average returns approaching well over 10 percent have only occurred in three decades over the past two centuries prior to the 1980s and 1990s: the 1860s, the 1920s and the 1950s (Figure 1.1). When adjusted for inflation, the 1920s and 1950s were the most stellar decades for stocks. Here's the even better news: It's almost certain that we will see another decade of strong stock growth of 10 percent or higher annually.

Stock Returns by Decade
1802 - 1995

Years	% Stocks Average Annual Return	% Annual Average Consumer Price Change
1802-1809	4.77	0.20
1810-1819	2.68	-1.15
1820-1829	5.31	-2.23
1830-1839	4.53	0.89
1840-1849	6.73	-1.91
1850-1859	0.45	1.27
1860-1869	15.73	4.68
1870-1879	7.58	-3.59
1880-1889	6.72	0.00
1890-1899	5.45	0.13
1900-1909	9.62	2.39
1910-1919	4.69	7.34
1920-1929	13.68	-0.94
1930-1939	-0.17	-2.04
1940-1949	9.57	5.36
1950-1959	18.23	2.22
1960-1969	8.17	2.52
1970-1979	6.75	7.36
1980-1989	16.64	5.10
1990-1995	13.00	3.33

That means three decades of stellar growth: the greatest boom in history!

In fact, we are on the brink of the most exciting boom period since the Roaring Twenties. I call it the *Roaring 2000s,* because it will usher in the kind of sweeping economic and social changes that turned post-World War I America upside down. This book is about understanding these changes for personal and business opportunities. These opportunities will be enormous for those that understand such changes, and threatening for those that don't, despite the boom ahead.

During the Roaring Twenties, new technologies, industries, products and services seemed to burst forth virtually overnight. Lindbergh's first flight across the Atlantic epitomized the soaring possibilities of the new technology, and the new spirit of optimism that accompanied it. Cars, phones, radios, electrical home appliances, movies, Coca-Cola, and so much more became affordable, mainstream, consumer items. At the same time, the entrepreneurial Henry Ford generation moved into their peak years of earning, spending and productivity. Like the baby-boom population today, the Henry Ford generation swelled to an unprecedented size, due to a massive wave of immigrants that only accelerated the boom. The Roaring Twenties saw high economic growth, a huge 5 percent gain in business productivity (on average), a zero rate of inflation, rising savings rates, and falling debt ratios. Sound like a great economy? It was! The Roaring 2000s will be even greater.

Now, new technologies, industries, products and services are again about to burst forth. This will mark the real beginning of the information revolution — *but it hasn't really happened yet!* Sure, a great many businesses have been leveraging the power of the Internet for the last few years, but we won't see the new era of network-based

---

Figure 1.1: Stock Returns from 1802 on, by Decades.

Figure 1.1 shows the decade averages in stock returns back to the 1802s. Inflation rates are also included, which puts the real stock returns in better perspective. The only decades with stock returns higher than 10 percent were the 1860s, 1920s, 1950s, 1980s, and 1990s. Adjusted for inflation, the 1920s and 1950s were the best decades, but never have we seen real returns higher than 10 percent for two decades in a row.

commerce and living until consumers move online in huge numbers, and use the Internet for more than casual information and entertainment.

Consider the recent explosion in Internet use, which has astonished almost everyone. What most of us don't realize is that this information revolution will not only change how we communicate, it will fundamentally alter how and where we live and work. It will create a new economic boom featuring a huge array of customized goods and services at increasingly affordable prices. It will create consumer conveniences that will begin to relieve the incredible time burdens of our careers, commuting, and the congestion of suburban living. As this unprecedented technological revolution emerges, the huge baby-boom generation (the largest in history) will reach its peak earning, spending, and productivity years. The confluence of these two highly predictable trends is about to ignite the Roaring 2000s. This boom will be even greater than the Roaring Twenties as it will be driven by a much larger generation and more powerful technologies. . . . the most powerful trends since the printing press and population explosion of the 1400s and 1500s!

The simple but powerful truth is that we can easily project long-term economic trends. Our economy is fundamentally driven by the predictable family spending cycles of each new generation and the predictable movement of new technologies and industries into the mainstream of our society.

40-YEAR GENERATION CYCLES

Ken Dychtwald, in *Age Wave* (Jeremy Tarcher, 1989), was the first author to show the profound effects of the baby boom generation as they aged. Every forty years, a new generation is formed through birth and immigration. This has been tracked as far back as the 1400s in extensive academic detail in two books: *Generations* (Morrow, 1992) and *The Fourth Turning* (Broadway, 1997), both written by William Strauss and Neil Howe. I will show how these new generations move through very predictable personal and family spending cycles that peak, on average, at around age 46 to 47 for the head of the household. This causes boom periods that last 26 to 29 years, followed by bust periods after the generation has peaked in its spending, that last 12 to 14 years.

The Henry Ford generation drove an economic and stock-market boom from 1900 to 1929 — the Era of Good Feelings to the Roaring Twenties. The extraordinary climax of that boom in 1929 was followed by the Great Depression. The Bob Hope generation drove up stocks and our economy from 1942 through 1968. Rising inflation and a series of recessions in 1970, 1974–75, 1980 and 1982 caused stocks to move into a 14-year bear market into late 1982. Now, the massive baby-boom generation is driving a bull market and economic boom that started in late 1982, which will last into 2008–9.

It is the enormous size of the baby-boom generation, augmented by a large immigration wave in the 1980s, which is driving the greatest boom in history and the unprecedented stock boom that almost none of our economists forecast. The best news: It will continue until about mid-2009, and the Dow will reach at least 21,500 and likely higher.

80-YEAR ECONOMIC REVOLUTIONS

Every eighty years, or every two generations, we see an economic revolution. This occurs because generations swing back and forth between being more individualistic or being more conformist, as Strauss and Howe have also documented. The individualistic generations are entrepreneurial and bring in radical new social trends and technologies, challenging the old status quo just as it is maturing and losing productivity. The conformist generation that follows, being more systematic and managerial, builds the new emerging companies and technologies into mass-market institutions. The last economic revolution revolved around cars, electricity, phones, and most of today's Fortune 500 industries. Although most of these technologies were invented in the late 1800s, it was the assembly-line revolution in mass manufacturing that launched the new industries rapidly into mainstream markets after 1914.

The Roaring Twenties represented the most exciting period of change and growth of the last revolution, as new technologies and industries suddenly moved mainstream while the Henry Ford generation that introduced them was moving into its peak spending years. The more conformist and civic-minded Bob Hope generation ushered in pervasive incremental technological innovations that extended such industries further into mainstream markets as they generated a boom into the 1950s and 1960s. They built the massive Fortune 500 and public institutions that rule today, and perfected the products and technologies of the last century. That's why we are being forced to usher in new technologies and trends — and the baby boomers have been doing that in spades.

Every 500 years, unusually large population explosions over the course of a century set off a tidal wave of change and progress. We are now undergoing the greatest economic revolution since the invention of the printing press, gunpowder and the tall ship, fifteenth-century technologies that inaugurated the Age of Science and Discovery.

The sudden emergence of information technologies, along with the peak spending years of the baby-boom generation, will usher in a new era of prosperity and sweeping changes. What was entirely predictable in the Roaring Twenties will happen on a much broader scale in the Roaring 2000s. We are almost certain to see the greatest economic boom in our country's history.

I'll show clearly and factually why these trends are inevitable, and why their convergence will have such an enormous impact. It would be naive to assume that what we're about to see happen will be easy on everyone. On the contrary: Just as in the 1920s, enormous gains mean tumultuous times. The Roaring 2000s, like the Roaring Twenties, will reward the people and companies that change, and change will only accelerate dramatically in the coming decades.

THE SIMPLE SECRET OF PREDICTING OUR ECONOMY

Let me introduce a simple principle that should change your outlook on the future. As complex as our economy is in its day-to-day workings, over the long term it is remarkably predictable. It is predictable for one simple reason: Our economy is driven by the family spending cycles of each new generation of consumers and workers.

It's that simple. In the short term, there are many factors that affect our economy: Interest rates rise and fall. Trade deficits expand and contract. The yen gets stronger, then the dollar gets stronger, affecting the competitiveness of our multinational companies in foreign markets. The one fundamental factor that drives the boom-and-bust cycles of our economy over time in a predictable manner isn't a matter of politics, interest rates, trade deficits or the strength of the dollar. It's consumption: how the average family spends money in predictable patterns over time. As a result, you and I can see the direction of our economy and the stock market over the next five decades with one simple indicator that plays on our own predictable spending habits.

Figure 1.2: U.S. birth rates in the twentieth century.

Figure 1.2 shows birth patterns since 1909, which is when birth data began being collected on a yearly basis. We can see that new generations emerge about every 40 years. For example, notice the size of the massive baby boom generation. The peak in the birth cycle of the baby-boom generation occurred in 1961, whereas the peak of the Bob Hope generation occurred in 1921. These two peaks are exactly forty years apart.

U.S. Births Per Year

© 1997 H.S. Dent Foundation, adapted from *The Great Boom Ahead* by Harry S. Dent, Jr.

THE BEST LEADING INDICATOR: BIRTH RATES

The best leading indicator for our economy is birth rates. That's how we form new generations. Simply put, people who consume in a predictable manner over the course of their lifetimes drive our economy. It expands as new generations of consumers and workers move through a predictable earning and spending cycle. It reaches its height when the greatest numbers of consumers reach their peak spending years. The economy will then decline until the next generation moves through its spending cycle. It is that simple!

Birth charts tell us decades in advance when new generations of consumers will move through predictable spending cycles. I prefer to

---

Figure 1.3: United States Immigration, 1820–1995.

Figure 1.3 shows immigration rates back to the early 1800s. Immigration was the driving factor behind growth and generation cycles before the early 1900s. The steepest spike from 1898 to 1914 caused the Roaring Twenties on a lag. The next large surge in immigration occurred from 1978 to 1991. These new consumers will contribute to the boom in the Roaring 2000s.

U.S. Immigration 1820 - 1995

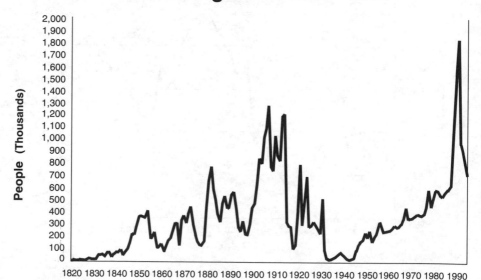

call the birth index "sexual activity on a nine-month lag!" If you remember nothing else, remember this: sex drives our economy — and that's precisely why economists have never figured it out, and probably never will!

The consumers driving the American economy include those born in this country and those who have immigrated to America. If we look at the immigration trends since the early 1820s in Figure 1.3, we can see how great an influence immigration has been in America's growth and generation cycles. Until the early 1900s, immigration

---

Figure 1.4: Immigration-Adjusted Birth Index.

Figure 1.4 shows the immigration-adjusted birth index for the U.S. The average immigrant enters this country around age 30. There was a peak in immigration rates, and a dramatic surge, into 1991. The average peak immigrant in 1991 would have been born in 1961, which coincides with the peak in the baby-boom births. Therefore, this recent immigration wave has even further exaggerated the enormous size of the baby-boom generation, making it more than four times the magnitude of a birth wave compared with the generation before it.

Immigration-Adjusted Birth Index

had a greater impact than birth cycles, and immigration waves peaked about every 40 years, similar to birth cycles.

Let's look at the impact of the largest immigration wave in United States history, which occurred from 1898 to 1914, right in the middle of the chart. This population surge was the biggest cause of the Roaring Twenties. Age statistics back to the early 1900s show that the average age of immigrants entering our country has been pretty stable —around age 30. These immigrants will peak in their spending in their mid-forties, much like the rest of us. There is a pretty clear correlation between economic booms and immigration rates on a 15- to 16-year lag back in the 1800s before birth cycles started to dominate more. The massive wave of immigration from 1898 to 1914 was dramatically curtailed in 1914 by World War I. After the war and the recovery period, this wave of new immigrants fueled the Roaring Twenties boom, along with the peak spending years of the maturing Henry Ford generation. That unprecedented boom climaxed dramatically 16 years after the peak immigration rates were reached in 1914. The economy plummeted from 1930 on, as that wave of immigrants didn't need to spend more money, as I will document. Immigration largely explains the Roaring Twenties and the Great Depression. As I have stated, immigration waves dovetail with birth trends in line with the 40-year generation cycles. Notice the peak of the most recent dramatic wave of immigration, from 1978 to 1991. If the average age of those immigrants was 30, then the average immigrant in 1991 would have been born in 1961: the same peak year of births for the baby boomers, as shown in Figure 1.2. Therefore, we have to adjust our generational birth cycles for immigration.

I calculated when these immigrants were born with a simple computer model and factored them into the birth statistics shown in Figure 1.4. The baby boom generation even more dramatically dwarfs the generations before it when immigration is factored in.

PREDICTABLE SPENDING CYCLES
FOR THE AVERAGE FAMILY

The average American family goes through very predictable spending cycles as shown in Figure 1.5. How do we know this? The U.S. Bureau of Labor conducts surveys of consumer expenditures

Average Annual Family Spending by Age
(5-year age groups)

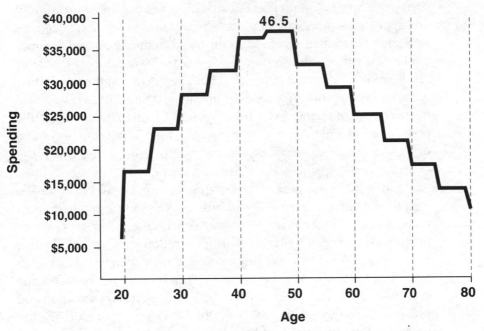

© 1997 H.S. Dent Foundation, adapted from *The Great Boom Ahead* by Harry S. Dent, Jr.

Figure 1.5: Average Family Spending.

Figure 1.5 shows the predictable spending cycles of the average American family. This data is taken from annual Consumer Expenditure Surveys conducted by the U.S. Bureau of Labor.

---

annually. We enter the work force, on average, at about age 19, get married, on average, at age 25.5 (age 27 for men and 24 for women). We buy our first car, move into apartments, and furnish them. This period of household formation represents the fastest rate in earnings and spending growth in the entire family life cycle. I will refer to this later when projecting economic-growth cycles. Two years later, at age 27.5, we have our average kid. The average person then buys a starter home around age 33 to 34, getting the first mortgage, and purchases all of the furnishings to go with it. By age 43, we trade up to the largest home we'll own, and fully furnish it by age 46.5, when most of our children leave the nest at age 19, making 46.5 the peak spending age today.

After age 46, average family spending decreases sharply. After children leave home, parents don't need a bigger house, more furnishings and appliances, more cars, or more car insurance. They don't need the refrigerator crammed with food, or the trendy tennis shoes and designer clothes. Parents typically mourn the loss of their kids, until they realize "Holy smokes, we've got it made!" These people are at the top of their earnings cycle, with a massive drop in financial obligations. They have the fixed costs of a home and furnishings for a lifetime, and their variable costs have suddenly dropped by as much as half! This is the beginning of high discretionary spending for the parents, but it is the end of the dramatic family spending that drives our economy.

Since there is a peak in birth rates about every 40 years, we see long-term economic expansions or bull markets lasting about 26 to 29 years, followed by economic contractions lasting 12 to 14 years, as mentioned earlier. The Henry Ford generation drove a bull market from 1900 to 1929. An economic collapse then followed, from 1930 into World War II. The Bob Hope generation drove the economy from World War II into the late 1960s. Fourteen years of inflation and worsening recessions followed. Now, the baby boomers are driving the economy, but the majority of baby boomers haven't entered their peak spending years yet. When they do, they will drive the economy into an extended and dramatic expansion that will take most people by surprise.

THE SPENDING WAVE

We can predict the health of our economy and stock markets over many decades to come simply by lagging the birth index forward 46.5 years. This tells us when a whole generation of consumers will reach its predictable spending peak, as shown in Figure 1.6.

I first used this simple forecasting tool in 1988, long before this raging bull market became obvious. At that time, in my first book, *Our Power to Predict* (self-published), I predicted a Dow of 10,000, and a boom that would last until about 2010, with falling inflation rates and a resurgence of America in world competitiveness. Adding immigration data to the original model has raised my forecasts much higher, but I was still forecasting the same basic scenario with one

The Spending Wave
Births Lagged for Peak in Family Spending

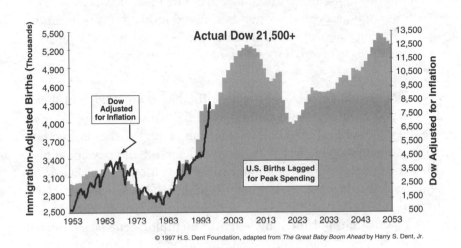

© 1997 H.S. Dent Foundation, adapted from *The Great Baby Boom Ahead* by Harry S. Dent, Jr.

Figure 1.6: The Spending Wave.

Figure 1.6 illustrates the spending wave, which shows how our economy correlates very closely with the birth index adjusted for inflation, moved forward 46.5 years for peak spending of the average family in the U.S. It allows us to see when the economy and stock market will grow and decline almost five decades in advance.

---

simple indicator. This proves that economics doesn't have to be complicated, if we focus on the long-term trends, not all the complex short-term workings of our economy. Let me explain a few refinements.

- The Bob Hope generation got married and peaked in its spending earlier than will later generations. Therefore, the birth lag starts at age 43 in the 1950s, and moves up about one year every decade, to reach 46.5 in the mid-1990s. This lag is projected to continue to move forward at the same rate, which means that the peak spending age for the top of the baby-boom spending cycle, in 2009, will be at about 47.5.

- I have also factored in, on a 25 percent weighting, the impact of new household formation and marriage into age 25.5 (starting at age 22 in the 1950s and rising toward 26.5 over the next decade) due to the strong initial surge in buying by these new sectors. This acts as a mild accelerator when household formation is rising and a decelerator when it is falling, but does not add to the long term trends set by the overall spending of new generations.

The spending wave begins with birth data from 1909, and shows how that data affects the economy from the early 1950s on. We can see the effect of peak spending by the Bob Hope generation into late 1968. After that, the S&P 500 (adjusted for inflation) went into a 14-year decline, losing over 50 percent of its value between late 1968 and late 1982 (the Dow lost almost 70 percent). We saw four back-to-back recessions (1970, 1974–75, 1980 and 1982) with ever higher rates of inflation and unemployment. Unemployment peaked at 10 percent in late 1982 and early 1983, the highest levels since the Great Depression. At that same time, however, the baby boom generation began to move through its predictable spending cycle, beginning in late 1982. Spending will continue to grow until around mid-2009, which is when the majority of this *massive* generation will reach the peak of their spending.

A PIG MOVING THROUGH A PYTHON

Here's how to understand our economy today, as well as all the extremes it is experiencing. Take a look at Figure 1.1 again. It shows you that the baby-boom generation is *three times* the size of previous birth waves. Now, factor in the high levels of immigration reflected in Figure 1.3, and you will see why the baby-boom generation has been called "a pig moving through a python." It is over four times the size of the previous generation—so massive that everything it does as it ages will stretch our society and economy to extremes.

This generation stretched the public-school system in the 1960s. Then it stretched inflation rates to extremes into the late 1970s. It elevated housing prices to extreme levels in the late 1980s. Debt levels then hit an extreme high in the early 1990s. The next surprise was a booming economy and an accelerated bull market in stocks between 1994 and 1997. How many forecasters predicted that? What many of them don't know and aren't predicting is the greatest wave of economic expansion still ahead of us.

This huge generation of consumers will drive the greatest economic boom in our history, with increased productivity, real-wage gains, rising savings and falling debt ratios. We should see a Dow of at least 21,500 and as high as 35,000, as the baby boomers and the recent wave of immigrants move into their peak spending years around the year 2009.

The baby-boom generation will continue to cause extremes in our economy. Baby boomers will eventually threaten to bankrupt the social security system during the 2020s and 2030s—after allowing the Bob Hope generation to be the only group in history to retire comfortably. So let's see these extremes for what they are and not view the debt ratio, for example, as a sign that our country is going to hell in a handbasket.

Three Waves of Expansion

If we look at Figure 1.5 a little more closely, we will see that the bull market economy caused by the baby boomers has and will continue to occur in three waves because there were three waves of baby boomers. The first wave (not officially classified as baby boomers) was born before World War II, the second just after the soldiers returned home, and the third wave was born in the glorious 1950s and early 1960s when the future looked so rosy—and before the pill was invented.

The first wave of baby boomers bought their houses, furnishings, and cars in growing numbers from late 1982 into mid-1990. Then, a sudden recession started in late 1990. The Federal Reserve did not cause this recession, nor did George Bush, although the brief Gulf War contributed a bit. It coincided with the peak spending of the first wave of baby boomers—and the sharp drop afterwards—when they no longer needed to buy durable goods.

The second wave of baby boomers drove our economy to higher growth rates from mid-1991 into late 1994. Growth rates slowed into mid-1997 with the tapering off of the second wave's spending.

From late 1997 on, the economy should again begin to grow

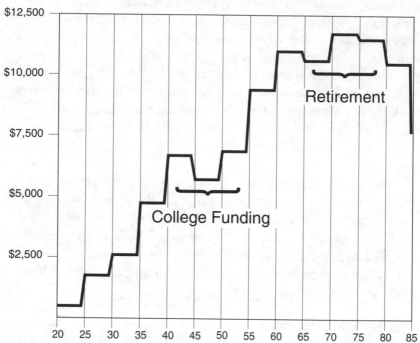

Figure 1.7: Average Family Savings.

Figure 1.7 shows that it is only after age 34 that people start to save significantly, and savings continue to grow until the late 60s or early 70s. Baby
boomers will be moving into the first accelerated stage of their savings cycle
in the coming decade in massive numbers.

---

more rapidly. This is when the third wave of the baby-boom generation begins to move into its peak spending years. Remember that the
highest rates of spending growth occur between age 19 and 25–26 in
the household-formation cycle? The third wave of baby boomers will
be joined by the strong acceleration from the next generation's household-formation cycle around 2002 on. As a result, we should see an
explosion in economic growth at around 2002 to 2003, leading us into
the greatest boom in history, which won't reach its peak until almost
mid-2009. This would correspond to the growth surge in the Roaring
Twenties that lasted from 1922 into 1929, on an 80-year lag or two-
generation economic revolution cycle.

For an in-depth look at the demographic and S-curve trends driving our new economy, read my first book, *The Great Boom Ahead.*

A Shift in Savings and Debt Trends

There were other consumer trends driving the Roaring Twenties, including rising savings rates and falling debt ratios. Let's take a look at the simple demographic logic behind these phenomena.

There is a predictable dynamic hidden in the average family spending cycle. At age 34, the average person buys his or her first home, and suddenly assumes a huge mortgage. Debt grows faster than spending and spending grows faster than savings, up to age 34. Age 34 also represents the peak debt-to-income ratios for the average family. After that, saving grows faster than spending and spending grows faster than borrowing. Saving begins to accelerate for the first time in the mid-thirties as we can see in Figure 1.7.

Let's look at one example to check our current assumptions about the danger of debt trends in our economy today—and see just how wrong they are. Approximately 80 million baby boomers, as they reached age 34 or so, bought starter homes in the suburbs in the 1970s and 1980s. What did this massive demand do to housing prices? They skyrocketed, of course. In fact, the price of housing went up at twice the rate of inflation in the 1970s and 1980s. In others words, we could have seen that incredible boom coming.

Who were the biggest beneficiaries of the real-estate boom? Members of the Bob Hope generation, who owned most of the real estate. Who were the biggest losers? Members of the baby-boom generation, who were forced to pay more than double the price for housing, even when adjusted for inflation, than the Bob Hope generation paid when they bought starter homes in the 1940s and early 1950s.

Housing, whether owned or rented, is the single largest cost of raising a family. But the biggest cost of housing is not the house, it's the mortgage interest. While the Bob Hope generation paid mortgage rates at around 4 percent, the baby boomers paid as high as 12 to 16 percent in the late 1970s and early 1980s, and still pay 7 to 9 percent today on 30-year mortgages—double to triple what their parents paid.

So, yes, the baby boomers went into more debt than any generation in history, individually to raise our families in an era very different from the 1950s, and collectively because we did so in much greater numbers. But the highest debt ratios in our country's history were caused by innocent parents simply buying homes for their families, not by a decline in moral values! In the coming decade, as baby boomers move into their forties and pass their peak years of debt assumption, debt ratios will plateau and fall while savings ratios will rise.

In the years ahead, savings rates for baby boomers will grow faster than their strong spending. As this money is fed into mutual funds and the stock market, it will only strengthen the bull-market economy. We will see less dependence on other countries for capital in the coming decades, and a lower cost of capital for our companies. In fact, we will soon become an exporter of capital to industrializing third-world countries. Eventually, economists will begin to complain that the baby boomers are saving too much and not spending sufficiently.

Figure 1.8: The S-curve for Radial Tires.

Figure 1.8 shows that it took seven years for radial tires to capture 10 percent of the market, yet within the next seven years, they had captured 90 percent of the market. The so-called sudden popularity of radial tires exemplifies how a new technology, product, or service explodes into the mainstream after a slow initial acceptance within niche markets.

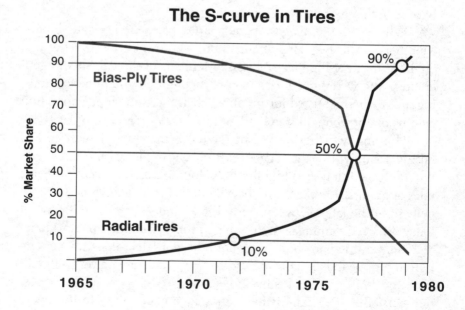

PREDICTING THE IMPACT
OF NEW TECHNOLOGIES WITH THE S-CURVE

Why do new technologies never live up to their promise in the early stages, and then surprise everyone by becoming suddenly indispensable? This was true with the automobile in the Roaring Twenties just as it's true today for the Internet. The biggest forecasting error people make is very simple. We think growth and change occurs in a linear fashion. The truth is, it's curvilinear.

I first came across the curvilinear model in the late 1970s, when I was given the task of predicting the growth rate of radial tires in U. S. markets. I looked at the data for Europe, where the transition from bias to radial tires had already occurred. The S-curve pattern was obvious.

Figure 1.8 shows what actually happened in the U. S. market for radial tires. Again, the S-curve pattern is unmistakable.

As I looked back, I saw that the S-curve has typically been the principle driving the emergence of new products, services, and technologies into the mainstream. It even predicts social trends! For example, hippies, environmentalists, and upscale baby boomers in California were trumpeting environmental issues in the 1960s and 1970s, but the green movement didn't go mainstream until the late 1980s. It's now so popular that recycling has become law in many cities.

Figure 1.9 shows the intuitive simplicity of the S-curve. New products and technologies move very slowly into niche markets as these products tend to be expensive, unfamiliar, and sometimes downright user-unfriendly, at first. Typically, younger, urban, and affluent sectors experiment first. The product gets tested and refined in this innovation stage. But then the growth stage suddenly hits. Once the product hits a critical mass of 10 percent of the potential consumers, it tends to explode into the mainstream at an accelerated rate until it penetrates 90 percent of the market. After that point, there is strong resistance by the most conservative sectors and marketing efforts hit increasing diminishing returns. The maturity stage, again, proceeds very slowly.

Automobiles and the Roaring Twenties

Let's look more closely at the incredible transformation that occurred in the Roaring Twenties, and get a feel for how dramatically
our economy and society can change in a period like this. We'll use
cars to illustrate what happened in a broad range of new technologies
and industries, the very same technologies and industries that have
driven our economy for the last 80 years.

Talk about new technologies suddenly emerging into the mainstream economy—take a look at the S-curve for the automobile! First
invented in 1886, the production of cars did not become a commer-
cially viable industry for more than ten years. In 1900, a tiny tenth of
1 percent of all urban households owned a car. That's where the
S-curve for the automobile starts. It took 14 years for the automobile

---

Figure 1.9: The S-curve.

Figure 1.9 shows the intuitive simplicity of the S-curve. It isn't necessary to
measure precisely the exact rate of market penetration of every new technology, product, or trend in our economy, but we easily can see that innovations
move very slowly into niche markets and then mushroom into the mainstream. In other words, it typically takes the same amount of time for a
product to reach 10 percent acceptance as it does to reach 90 percent acceptance.

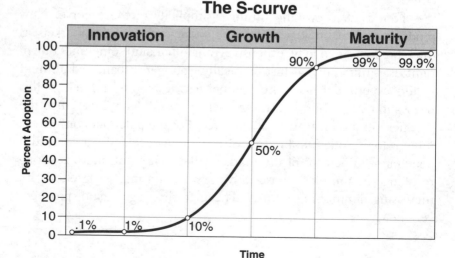

to penetrate 10 percent of the urban market. In other words, three decades after their invention, cars were only affordable to a small, niche market. They were clearly luxury items, beyond the means of the average person.

Within the next 14 years, the same amount of time it took for cars to reach 10 percent market penetration among urban households, they grew to a staggering 90 percent! Largely propelled by the incredible productivity of the assembly-line revolution pioneered by Henry Ford in 1914, and by the introduction of installment financing by

---

Figure 1.10: The S-curve for Automobiles.

Figure 1.10 shows the S-curve for the automobile from the years 1900 to 1928. It illustrates the principle clearly: It took the same amount of time (14 years) for cars to penetrate 10 percent of the urban household market as it did for cars to penetrate 90 percent of that market. There was a clear explosion in their popularity, so that by 1928, the automobile was an affordable, indispensable part of the urban household.

The S-curve in Cars

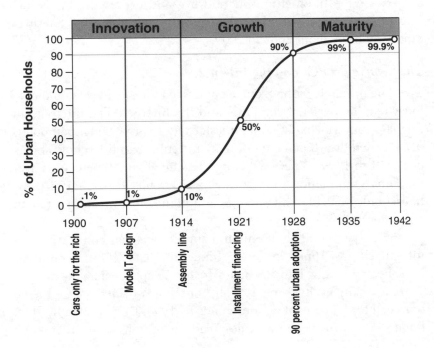

General Motors in the early 1920s, an overwhelming majority of urban households owned a car by the year 1928, as shown in Figure 1.10.

The automobile is just one example of the kinds of products that were suddenly available to, and affordable for, the average family. Consumers just after World War I had no idea that within a decade they would be able to afford a new host of luxury goods. Of course, economists did not see the Roaring Twenties coming. Like the Internet today, cars were one of the accelerators of the last economic revolution that emerged so strongly in the Roaring Twenties. Home electrification and phones took from about 1900 to 1928 to go from 10 to 90 percent penetration. Cars, electrical appliances, movies, and radios moved much faster into the mainstream (10 to 14 years to go from 10 to 90 percent) and gave consumers what was most important to them: mobility, convenience, and entertainment.

The greatest part of a new economic revolution occurs when it finally moves into the mainstream of the consumer marketplace. Electricity, phones, and motors moved into businesses much faster than into consumer households, just like computer technology today. But the information revolution — when mass numbers of average consumers use the Internet to work and live — is just around the corner. Expect it to cause sweeping changes in every aspect of our lives, especially from about 2002 to 2009.

The S-curve for PCs and the Internet

The principle of the S-curve applies to radically new technologies today like the personal computer and the Internet. The Internet, hitting later but moving at a much faster rate than personal computers, just reached the 10 percent of urban and suburban households breakout point in 1994, as personal computers hit about 50 percent. This is the same conjunction we saw as when cars hit 10 percent of urban households in 1914, while phones and home electrification hit about 50 percent.

The first genuinely useful and simple personal computers were introduced by Apple in 1977. Since the late 1980s, computers have been moving into the mainstream at an accelerated rate. By 1996, as many as 40 percent of all households owned a PC. Predictions call for 50 percent of households by 1998. I expect that by 2006, home PCs will become widespread, common, consumer prod-

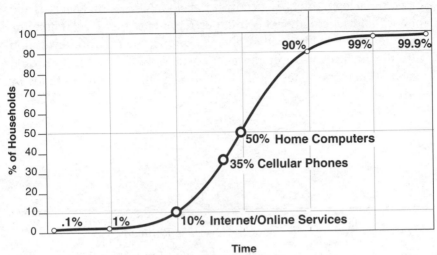

Figure 1.11: S-curve for Household Computing (Nonrural).

Figure 1.11. shows the S-curve for personal computers and other devices that are feeding the information revolution. Home computers were at 50 percent adoption, cellular phones at 35 percent, and the Internet at 10 percent as of the mid-1990s.

___

ucts like TV and cable, reaching 70 percent to 90 percent of all households.

But, like cars in the early 1900s, it would probably be more appropriate to define the S-curve for personal computers as inclusive of urban and suburban households only, which accounts for about 70 percent of the population. If we do that, then we see that household use of personal computers reached the 50 percent mark in 1994 and grew to 57 percent by 1996. The same is true for the Internet. If we include only urban and suburban households in our calculations, Internet usage reached 10 percent of the market in 1994. The figures for cellular phone usage falls between PC popularity and Internet popularity. They have reached about 25 percent of all households, but exceed 35 percent when we consider only urban and suburban areas.

History suggests that, once a new technology reaches 50 percent market penetration, it starts to have a noticeable impact on the economy and on productivity. This happened with electricity and phones in the home around 1914, and with cars in 1921. The S-curve pattern of personal computers is occurring at about the same pace as did phones and electricity. The Internet represents the accelerator, the consumer-oriented innovation that will propel the network revolution into the mainstream over the coming decade. The Internet should reach 90 percent penetration of urban and suburban households by 2010, at the latest.

Figure 1.12: Passenger Traffic: Cars Overtake Railroads.

Figure 1.12 shows the effect of the emergence of the automobile as a mainstream consumer product in the years between 1916 and 1933. Passenger traffic on the railroads fell, despite a booming economy. The fate of the railroads is not an isolated phenomenon. Many other mainstream industries were decimated during these decades, while new industries suddenly emerged as huge contributors to the booming economy.

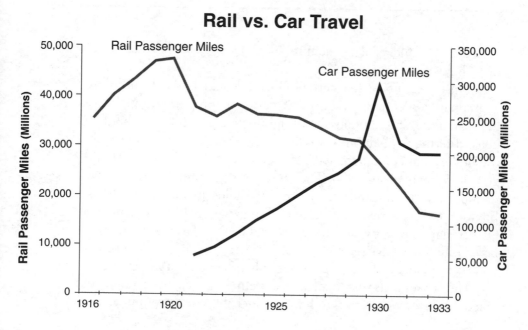

MAKING WAY FOR THE NEW

Most of our mass-market, brand-name products, technologies, and Fortune 500 companies first joined the mainstream in the Roaring Twenties. It was, in fundamental ways, the invention of an entirely new economy. Whereas the hallmark of this new economy was an array of products and services that had been unimagined, let alone unheard of, fifty years before, the foundation of this change was a new style of production and business management. To make way for the new, old industries and practices had to give way. For example, the mature railroad industry for passenger traffic was decimated in the Roaring Twenties, while the youthful automobile industry was growing at a furious pace. Figure 1.12 plots the fate of these two industries during this time.

The lesson that the Roaring Twenties teaches us is that: An old economy must die for a new one to emerge.

The necessary death of outmoded industries, products, services, and business practices is the source of the incredible confusion, anxiety, and pessimism we have witnessed in the past two decades. Even the largest, most stable corporations have re-engineered themselves by laying off massive numbers of workers, some for the very first time in their corporate history, and contrary to tradition and formal company policy. Some of what were once considered essential jobs in blue- and white-collar professions have been assumed by computers or exported to third-world countries. Many more jobs will be automated in the coming decades. In the 1970s, we struggled with the highest inflation rates in history and, by the 1990s, our debt levels have risen to their highest rates ever. Real-estate prices have stalled in the suburbs (where most of us live), while congestion and taxes continue to rise.

The social consequences of these huge changes have been dire. We have seen our school systems failing for both lack of funding and lack of consensus as to how to prepare children for the world they will inherit. Private institutions and public ones, including (and perhaps especially) our government, have cultivated no genuine leaders and have lost the respect of most citizens. Family relationships have suffered under these stressful changes, and a sense of genuine community comprised of family, neighbors, and friends is all but gone. The structures and traditions that our grandparents could rely on to see them through the economic and social crises simply don't exist anymore. There's tremendous freedom in this chaos but also tremendous anxiety.

These are not signs that our society and our economy are failing. The very successful technologies and institutions of the past are failing, but new, better ones are emerging to take their place. The process of innovation is painful—that's how we advance our standard of living! Did you know that in the last economic revolution, between 1876 when phones were first invented to today, the average family income increased *nine times* even when adjusted for inflation? Did you know that this was the direct result of automating most of the jobs and destroying most of the major businesses and institutions of the time? Do you think anyone then liked it any better than we do now? I'm sure they didn't. At least we benefit from their hard-earned insights.

In the last decade, most mainstream economists and academic forecasters have painted a dismal picture of our situation. They say that new technologies will reduce our standard of living, reduce our level of consciousness, and eliminate jobs while not creating any better ones. *This has never happened in history and it's not about to happen now!* We are about to emerge from the chaos to see the enormous benefits of the greatest technological, social and economic transition in history. In the coming decades, we will see strong, clear opportunities for business creativity and growth, and substantial lifestyle gains.

The Internet: Key Productivity Lever

The mass acceptance of Internet technology will leverage the new economy, which we have begun to see emerge into the mainstream in recent years. New industries or growth segments of old industries will continue to ascend into the mainstream as the economy continues to boom into 2009, when the baby boomers will reach their peak spending years. The booming economy, the Roaring 2000s, will parallel the Roaring Twenties on a two-generation or 80-year lag, from about 2002 to 2009. Why? Every 80 years, those highly ingenious, individualistic generations produce radical innovations that *spawn* a new economy. Their spending power brings those new innovations into the mainstream economy just as they begin to move into power in management and politics, ushering in a work revolution like the assembly line from 1914 on, and the network revolution that is just beginning to accelerate productivity and earnings in the mid 1990s.

The Internet is to the coming economic boom, the Roaring 2000s, what the moving assembly line was to the Roaring Twenties. It is the key productivity lever that will rapidly feed new technologies, products, and services into the mainstream economy.

As Steve Jobs succinctly put it in an interview with *Wired* magazine in July 1996, "picture the Internet as a direct producer-to-consumer distribution system." Widespread use of the Internet and allied technologies will fundamentally change the way we handle our business at home and at the office. It will collapse the many expensive layers of administrative, marketing, and distribution bureaucracy, much as the assembly-line revolution greatly reduced production costs. Electronic communication and commerce will also allow companies to tailor products and services to individual needs for what standardized goods cost today. Customized goods and services, once luxuries, will increasingly be affordable for the average consumer. The result is that consumers will get better products at better prices because businesses will be able to customize and cut costs.

THE COMPANIES TO WATCH

David Birch of Cognetics in Framingham, Massachusetts, has carefully documented the changes in growth and jobs in the past decades. Between 1990 and 1994, high-growth (20 percent or more per year), small- to medium-sized companies created 5 million new jobs. At the same time, the economy as a whole created only 4.2 million jobs. Weird math? Nope. Every company in America other than one of these high-growth gazelles, or new-growth companies — such as the Fortune 500 corporations and mom-and-pop businesses — created a net loss of 800,000 jobs. Between 1991 and 1995, the gazelles created 80 percent of the new jobs, whereas the other companies created 20 percent. That's why downsizing the corporate behemoths is not the key to our country's economic health. The new economy is already creating more jobs than the old one is losing.

It is these gazelles, as David Birch calls them, that will usher in the greatest economic boom in history. These companies will bring their technologies, products, and services into the mainstream market-place in the coming decade. A fraction of these companies, like Micro-soft or Starbucks Coffee, will join the Fortune 500. Some large, established corporations that make radical changes in organizational structure, work, and management may capture the new, growing mar-kets. The best older companies with a strong mature product or ser-vice, such as McDonald's, Coca-Cola, Gillette, and GE, will continue to grow by moving aggressively into markets in developing countries around the world.

The companies you should watch, work for, or invest in are the gazelles. These are the 3 percent that have thrived during the last decade, or the companies like GE, Coca-Cola, and Gillette that are dominating emerging new markets overseas with proven products from the past.

The new economy means new technologies, new growth compa-nies, new career opportunities, new public institutions, new lifestyles, and new hot areas of real estate. We can't just work harder in outdated jobs. We can't just keep re-engineering outdated organizations. We can't just fix up our suburban homes and expect the same rates of appreciation we enjoyed in the past.

Instead, we must face our need to change, personally and collec-tively, and find the new companies that are taking advantage of the extraordinary opportunities the nascent new economy is already offer-ing, and move with them into the Roaring 2000s. Visionary individu-als, entrepreneurs, and leaders will spearhead this change, not institutions, committees, and bureaucrats.

THE NEW NETWORK ORGANIZATION

The first assembly-line system revolutionized productivity 80 years ago. It was a top–down, command-and-control, producer-driven economy. Just as employees were told how to work, consumers were told what to buy. Standardized products and services at lower and lower prices were the result. It allowed millions of largely unskilled workers to migrate from farms to factories. It also allowed expensive information to be concentrated at the top, in the hands of a few highly educated people.

Now, our world is growing more complex every day. Smart consumers expect choice and personalized service. Technologies are changing at a much more rapid rate. The companies that will be able to respond efficiently to these expectations are those that literally run from the customer back, like the Internet, and not from the top down, like a traditional bureaucratic hierarchy. The network principle, not the assembly line, will drive the next 80-year cycle of productivity and economic advance. Companies who retain their old organizational structure simply will not be able to respond quickly enough, no matter how much they streamline their bureaucracies. Network organizations don't have a sluggish bureaucracy. A premium is placed on delivering customized information, goods, and services at light speed, when and where they are needed. The new network model is a wholesale change in business structure and practice that changes the role of every person within the organization.

The Internet Shows How Different Network Structures Are

The Internet demonstrates the very principle of networks, even in its chaotic infancy. Here's a great question for all of the managers trying to re-engineer their companies using top–down initiatives: "Where is the management of the Internet?" Isn't that a good question? Have you ever seen the CEO? Is there a board of directors guiding it? The real answer is obviously that end-users drive the Internet. It operates from the customer back, not from the top down. It is growing and changing so rapidly that even our most nimble high-tech companies have a hard time keeping up with it. In Part III, I will show how the network principle — how we organize our human talent, not just computers — will be the key to a productivity explosion and the acceleration of the new economy of customized goods and services into mainstream affordability. Re-engineering is not the key trend in business. It is simply the last extension of top–down strategies in a world that is moving too fast for any top–down strategy to be sufficient.

The Financial Markets Can Change at Light Speed, Why Can't Our Corporations?

A much better example of the power of network structures to grow, change, and respond rapidly is the financial markets. They put a price on every commodity; stock; bond; mutual fund; and currency, cash, and futures, every second of the day in most countries around the world. Now that's a phenomenal pace of change and response. Do you think that a committee of the best financial experts could even begin to do that? Or would they be behind two months in the first two seconds of trading? The point is clear: Complexity, customization, and fast-paced change cannot be managed from the top down.

Where is the management of the New York Stock Exchange? What we do see is that some guy runs up at 9:30 A.M. Eastern time, rings the opening bell, and then runs and gets the hell out of the way! Who runs the financial markets? They leverage the collective intelligence of all investors in the world . . . millions and millions of people buying and selling in their own interest. The real-time information systems allow us to set these prices and have them reflected almost immediately on our televisions or computer screens. Nonlinear, network systems can handle customization, complexity, and fast-paced change with the greatest of ease if designed properly. However, the result is that they end up running from the customer, user, investor, or citizen back. That is the real future and the real revolution yet to be seen. Approaching business or public changes from the old assembly-line or re-engineering method will be even more fruitless and frustrating as the network principle is bolstered by the majority of consumers moving online in the coming decade. The real Information Revolution will begin to mushroom in the Roaring 2000s just ahead.

SUMMARY

How and where we work and live is about to change more than at any time in our history. There will be unprecedented opportunities for investors and entrepreneurs, great buys in real estate, and a wealth of high-quality lifestyle choices for the savvy people who anticipate these changes instead of dreading them. It's time to start thinking differently about the future: how you manage your finances, where you invest your money, how you design and run your company, how you serve your customers, where you live, how you shop, and how you stay in touch with family, friends and business associates.

CHAPTER 2

How New Generations
Drive Economic Revolutions

THE ANXIETY WE FEEL right now, in the midst of the current economic revolution, creates a nostalgic longing for the good old days. Is this sentiment born of naiveté? Just how good were the good old days, anyhow? To appreciate the importance of the economic revolutions that emerge every 80 years or so, let's take a realistic look at life before the dawn of the automobile and assembly-line revolution.

THE GOOD OLD DAYS?

In the 1890s, America was largely a nation of struggling farmers, household servants, shopkeepers, trappers, and miners. Most of us did hard physical work 60 to 80 hours a week. Comfortable offices, job security, human rights, and medical and pension benefits were unknown. Mental work was the exception, not the rule. Who would stand in line for those jobs today?

It required almost half the American population, 43 percent, to produce all the food needed. Today, it requires a mere 1.9 percent to do the same, and that number is shrinking. That's an enormous gain in productivity! As late as the 1940s over 40 percent of the workforce was employed in factory work. Now factory jobs are at 15 percent and falling.

In the 1890s, America wasn't an educated nation. Two percent of the population attended college and 14 percent attended high school. Most children went straight to work on the farm when they reached puberty. Most people could not have done basic clerical work, not to mention the more complex forms of left-brain work like technical, professional and managerial functions.

In the 1890s, we Americans had very few of the conveniences that make our modern life comfortable. We didn't have cars and paved roads to drive anywhere we chose. We didn't have telephones to stay in touch with family, friends, and associates. We didn't have indoor plumbing, or electricity in our homes to run lights, home appliances, television, stereo systems, and power tools. We didn't have movies to watch or radios or TVs. We didn't have air-conditioning. There were no skyscrapers. We didn't have synthetic fibers or plastics. We didn't have propeller or jet airplanes to shoot around the world. We did not have the variety of canned, frozen, and prepared foods that fill the aisles of today's supermarkets, or fast-food restaurants, department stores, or malls. We didn't live in the suburbs. We didn't even have a broad array of everyday items from aspirin to razor blades to tea bags to ice cream cones to Coca-Cola! Life without Coca-Cola? At least we had whiskey and beer!

If the bucolic farm life was such a pleasure a century ago, why did people rush off those farms and move to the city when factory jobs became available, like many people are doing in China and other emerging countries today? Even the few farmers left in America today have put the good old days behind them. They are often quite wealthy, large-scale businesspeople, and harvest the fields in large, air-conditioned combines with eight-speaker stereo systems, accessing a satellite-based global positioning system via laptop computers to analyze their planting and harvesting down to the square inch.

The truth is, the American standard of living in the 1890s was closer to that of Mexico today. Perhaps the most genuine measure of standard of living is that we are now living much longer, healthier lives. In the 1890s, the average life expectancy was in the mid 40s. In fact, for centuries, life expectancy hovered around the mid-thirties and didn't begin rising until 1820 or so. In a little over a century, our life expectancy has more than doubled, to the mid- to late seventies and is still rising!

Pessimism, the Predictable Response

Our world today is so different from what it was a century ago, that if a turn-of-the-century futurist had envisioned the new technologies that have transformed our standard of living, people would have thought he or she was crazy. Even as late as World War I, virtually everything we now take for granted was not affordable to most people. But instead of imagining the best, we imagine the worst.

We were pessimistic during that war and immediately afterwards, and along came the Roaring Twenties. We were pessimistic during the Depression and World War II, and along came the booming economy of the 1950s and 1960s. In the last two decades, beginning in the early 1970s, we have seen the advances in our standard of living slow down. During the 1990–1991 recession, pessimism was once again rampant. Best-selling books predicting a dire future competed with one another on the *New York Times* bestseller list. The economy, particularly the stock markets, have been booming ever since.

When everything that is familiar to us starts to change or disappear, we become fearful and anxious about the future. That is precisely why most people, including the experts, have been so pessimistic in recent years. Our own history teaches us that we are on the threshold of a new economy, and the pessimists have been proven wrong. The stock market has been recognizing something for many years that economists have not.

What we have seen in the last two decades is exactly what occurred about 80 years ago. An old economy of products, services, technologies, and production methods has matured while the new economy has not yet fully taken its place. It is the growth of the new economy that creates the next boom, not the re-engineering of the old economy. While it is alarming when AT&T or U. S. Steel announces another round of massive layoffs, when viewed in the long term such displacement is not significant to the future of the economy. These mature industries simply don't make the same contribution to overall wealth that they once did and in the future their impact will only decrease.

After the mild slowdown in economic growth from late 1994 into early 1997, we should see the economy begin to surge again from late 1997 on. It will be a healthy surge but with challenges from the Asian crisis to tensions with Iraq to a likely mild near-term rise in inflation. But you can expect even more dramatic growth around 2002 to 2003, as I explained in the section on the spending wave.

We've talked thus far about how new technologies moving mainstream and the peak spending years of new generations create the explosive emergence of new economies, as in the Roaring Twenties. In this chapter, I will show how predictable that process is, how it is driven by new entrepreneurial generations that appear every other generation or about every 80 years, and how the information revolution will move much more rapidly into the mainstream in the coming decade.

ALTERNATING GENERATION CYCLES

Generations alternate between two extremes: from individualistic, entrepreneurial, inner-directed generations to conformist, civic-minded, outer-directed generations. This cycle has been established in great detail in the book *Generations,* and in its sequel, *The Fourth Turning.* Strauss and Howe point out that each successive generation reacts to the qualities of the one before it in its rebellious, adolescent years, and that this causes the swing in generational personalities and in the generation gap that naturally exists between parents and children. It's not just an age difference, it is a difference in personality, outlook, values, and approach to life. It is a difference in the times and the environment that shapes each generation.

The importance of this phenomenon for the economy is very critical and very practical. Individualistic, entrepreneurial generations usher in radical new technologies, economies, and social trends. The conformist generations, like the Bob Hope generation of World War II, bring the innovative products into the mainstream, making them affordable to the average consumer, thus saturating the market to the point in which there is a diminishing return on gains in growth and productivity. As a result, a new wave of innovative products and technologies is needed to stimulate growth and progress again.

However, it takes a few decades for such innovations to join the mainstream economy and bring the next new productivity revolution. In the meantime, the productivity of the old economy declines, as companies downsize, industries consolidate, and the new, innovative companies are not yet fully able to take up the slack. The sense of chaos is fueled by the confusing transition from the old to the new, exactly as we've seen in the last few decades.

The individualistic baby-boom generation dominating our economy now, like the Henry Ford generation that dominated the early 1900s and Roaring Twenties, is in the midst of the experimentation that will give birth to the new economy. This economic birth is always a messy process, just like human birth. That's one reason innovative generations always look a little crazy, indulgent, and reckless to their conformist parents.

Thus, we see that new economies emerge every two generations. The first generation consists of the entrepreneurs and innovators who create new industries. The second generation is made up of the institution builders who systematically help the innovative industries to mature, so that they reach full mass-market penetration. Their roles and personalities are very different — and they're supposed to be.

It is a very fruitful dynamic for the economy, but it's difficult for those who see themselves on opposite sides of the fence. Such generations never understand each other or respect each other's values. In particular, this dynamic explains why the conformist generations always think the world is going to hell in a handbasket as they age. Every aspect of their perfect "Lawrence Welk, Leave It to Beaver" world gets attacked and threatened, including moral values, institutions, management, and work methods.

THE GENERATION WAVE: THREE STAGES TO AN ECONOMIC REVOLUTION

Every 80 years, a new entrepreneurial generation ushers in a new set of technologies, social trends, and industries in a predictable three-stage process. The waves, illustrated in Figure 2.1, are an innovation wave, a spending wave, and a power wave.

The first stage, the *innovation wave,* occurs as the new generation enters the work force. Young people are society's innovators. As they enter the work force and become the new consumers and the new workers, they bring radical changes in technologies, social values, and consumer trends. Such entrepreneurial generations do not respect or follow past traditions, but experiment with new approaches, often

The Generation Wave

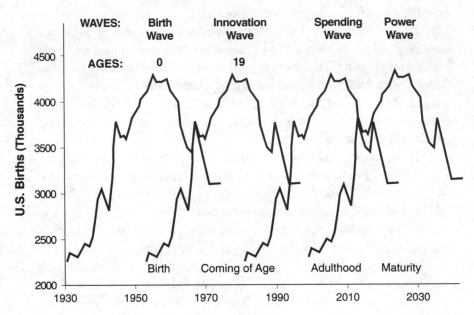

Figure 2.1: The Generation Wave.

Figure 2.1 shows the three predictable waves of the innovative process that happens when an entrepreneurial generation initiates new technologies, industries, and social trends.

---

foolishly. Imagine you are Orville and Wilbur Wrights' parents and your kids are in the back yard trying to fly! What would you think? Yet we know that this is the only way to innovate: You experiment in a chaotic process until a breakthrough occurs!

It's not that members of conformist generations don't innovate, especially in their youth. They do, but their innovations tend to be incremental. They extend the industries and technologies of the previous generation, rather than direct them in entirely new directions. In this way, they improve the best ideas of the radical generation by helping them to achieve mainstream popularity.

For example, the last entrepreneurial generation, the Henry Ford generation, brought unprecedented products and services into the economy: cars, electricity, phones, airplanes, movies, Coca-Cola, and

aspirin, to name but a few. The Bob Hope generation, which suc-
ceeded them, introduced the jet engine to make air travel faster. They
developed power brakes, power steering, and automatic transmission
to make cars easier to drive and more comfortable. They added many
new types of home appliances, like TVs, clothes washers and dryers
and dishwashers. These were significant additions to innovative products, which greatly extended the airplane, automobile, and electri-
cal-appliance industries to help them capture much more of the
mainstream market.

THE LAST ECONOMIC REVOLUTION:
THE HENRY FORD GENERATION

We can clearly attribute the dramatic advance in our standard of
living over the last two generations to the radical innovations of the
Henry Ford generation. Not only did most of our modern products,
services, and conveniences — things that we take for granted today —
emerge only in this last revolution, but our standard of living, adjusted
for inflation, has grown nine times since the first phone was invented.

Let's take a closer look at that economic revolution. We'll see
that it unfolded in a predictable three-stage fashion:

- The *innovation wave,* when new products and services make their
  way into niche markets.
- The *spending wave,* when the economy booms and the race for
  leadership in emerging new industries heats up.
- The *power wave,* when organizational change and a revolution in
  work secure the mainstream position of the new economy and
  create a productivity surge.

The Innovation Wave: A New Economy Dominates Niche Markets

Between the invention of the first phones in 1876 and the Model
T in 1907, there was a surge in innovation that created most of our
Fortune 500 companies, and the mass-market brand-name products
and services we recognize instantly today. Figure 2.2 shows a graph of
a broad sample of such companies and brand names. It's reproduced
from *Entrepreneurs,* a book that traces the history of the corporate

giants to their origin as entrepreneurial start-ups. The peak of that innovation wave occurred at about the turn of the century, approximately 80 years before the peak of the incredible start-up and Initial Public Offering (IPO) boom into the late 1970s and early 1980s that launched many of the companies driving our new economy. Those were the peak years of work-force entry of the Henry Ford generation.

In the last chapter, I gave the specific example of the S-curve

---

Figure 2.2: Birth of Mass Market Brand Names.

Figure 2.2 shows a broad sample of the companies and brand names that trace their origins to the innovative Henry Ford generation.
Source: *Entrepreneurs,* Joseph and Suzy Fuchini.

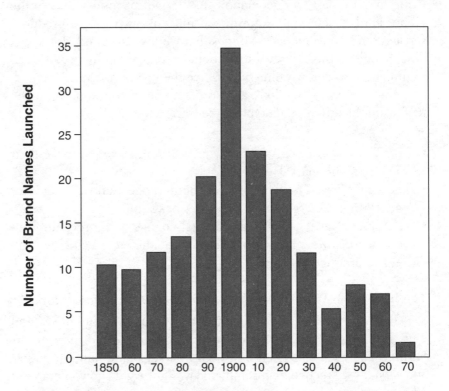

Birth of Mass Market Brand Names

progression of the automobile industry. Cars exploded in popularity, becoming mainstream consumer items, after World War I and into the Roaring Twenties. Now, imagine all of the numerous innovative products, services, and industries — from cars to phones, from electrical motors and appliances to movies and cameras, from skyscrapers to indoor plumbing — moving into the economy on a similar S-curve progression from the early 1900s into the Roaring Twenties. Imagine them suddenly becoming affordable to the average consumer, followed by the fervor to buy! That's exactly how approximately 3 percent of the companies can create a booming economy — more than compensating for the losses generated by the old industries which are downsizing at an accelerating rate. It happened in the Roaring Twenties, and it's beginning to happen again, 80 years later.

The Spending Wave: The Race for Leadership in the Emerging Industries Stimulates an Economic Boom

Chapter 1 showed how the economy booms when the new generation begins to form families and spend their incomes in greater amounts. The key insight we gain from this fact is that the new generation's spending power drives the new technologies, products, and industries out of niche markets into the mainstream. Such products, once only affordable to the most affluent segments of the new generation — the yuppies of today — move within reach of the average consumer. The cachet of these innovative items, gained from their niche-market appeal, makes them desirable. The reduced production cost achieved through the application of new technology makes them affordable.

This trend clearly occurred for cars and many new products in the early decades of this century, peaking in the Roaring Twenties. The spending wave of the Henry Ford Generation that first drove today's Fortune 500 and mass-market products into the mainstream lasted from about 1900 to 1929. As new products and services move rapidly into mainstream markets, companies compete for leadership within their industries. The more each leading company grows, the more it will enjoy greater economies of scale and brand-name advantages, making it impossible for marginal companies to compete. After the spending wave peaks, the downturn in the economy will shake out the few inefficient competitors that are left.

Let me return to the car industry to show how the race for leadership played out in a way very different from that which most experts forecast. Ford dominated the innovation wave in cars, developing the Model T in 1907, which was the first car designed from standardized parts. Ford pioneered the first successful assembly-line production plant in 1914. As late as 1921, well into the spending wave, Ford dominated cars almost as much as Intel and Microsoft dominate high-technology markets today. In 1921, Ford had captured 50 percent of the market for cars, while General Motors was a distant second with only a 12 percent share.

Yet who is the leader in cars today, both in the U.S. and worldwide? GM. This can't possibly be attributed to their incredibly inept, overly bureaucratized management of the past few decades. It all happened in eight years, between 1921 and 1929. In 1921, Alfred Sloan took leadership of GM while the company was in crisis. He completely revamped the organization by extending Henry Ford's assembly-line concepts far beyond the factory floor and applying it to all departments. Sloan created a broader line of trade-up brands to exploit the rising purchasing power of a new generation of consumers. By 1929, General Motors had 50 percent of the car market, and has dominated it ever since. The company made a profit in every year of the Great Depression, the shake-out period, due to its absorption of market share from failing competitors, its superbly responsive management, and the soundness of its financial structures.

Most of our present-day Fortune 500 companies were established around the turn of the century during an incredible surge in innovation. The leaders of such new industries that rapidly, and unexpectedly, emerged in the mainstream economy had established their top position in the Roaring Twenties. In our own time, we will see the same thing: The next decade will establish the leaders in the vital industries of the new economy for many decades to come.

In the race for leadership characteristic of the spending wave, success becomes less a matter of who has the best product or technological innovation, and more a matter of who can bring the new products into the mainstream the fastest.

The Power Wave: A Revolution in Management and Work

The real productivity revolution that finally secures the mainstream position of the new economy only occurs in the third and final stage. When the new generation moves into the corporate power structure, it stimulates a revolution in business practices that truly exploits the economic advantages of the new technologies. This revolution catapults the new technologies and industries into the mainstream, making them affordable to the average consumer.

It was the assembly-line revolution beginning in 1914 — just as the Henry Ford generation was first moving into its power years — that made cars and many other commodities affordable for most people. In the first year of assembly-line operation alone, Ford cut the price of the Model T in half while doubling the wages of his workers. The assembly-line organizational model was a radical departure from the job shop and craft production systems. It proliferated throughout the economy from 1914 to 1945, transforming a multitude of industries and institutions in its wake. Manufacturers, retail stores, service companies, schools, hospitals, and government agencies all adopted the segmented, hierarchical approach that was characteristic of Henry Ford's assembly line.

The power wave of the Henry Ford generation created the unprecedented productivity rates that initially averaged 5 percent in the Roaring Twenties and 3 percent into the 1960s, dramatically raising both corporate profits and wages. The assembly-line revolution also determined who the new Fortune 500 would be in the race for leadership into 1929, as it quickly became the key competitive weapon in business. Henry Ford started that work revolution, but General Motors finished it. By 1929, GM beat Ford at his own game.

Are you wondering what the next version of the assembly-line revolution will be? You need look no further than the personal computer and modem you use every day. The vast, powerful, and intricate electronic communications network known as the Internet represents the key productivity lever that will drive the new economy. In the coming decade, we will undoubtedly see an even greater productivity revolution than that of the Roaring Twenties.

THE BABY-BOOM INFORMATION REVOLUTION

Today, we are witnessing an even greater revolution than the one that fueled the Roaring Twenties. Unusually large, young, entrepreneurial generations emerge every 500 years or so. The baby-boom generation is the largest generation by far to enter the American economy. The birth and population explosion worldwide was even greater. These massive generations create massive revolutions that are far more extensive in scope and intensive in effect than the 80-year *technology* revolutions.

The Information Revolution inaugurated by the baby boomers is just about to enter its most powerful stage. This is the confluence of two trends: the peak of the spending wave of the baby-boom generation and the first emergence of the power wave, which will create a huge surge in productivity. The 15 years from 1994 to 2009 will be much like 1914 to 1929, but on a much larger scale. The enormous baby-boom generation, much larger than the Henry Ford generation, has enormous buying power. And the new communications technologies are truly amazing. If history considers the assembly line to be a dramatic innovation, just imagine how it will judge Internet technology and network organization structures decades from now!

Let's trace this new Information Revolution in the three stages of the generation wave. We'll see how it is unfolding just like the last one, on a much broader scale.

The Baby Boom Innovation Wave: The Revolution in Technology and Society from 1956 to 1983

In the three decades from 1956 to 1983, we witnessed two profound revolutions: a technological revolution and a social revolution. The first serious mainframe computers were introduced in the mid-1950s and, within 30 years, the first serious personal computers were introduced by Apple: the Apple II, in 1977, and the Macintosh, in 1984. This technological revolution coincided with a sweeping social revolution: Elvis and the beatniks were the icons of popular culture in the mid-1950s, the Beatles and hippies were the next wave from the late 1960s into the 1970s, while affluent and acquisitive yuppies became the icons of pop culture in the mid-1980s.

Almost every company in the top 3 percent growth companies, the companies that are now fueling our economic growth, were innovative start-ups in this period of rapid transition — from Intel to Apple to MicroSoft, from Starbucks Coffee to Celestial Seasonings to Ben and Jerry's, from the Sharper Image to the Nature Company to Smith and Hawken, from Levis to Benetton to Giorgio Armani . . . and even the larger-scale discount competitors in many older industries, from Wal-Mart to Home Depot to Charles Schwab to Nucor Steel.

This new economy is now emerging into the mainstream very rapidly on the predictable S-curve path described in Chapter 1. Have you noticed all of the Starbucks and specialty espresso and coffee shops everywhere in just the last 5 years or so? And, of course, more basic new technologies like personal computers, fax machines, and cellular phones are also proliferating. They're in the growth phase of the S-curve, just as cars, electricity, and phones became ubiquitous during the Roaring Twenties.

THE BABY-BOOM SPENDING WAVE: THE ECONOMIC BOOM FROM 1982 TO 2009

Baby boomers started driving the bull economy and stock markets beginning in late 1982. They will continue to do so until around mid-2009, as discussed in Chapter 1. This new generation, which has the purchasing power to dominate the consumer market, is popularizing all of the innovative products and social trends introduced in the 1960s and 1970s. By the top of this economic boom, we will see a new set of corporate leaders, as new companies race for the leadership position of new markets. After 2009, we will see an extended economic contraction that will further cement the positions of the leading companies, and weed out the few remaining contenders that aren't strong enough to go the distance. This is exactly what occurred during the Great Depression.

Many people will be surprised to see more large, established companies suddenly in trouble — not merely downsizing, but rapidly losing market share. On the other hand, the nimblest of our larger companies will see the urgency of moving into new markets and adopting the network organizational model that will sustain their leadership. The best will continue to realize the urgency of moving their more mature, standardized products and services into the international markets, especially into the emerging third-world countries that are successfully industrializing.

The Baby Boom Power Wave: The Network Revolution from 1994 to 2021

As the baby boomers attain the most powerful positions in society and industry, and as computers and online services become mainstream consumer items, we will finally see the beginning of the real Internet age, summarized in Part 2. Astute economic observers may have already noticed the accuracy of the 80-year generation wave: The Internet gained public prominence and seeped into the top management ranks of Microsoft in 1994, exactly 80 years, or two generations, after Henry Ford constructed the first successful assembly-line plant.

The Internet will facilitate the introduction of the network organizational model in our companies and institutions in the coming decade and beyond. This new organizational model, and the technology it is based on, will change how we work and live more than at any time in history. The network model will create companies that truly run from the customer back. Every customer will be a market, and every employee will be a business. Expect to see phenomenal productivity gains in the coming decade. These gains will not only raise business profits, but push wages to new highs. For the first time, middle class workers will begin to share the rewards, since wage increases won't just go to the highly educated and technologically literate, as they have in the past two decades.

The companies that most effectively and most rapidly adopt the new network organizational model will win the race for leadership in their industries, just as GM eclipsed Ford in the Roaring Twenties. Therefore, we could see a whole new set of leaders in the growth sectors of older industries, such as specialty coffees, and in the new industries, such as personal computers and software. These leading companies will be the ones to work for and to invest in if you want to be one of the first to profit from the next information revolution. Ultimately, we will all work for such companies because those left behind — the sluggish, conservative, corporate giants — will continue to downsize at an accelerated pace, while many expand dramatically overseas.

THE NEW CUSTOMIZED ECONOMY

Figure 2.3 shows that we are about to see an entirely new economy emerge that will change virtually everything—from the types of products and services that thrive, to essential jobs and skills, to organizational structures and management practices, even where we live and play. This paradigm shift can be summarized this way: We are moving from a standardized economy powered by assembly-line organizations that used powered machinery to automate physical

Figure 2.3: The Customized Economy Emerges.

Every two generations, or about every 80 years, we make the transition to a new economy. Soon, information technologies and the network organizational model will catapult us into an economy of increasingly affordable customized goods and services, just as powered machinery and assembly-line organizations made standardized products and services mass affordable in the last century.

The Emerging Customized Economy

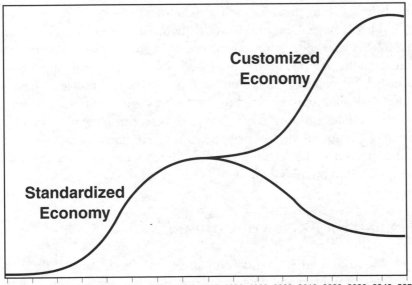

work, to a customized economy powered by network organizations that use computers to automate routine thinking work.

The real revolution will not be technological. Computers, software, and the Internet are only the infrastructure that will facilitate substantive changes in how we work and live. Oddly, these technologies will return us to the intimacy of personalized customer service and craftsmanship that were swallowed up by huge assembly lines, while retaining the incredible economies of scale of the past era.

In work, we will see a return to customer focus (as opposed to an emphasis on functional skills), the resurgence of small, dynamic work teams, and more value placed on creative, right-brain, entrepreneurial skills. The result will be that customized quality in products and personalized service will become the norm, and increasingly affordable for the average consumer. In our lives, we will see a high-tech return to small-town living, with increased political participation and decision-making in our local communities, more diverse lifestyles, and a lower cost of living with higher quality, due to less congestion and pollution. More rural areas will be linked into global information and entertainment that provide access to the larger world.

The sophisticated communication technologies that are driving the current information revolution will make our world more human: creative, interactive, and intimate. It won't make our world more machinelike, bureaucratic, and overwhelming.

This is hardly the future world pictured in most movies. They depict Schwarzeneggerlike superhumans fighting giant robotic machines in the polluted haze of destroyed cities. These horrifying visions overlook the fact that computers (and most new technologies) have a unique attribute as compared to the technologies introduced during most of modern history: They get more powerful by getting smaller. Small is beautiful in the new economy. Human interactivity and creativity will come to the fore while bureaucracy and technocracy disappear into the background.

FINDING HIGH-GROWTH COMPANIES

Microsoft and Intel are companies that create large-scale standards for computers and networks. True, they have grown very rapidly and are enormously successful, but they don't epitomize the companies that will thrive in the new network economy.

Starbucks Coffee, on the other hand, does. It offers a specialty or customized product, and makes it available and affordable to everyday consumers. Companies such as Starbucks focus on meeting the needs of specialized or more quality-sensitive markets. They don't tend to face extreme competition or get the media coverage that the high-tech and entertainment sectors do, but they tend to practice the principles of the new network corporation and, hence, give workers and suppliers the ability to move into the new economy.

It is the high-growth companies, just 3 percent of the companies in both high-tech and low-tech industries, that will retrain our work-

Figure 2.4: Standard, Premium, and Discount Trends.

You can find these promising companies in any industry by using Figure 2.4. Always look for job and investment opportunities in the industries you're familiar with first. There is typically far less competition outside the well-known high-tech and glitzy entertainment industries.

Standard, Premium, and Discount Trends

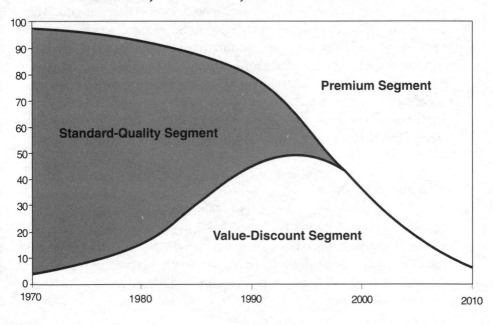

force. It is this tiny fraction that will usher all of us into the network world that encourages right-brain, entrepreneurial skills. These companies will also see the greatest gains in stock value over the next 10 to 12 years, especially the ones that become the large new leaders.

In most industries, you can identify the more promising companies for work and investment by using Figure 2.4. As we have been moving from the old standardized economy to the new customized economy, a predictable dynamic has and will continue to occur among three types of companies. These include:

- Standard companies, such as General Motors, Coca-Cola, McDonald's, and Sears
- Discount companies, such as Wal-Mart or Domino's Pizza, or Charles Schwab
- Premium companies such as Giorgio Armani and Starbucks Coffee

Standard Companies

The standard companies, or mass-market leaders of the 1960s — General Motors, Ford and Chrysler, Sears and Montgomery Ward — have typically been shrinking and losing market share since the early 1970s. Their success in the 1950s and 1960s left them vulnerable: Management grew complacent, and they had invested huge amounts of capital in technologies and organizational systems that were quickly becoming obsolete. Some of them, such as Sears and Pizza Hut, have revived in recent years and are gaining market share again. They are still the most likely candidates for becoming the railroads of the next era, as the customized economy and information technologies move mainstream for the first time, unless they make bold moves like Sears into specialty retailing. The most successful leaders are booming in international markets selling to 5 billion new customers in emerging countries.

Discount Companies

The discount or mass-market price leaders like Wal-Mart, Toyota, Domino's Pizza, or Charles Schwab have gained market share in maturing markets. They have accomplished this by re-engineering, or by adopting the best in new technologies and management practices. As a result, they are able to offer consumers standardized products or services at lower prices, and often with better service to boot.

These discount companies created most of the jobs and the greatest collective increase in investment profits in the 1970s and 1980s. Since 1992, companies like Wal-Mart and Home Depot have seen flat stock prices. Traditional standard companies have become more competitive and the market has become more saturated. For example, the period between 1979 and 1992 represented the 10 to 90 percent S-curve growth for Wal-Mart.

The discount and re-engineering trends have already largely transformed the maturing, standardized sectors of our economy. This was the key economic trend of the past two decades and created the greatest opportunities in employment and investment.

Premium Companies

The most important trend in the coming two decades will be that the new, high-tech and customizing companies will rise more rapidly on the S-curve. Many companies in this premium segment will reach the mainstream market, expanding beyond the niche markets they carved for themselves in the 1970s and 1980s. This is where the real opportunities for both employment and investment will mushroom in the future.

Most people tend to think that premium companies are high-tech companies. Some of them are, but there are many more areas of growth outside the high-tech field. These include health care, entertainment and communications, specialty restaurants, outsource and consulting services for business, specialty manufacturing components, energy and plastics, quality and testing equipment, and aerospace. To create a strategic advantage in customization or quality, these companies tend to embrace new computer technology and network organizational principles; they heavily decentralize information and decision-making. This makes these companies the best for which to work. Not only are they prospering, they also offer plenty of opportunity for training in new skills and responsibilities.

Many premium companies won't remain confined to their small, niche markets for much longer. They will become mainstream industries, becoming the dominant source of new jobs and investment profits in the Roaring 2000s.

Here is a list of some of the best and more notable companies that have already moved out of niche markets into the mainstream or are in the process of doing so. Use this partial list to investigate compa-

nies in your area of expertise for career and investment opportunities.
Remember, there are many more local or regional growth industries
with consumer visibility. But there are far more less-visible specialty
manufacturers and service companies to choose from, too.

PREMIUM HIGH-TECH COMPANIES: Microsoft, Intel, Dell, Gateway
2000, Cisco Systems, Hewlett-Packard, Compaq, Acer, Sun Microsystems, Oracle, Netscape, Nokia, Novell, Apple, Toshiba, NEC,
Sega, 3Com, Broadband, IBM, Teledisc.

PREMIUM CONSUMER COMPANIES: Starbucks Coffee, The Coffee
Beanery, Häagen-Dazs, Ben & Jerry's, The Nature Company, Celes-
tial Seasonings, Mrs. Field's, La Petite Boulangerie, Blockbuster, Ar-
mani Exchange, Donna Karan, Sunglass Hut, The Monterey Pasta
Company, Odwalla Juices, Snapple, Evian, Tea Java, Arizona Iced
Tea, Calistoga Waters, Hansen's, Panda Express, Sharper Image,
Benetton, Mondavi Winery, *Investor's Business Daily* newspaper,
Wired magazine, *Worth* magazine, *Condé Nast Traveler* magazine,
The Wine Spectator, Afficionado (cigars), CNN, CNBC (financial
news network of CNN), TCI (cable TV), Boston Brewing Company
(Samuel Adams beer), Nordstrom, Barnes and Noble, and Borders
bookstores and cafes.

The key to prosperity in careers and investments is simply to find
the *growing 3 percent*— those companies generating new jobs in our
country and a higher rate of investment return. Most people only
look to the prominent companies of the past, which may be a good
investment especially if they are doing business overseas, but that
aren't creating new employment opportunities in this country.

THE REAL CAUSES OF INFLATION

There is another important economic variable that we can attribute to the generation wave and to the emergence of new economies:
inflation. Before we understand this, there are two myths about inflation that need debunking. The first is that growth causes inflation and
the second is that debt causes inflation. Neither is true.

Economists think that growth causes inflation. This is simply not the case, except in some short-term economic booms where scarcity in capacity, materials, and labor will cause inflationary pressures. However, in many boom periods like 1982 to 1986 and 1993 to 1997 this did not occur. In fact, if you look carefully at the course of history for the last 3000 years, it is clear that great boom periods do not tend to be inflationary. This is evident just in the last century. The greatest three boom periods were 1921 to 1929, 1950 to 1965, and 1982 to 1990. The Roaring Twenties saw a zero rate of inflation for the entire decade. The 1950s and early 1960s saw a zero to 2 percent rate of inflation. The 1980s saw dramatically falling inflation rates! Growth clearly does not cause inflation.

There is the other popular argument that debt and government deficits cause inflation. According to this notion, we borrow from our

---

Figure 2.5: Growth in Nonfinancial U.S. Debt.

Figure 2.5 shows the growth of debt in the U.S. economy from the 1960s through the early 1990s.

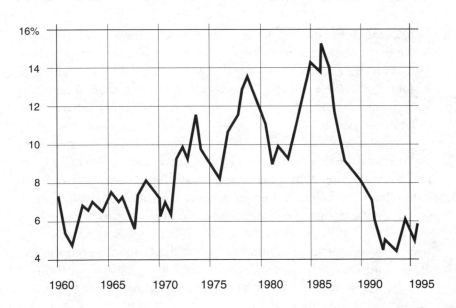

Nonfinancial U.S. Debt
Annual Growth

1000 Years of Inflation

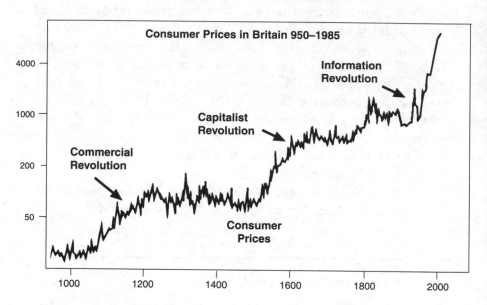

Consumer Prices in Britain 950–1985

Figure 2.6: 1000 Years of Inflation.

Figure 2.6 illustrates the coincidence of periods of massive inflation and periods of major technological innovation.

---

future and, in the process, destroy the financial system and the moral fabric of our society. Sounds logical, but this one is also easy to refute. For example, Figure 2.5 shows the growth of debt in recent U.S. history. From 1980 to 1986, debt accelerated more than at any time in U.S. history. But during the same period of time, inflation fell dramatically.

What *does* cause inflation? The development of radical new technologies and the entrance of the young new generations that bring them into the workforce. Other than war periods, the greatest periods of inflation have coincided with major periods of technological innovation.

Figure 2.6 illustrates how broad-scale inflation hits the economy every 400 to 500 years. We can see the inflation wave that accompanied the commercial revolution following the Crusades from the late 1000s into the early 1200s. It also shows the massive inflation in the late 1400s and 1500s that accompanied the capitalist revolution following the invention of the printing press. That was clearly the greatest inflationary period prior to this one. It has been exceeded only by the inflation of the twentieth century, which coincided with the beginning stages of the information revolution. Following the inflation of the fifteenth century, there was also moderately strong inflation in the late 1700s, just after the invention of the steam engine. It should come as no surprise that this period of inflation coincided with the beginning of the Industrial Revolution in England.

The lesson? Inflation is a sign of progress in the making, not the destruction of our monetary system and our moral fiber. Inflation is our economy's means of financing an economic revolution. The higher the inflation, the greater the revolution and growth to follow. We have just witnessed the greatest relative inflation rates in history. The massive inflation peaking in the late 1970s was just another clear sign that the greatest economic boom in our history was just ahead.

Think about it for a minute. Doesn't it take a huge investment to raise children before they become productive members of society?

Figure 2.7: The Inflation Indicator.

Figure 2.7 shows how closely the rate of inflation tracks the growth in the labor force, which is a reflection of the incorporation of a new generation and its innovations into the economy, entailing massive investments in new infrastructures.

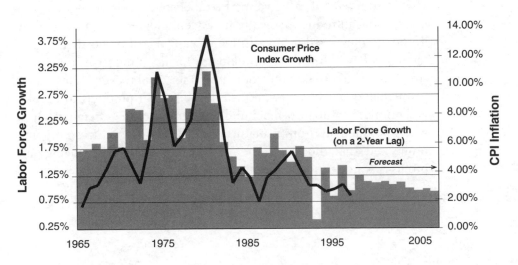

Doesn't it take a huge investment to launch a new business before it generates its own cash flows to sustain itself? Then, why wouldn't it take a massive investment to launch a whole new economy? It does every 80 years, especially every 500 years, when massive revolutions occur.

Figure 2.7 shows that inflation correlates very closely with changes in the growth of the labor force. The labor force naturally expands during the innovation wave that occurs when a new generation enters the job market. That's why President Carter was no more responsible for the highest inflation rates in history than President Bush was responsible for the recession of 1990 to 1991. Baby boomers created both the inflation and the recession.

Three basic factors conspire to create expanding inflation when an entrepreneurial generation is entering the work force.

- First, the new technologies they introduce force organizations of all sizes to retool to remain competitive, which requires capital investment.
- Second, the new generation launches many new companies, which require an infusion of capital before they become self-supporting.
- Third, and most important, the new generation of workers suddenly elevates the demand for commercial infrastructures — from office space to factories to warehouses for work, and malls and stores of all kinds for personal shopping and entertainment — which requires a huge capital investment by businesses and government.

In summary, it is the young members of an entrepreneurial generation that introduce radically new technologies into an economy. To do so, they need a huge influx of capital just when their rate of savings is low. They drive up demand for investments in new infrastructure, which makes the competition for capital even stiffer. These two demands for capital — from innovators with products to develop and from the companies that build the infrastructure — occur at a time when productivity from a maturing old economy reduces corporate profits and wage increases. The result is that capital from savings and profits is scarce just when it's needed most.

THE THREE PHASES OF AN EMERGING NEW ECONOMY, AND THE FAMILY SPENDING CYCLE

The emergence of a new economy also coincides with the family-spending cycle. This gives us yet another view of what causes inflation.

The First Phase

In the earliest phase of innovation, inflation is like an equity investment, or a forced public-savings program. The business sector's need for cash flow imposes an inflation tax on consumers. We pay to retool our economy now, and benefit from the rewards, which include more jobs and greater productivity, later. Similarly, in the earliest phases of household formation when young people are getting married, entering the workforce, and moving into their own apartments, they don't have the option to borrow money to finance their basic living needs. Finally, new businesses who need to raise venture capital can't borrow much in the earliest stages of the company's growth because the business has not yet stabilized and demonstrated a predictable growth pattern.

Debt financing in this first phase is not a viable means for either new families or new businesses to finance the huge capital investments required to launch a new economy and incorporate a new generation into the workforce. High inflation at such a time forces an equity investment in new ventures through venture capital and in consumer infrastructures through inflation. We see moderating real growth and low levels of productivity.

The Second Phase

The second phase sees falling inflation and rising debt, due to finance growth and investment. As members of the new generation age into their late twenties and thirties, they begin to finance their investment in housing and durable goods with debt because they can. They are more established financially, and have an easier time qualifying for loans and credit cards. The new companies become more established and can borrow to meet much of their needs for capital to grow and retool. Junk-bond financing by Michael Milken and others fueled the growth of many of the very companies that are creating our growth and jobs today, and will dominate our economy even more in the coming decade.

Let's not forget the role of the government. It sees a booming economy and falling inflation rates as consumers are spending and borrowing, as occurred in the 1980s. This makes it more politically attractive to borrow money instead of raising taxes, money which the government needs to fund its growing infrastructure and to finance the transition to a new economy. For example, some of the costs we can attribute to an economy in transition include a higher welfare budget to accommodate individuals who are losing their jobs. It also includes the mushrooming military budget in an age when technological shifts aggravate military tensions and produce a cold war as occurred increasingly in the 1970s. The growing economy, expanding tax base, and falling interest rates make this approach feasible, at least up to a point.

The second phase of an emerging new economy sees rising debt to finance investment and growth, falling inflation rates, and continued low but improving productivity rates. This is exactly what happened in the 1980s.

The Third Phase

In the third phase, as we'll see in the coming decade, productivity surges as the new technologies move mainstream, following the S-curve pattern. At the same time, a revolution in business organization and management leverages the new technologies to increase productivity, wages, and profits. The high profits in the new growth companies and the wage gains earned by families as they enter their peak spending years create high cash flow for investment and growth, with less need for equity or debt financing.

The third phase sees very high rates of productivity, low or flat inflation rates, and falling debt ratios. This is attributable to the coincidence of the maturing phase of the family spending cycle and the business life cycle, which together generate ample cash flow for growth and investment.

It should be obvious at this point that a simple understanding of the generation wave is critical. It helps us put history in perspective, and makes it possible to confidently forecast the future. When we will spend, save, go into debt, experience inflation, spawn new technological and social innovations, and reinvent work and organizations is all entirely predictable.

THE INTERNATIONAL BOOM
IN THIRD-WORLD COUNTRIES

The customized economy will become the dominant growth path in the most developed countries. These countries already have high standards of living, and already have saturated their markets with standardized products and services. This new economy has and will continue to emerge faster in the United States, and to a slightly lesser degree in Canada, due to a stronger entrepreneurial ethic and the more rapid adoption of computer-network technology. The regions where customization and high tech will begin emerging include Western Europe, Israel, Japan, Australia, New Zealand, and the most affluent sectors of the newly industrialized countries of the Pacific Rim, such as Hong Kong, Singapore, Taiwan, and South Korea.

The baby-boom generations in Canada, Australia, New Zealand, and the Pacific Rim countries, excluding Japan, are very similar in relative size and approximate spending peaks. Therefore, those economies will follow our trends closely. Australia will experience a much milder downturn, because of their sustained birthrate and immigration figures after the early 1960s. The rates at which Canada, Australia, and New Zealand are adopting high technology will give their economies a productivity and growth advantage. Canada's proximity to the U.S., and Australia and New Zealand's proximity to the booming Pacific Rim, also gives these countries strong growth potential. However, their governments are typically more protective of older industries, with the exception of Great Britain. As a result, these countries have a less dynamic entrepreneurial sector and higher unemployment rates, something like Europe, which has similar protectionist policies.

Japan's generation trends are very different, due to World War II. Japan had a baby boom into World War II, but not afterward in the 1950s. Its generation cycle is directly counter to that in the U.S. — out of phase by about 20 years. Japan had something like our conformist Bob Hope generation, which excelled at hierarchical organization and management, that peaked in its spending around 1989 to 1990. That is why Japan's stock market collapsed, and its economy has been much weaker ever since. Generational spending trends won't turn up strongly for Japan until around 2008, and then they will be booming again when growth in the U.S. turns down after 2009.

Japan will provide an area of equity growth and diversification for investors when trends turn down in the U.S. equity markets after 2009, as will Europe, to a lesser degree.

Most of Europe was thrown off cycle by World War II, but not for as long a period of time as was Japan. It took 5 to 8 years for the baby-boom cycles to kick in. European countries did not have as strong a baby boom. Their birth rates per capita tend to be smaller, on average, than those in the U.S.

France has little growth potential from baby-boom demographics, Germany has mild potential for growth, and Great Britain and Spain have the strongest growth potential. Northern Italy boasts leadership in the high-fashion industry and a rising standard of living, but its economy is being dragged down by southern Italy. Great Britain is likely to be the strongest major growth country in Europe due to its greater fiscal discipline and deregulation, and to its high-technology advantage as an English-speaking nation. Economic trends in the next two decades should be positive for Europe, though not nearly as strong as in the U.S. Many European countries will still be booming mildly after 2009 into 2013 to 2017, after the U.S. peaks.

Thus, the new economy will emerge in the highly industrialized, developed countries. The U.S. will be the leader in high tech and customization. Baby-boom demographics will strongly favor countries like Canada, Australia, New Zealand, and newly industrialized countries of the Pacific Rim. Demographics will not favor Japan in the coming decade, and will see only mild growth in most of Europe. Europe and especially Japan should outperform the U.S. after its peak in 2009.

INDUSTRIALIZATION IN DEVELOPING COUNTRIES

While more than 1 billion people in the developed countries move into the new customized, information-driven economy, much of the rest of the world will be moving into the standardized economy we entered in the last century. The major difference is that industrialization will tend to happen faster for these countries because they can benefit from our management skills and experience, new technologies, and an influx of capital.

Since these countries are growing from very low standards of living and per capita incomes and they have much larger populations, their growth will continue to be higher on average than countries in the developed world. But these countries will see more political and economic volatility, which makes for a trickier investment choice.

The greatest growth and opportunities will come from emerging countries in the Far East, South America, East Europe, and select areas of Africa, roughly in that order of potential. These countries will provide renewed growth opportunities for the maturing multinational companies that dominate these new markets like Coca-Cola, McDonald's, Gillette, and General Electric. However, these countries will also experience greater political volatility as we have seen in Asia recently and in Latin America earlier. Think of them as the adolescents of the booming world economy. They will create fewer jobs in this country and offer riskier investment opportunities, although some of this volatility will be mitigated by our largest multinationals, who can provide diversification and currency risk management.

For most of the emerging third world, generation cycles are not the key to growth and development. Why? The standard of living and health care are so poor that only a fraction of the population lives long enough or earns enough to follow the middle-class spending cycle common in developed countries. Therefore, the first task of these countries is to industrialize and develop a middle-class living standard for broader segments of its population.

So, what you should look for in the developing world: political systems moving more towards democracy; development in free-market economies; investments in infrastructures such as power plants, roads, canals, and airports; and a growing middle-class population with living standards closer to the developed world.

China is a great example of this. It has a policy of low birth rates and zero-population growth, yet it has very high economic growth rates, but such growth is centered largely in southeast China, emanating from Hong Kong. There, people have immigrated from rural areas into cities where there are good economic infrastructures and a strong entrepreneurial spirit, while most of China still lives in rural areas with very low standards of living. Now that over 10 percent of China's population has achieved a high standard of living, the rest will follow on an accelerated S-curve trend.

What Three Millennia of Innovation and Migration Can Teach Us

Most experts cite the large populations and the strong work ethic for the unprecedented growth in Far East countries. Let me cite another reason, one of the most obvious when we take a long historical view:

The peak of civilization, which includes social, economic, technical, cultural, and political hegemony, has slowly moved over time from east to west, while remaining in the more temperate climate zones of the northern hemisphere.

Now, I don't want to raise cultural or political tensions here, but history is clear on this matter. The peak of civilization has moved in the last 3,000 years from Mojen Dari, in northern India, to Babylon and the Tigris and Euphrates Rivers (modern-day Iraq) to Egypt to the Persian Empire (including Iran and Turkey) to Greece to Rome to Spain to Great Britain to the eastern U.S. to the western U.S. Next, it will predictably migrate to the Far East, likely even more to China than Japan, and eventually back to northern India. We also saw a very advanced civilization in northern China, while Western culture was exploding.

Why the northern hemisphere? I would say due to the larger land mass and population, especially in areas with predominantly cooler temperatures. We tend to vacation in more tropical areas precisely because it counters our busy work ethic. One evolutionary theory says that since human life appears to have originated in the southern hemisphere, all or most in Africa, it's likely that the most innovative populations tended to migrate, the greatest numbers moving to warm climates in southeast Asia, smaller numbers moving north into Europe and Russia. They had to be more creative and ingenious to survive in colder, more adverse climates; hence greater technological advances. Even in the more temperate and colder climate areas of the southern hemisphere we see high standards of living in countries like Australia, New Zealand, Argentina, Chile, and South Africa. However, there is too little land mass and population in the cooler areas of the southern hemisphere for such areas to be likely to dominate world population or power. However, with the advent of air-conditioning we are starting to see booming urban societies in tropical areas from Kuala Lumpur and Singapore to southern India.

If we look at such megatrends we could have foreseen that the next explosion in standard of living and economic growth was certain to occur in the colder, more temperate zones of the Far East: Japan, China, Korea, Taiwan, Singapore, and, ultimately, northern India. That's what we see happening. This growth will occur for centuries to come, not just in the next decades. The more developed sectors of such countries, with the exception of Japan, have age demographics very similar to those of the U.S. With expanding middle-class populations that live to ages similar to the U.S., they will enjoy similar economic booms in the coming decade.

As these more temperate areas develop into strong industrial economies and middle-class demographic powerhouses, they bring growth to warmer and more southerly agricultural economies including Indonesia, Malaysia, Thailand, Vietnam, Cambodia, Burma, the Philippines, and, ultimately, to the whole of India. These countries have also begun to industrialize. They will specialize in agricultural and textile-oriented industries and in others on a selective basis. As a result, they will begin to achieve the lower ranges of middle-class living standards.

The most explosive trend in the Far East is simple. People are migrating from rural areas that offer only subsistence living to cities. This is what Americans did in the late 1800s and early 1900s as the United States was industrializing and becoming a developed country. A study by Dean Witter estimates that 1 billion people in the Far East will move from farms to cities over the next three decades. Even if only a fraction do so it will represent an enormous economic advance, bringing incredible environmental strains and demands for basic infrastructure as well.

My study of population shifts, such as American migration from the farms to the cities and from the cities to the suburbs, suggests that at least 20 percent of the population relocates during a three-decade period. This would mean that at least 650 million in Asia could be expected to move during the next 30 years. This will create a massive rise in jobs and a dramatic expansion in the basic infrastructure needed to support an industrialized economy. There will be very strong growth in local companies and in those multinational companies that can build the roads, airports, power plants, water systems, and factories. Large companies from General Electric to Enron will benefit. There will also be very strong growth in the demand for brand-name consumer products from Coca-Cola to Levi's to McDonald's.

The very same multinational companies that have dominated the mature and declining markets in the U.S. will, in the future, have the greatest ability to move standardized products and services into the expanding Far East and emerging countries around the world. The race for economic leadership in these countries will be won or lost in the coming 10 to 15 years — at exactly the same time as the race to see which companies will dominate the customized economy in developed countries will be won or lost.

A General Economic Forecast for Four Developing Areas

I've identified four developing areas that you will want to keep an eye on for investment and business-growth opportunities. The four areas are South America, Eastern Europe, Africa, and the Middle East.

South America

This continent will continue to boom, and benefit from the growth of North America, which will lead the world's transition to a customized network economy. The stock markets here have performed very well in 1996 into mid-1997. These countries have already seen a substantial population migration to major cities, from Mexico City to São Paulo. The growth will tend to be highest in the countries that offer the most temperate climate and that have made the most political progress: Argentina, Chile, Brazil, Paraguay, and Uruguay. These countries are moving increasingly into a common-trade pact and should, in the next decade, join the North American Free Trade Agreement.

Mexico will also benefit from its proximity to the United States, from NAFTA, and from its low wage rates, which make it an attractive subcontractor for certain industrial products. There is also strong growth emerging in Colombia and Peru. South America will not grow as fast as the Pacific Rim simply because of differences in the work ethic, in the adoption of high technology, and in the slower migration to urban areas at this point.

Eastern Europe

The social and political devastation in eastern Europe, which affects working conditions and management practices, is making it difficult for this area to move as fast as other areas into a free-market economy. I predicted in *The Great Boom Ahead* that there would be years of turmoil in the countries of the former Soviet Union before they turned the corner. But now the beginnings of positive trends are emerging. However, I don't recommend investment in this part of the world unless you are expert in Eastern European affairs and are willing to take strong risks. But it is where the smart money is starting to migrate. The countries that appear to have the most intermediate-term potential are Turkey, Hungary, Czechoslovakia, Poland, Russia, and, to a lesser degree, Romania.

Africa

South Africa is showing enough political progress to become a booming country in the coming decade, but there will continue to be some strife and weak sectors in the economy. Capetown is becoming a fashion center for models and the jet set. The remainder of Africa has potential to grow but is still a question mark to me. Uganda is an example of a country that was quite backward and under the rule of a tyrant, and is now showing good signs of growth and progress. Again, I would be more selective in Africa unless I was familiar with the situation.

The Middle East

I see the Middle East continuing to slowly lose power, as oil becomes less significant in our information-intensive world and as other countries, such as Russia, eventually bring new oil reserves onto world markets. The Middle East will continue to be the political powderkeg of the world for many years to come, which makes investment trickier. Saddam Hussein is almost certain to cause trouble again in the next few years. Other than Israel, which has strong positions in many niche and high-tech industries, I would be cautious about investing in the Middle East.

The coming economic boom will be worldwide, as many emerging countries move rapidly into industrialization and middle-class living standards. The Far East and Pacific Rim will still dominate world growth, but much of South America and some countries in East Europe and Africa will boom strongly. Above all, diversify your investments! This is the best way to protect yourself from the intense volatility that arises from unstable political structures and the strains of high rates of growth.

Opportunities for Work Overseas

In addition to the strong investment opportunities overseas, there will be strong job opportunities for people who are willing to work in these high-growth countries. Many will be consultants or will work for large multinational companies. Consider mastering a foreign language and taking a several-year stint in a country that interests you. For example, I recently met two people that were very happy living in Prague, Czechoslovakia, and managing The Gap there. Prague is a trendy center for arts and culture in eastern Europe.

There will also be career and investment opportunities in resort areas around the world as baby boomers move into their peak vacationing and vacation-home buying years. New technologies that will revolutionize travel and communication will make resort areas even more accessible and affordable in the coming decades.

SUMMARY

We can easily see that we are on the brink of the next information revolution, the huge and incredibly important 500-year cycle that will result in the greatest economic boom in history. The Internet represents the key innovation fueling this revolution. In the coming decades, it will support an era of unprecedented productivity, and just in time, too! In the coming decades we will move into the most powerful stage of the generation wave: the confluence of the peak spending wave with the beginning of the power wave. While this occurs in developed countries like the U.S., most of the third world will be emerging into industrialization or the standardized economy we are leaving behind. This will mean the continuation of a strong worldwide boom as well.

PART 2

Life in the
Internet Age

CHAPTER 3
The Real Information Revolution

THE STORY OF HISTORY is simple: New technologies advance our standard of living by changing how we work and live. So, the obvious question today is this: If information technology is so powerful, why hasn't our standard of living improved in the last 25 years? Hasn't it benefited only a privileged few, the most educated, the most entrepreneurial and the technologically sophisticated? The answer is yes. . . . and no.

Yes, the gap between rich and poor has grown, as it always does in the first stages of technology revolutions. For instance, the measured standard of living for the top 20 percent of society has increased substantially since 1970, that of the middle 60 percent has increased only slightly, while the standard of living of the bottom 20 percent has decreased dramatically. But, no, these measurements do *not* reflect the real gains in the quality, selection, safety, and convenience of the growing array of products and services available to most of us.

Nonetheless, it would be safe to say that the average person does not feel much better off. In fact, most people feel overwhelmed by the enormous changes in society today. In part, this is a reflection of reality: We are undergoing an enormous period of transition. In part, however, this feeling is based on our perceptions of ourselves and our economy. It's based on what information we have and what information we hear. Many people in my profession have contributed to this perception by underestimating the considerable advances in our overall standard of living. And the media has really overplayed the negative symptoms of this economic transition. In this chapter, you'll hear another view of what's happening right now. You'll hear why I predict that we're soon going to see the greatest economic boom in our history.

The principle of the S-curve, which I discuss in my book, *The Great Boom Ahead,* assures us that the trends of the past two decades will not only continue, they will accelerate. The result? The technology that has already changed a minority of lives will reach many more consumers. Attracted by products that save them time and make their lives easier, consumers will leap online. *This* will mark the beginning of the real information revolution, changing not just our social interactions but our own work as well as our interactions with the businesses that provide us products and services. In fact, the computer information revolution that's just beginning now will change our lives far more than the assembly-line revolution of the last century.

When will this begin? Just after the turn of the century, by 2001 to 2002. In the short term, we've heard a lot of hype about the Internet, exactly the kind of promotion that makes the vast majority of people question its real impact or value. But most of us, even those already on the Internet bandwagon, are greatly underestimating its impact over the long term. We won't see its real value until important innovations in ease of use reach the customer, nor will we see its real power until the *bandwidth* of the information highway, a technical term for its capacity to deliver data in a given period of time, greatly increases. These two changes, ease of use and bandwidth, are what this chapter and the next are all about. I want to give you a glimpse of the greatest technological revolution in history—and prepare you for some of the huge changes that will follow in its wake.

You might ask, "We haven't seen the information revolution yet?" Computers have been around since the 1950s! Most businesses are computerized and a majority of employees, from farmers and factory workers to clerical, sales, technical, professional, and managerial personnel, use computers in their work, but this so-called information revolution has yet to restore broad-based productivity. Nor has it dramatically improved most of our lives.

The secret to understanding technological change and how technology changes us is to understand how innovative products and services become mainstream. Or, more to the point, how we adopt new technologies in a *predictable* way. For example, some of the first industrial products of the late nineteenth century, including electricity, lighting, cars, telephones, and electric motors, were used in businesses long before they were used in the home. There was no dramatic economic boom or productivity gain until the Roaring Twenties, when these innovations became consumer products, ubiquitous in home and business. The lesson: Revolutions in productivity and our standard of living lag behind the introduction of new technologies. It takes three to four decades for innovative products and services to become popular mass-market consumables. When they do, prepare yourself for big changes fast!

AN ECONOMY IN A DIFFICULT TRANSITION

We are in the midst of a huge transition from an old economy to a new one. Human beings accept change grudgingly under the best of circumstances and, since we are facing such massive change today, it is even harder to swallow. When we look at where we stand, though, it's important to remember that there are two sides to this story.

In the last two decades, the standard of living for most has been static, while for some people and industries, things are positively worse. An old economy of products, technologies, and methods of work has reached its maturity. To remain competitive, this economy is struggling to re-engineer itself, to change its time-honored practices and philosophies. Though this is a good move in the long run, right now it only adds to the confusion and anxiety.

This is why we must tell the other side of the story: The new economy, which will create the next boom and stimulate rapid growth in standards of living, is alive and rapidly expanding. Sure, it's showing the awkward fits and starts of any young venture, but it is also ripe with opportunity. In fact, the next economic boom will get its start in two predictable trends we can see right now: the peak spending years of the baby-boom generation and the emergence of simpler home computing devices which will make the Internet an indispensable mass-communications technology.

Before we look at these trends, let's see what the last information revolution can tell us about the end of this millennia and the decades ahead.

THE LAST INFORMATION REVOLUTION

Gutenberg's printing press was the technology that inaugurated the first mass information revolution. In subsequent centuries, new methods of communication and commerce revolutionized productivity and stimulated a long-term economic boom. First, capitalism, and then, industrialization produced huge changes in standards of living. The way people lived and worked would never be the same. Let's take a closer look at the hows and whys.

The real origins of the Industrial Revolution can be traced back to the printing press. It was one of the first inventions dedicated to mass production, in this case, the mass production of the printed word. It was preceded only by the first mass production of long-range ships in Venice, which we could also broadly view as a communications technology in that it facilitated contact between medieval Europe and other parts of the world. Before Gutenberg invented movable type in the mid-1400s, only a very tiny fraction of the population was literate, fewer still had ready access to printed books and materials, and private libraries were almost nonexistent. Did you know, for example, that there were only 300 Bibles in the world when the printing press was invented? Within forty years of Gutenberg's invention, more than twenty million books were in print, and literacy rates began steadily rising. In the decades following, the world underwent enormous changes, many of which can be attributed to this first information revolution and the adoption of a number of critical technologies. For instance:

- Spectacular advances in celestial navigation and ship design helped Europeans to discover a whole new world—the Americas—and, ultimately, to explore the rest of the globe.
- The invention of gunpowder and the technologies of warfare transformed the meaning of military power and assisted in the consolidation of great nation-states.

- The scientific revolution, begun with Copernicus and Galileo, initi-
ated the greatest expansion of scientific knowledge in human history.
- The opening of more trade routes allowed the exchange of products
such as food, spices, and textiles between all parts of the globe,
stimulating commerce and communication between the old world
and the new.
- At the same time that the known world was expanding, the population in the old world quadrupled in less than a century.
- The power centers in the world shifted suddenly from the Mediter-
ranean (Italy, Greece, and France) to the Atlantic coast of western
Europe (Spain, Portugal, Netherlands, Belgium, Germany, and England) and eventually to the west toward the new American colo-
nies.
- The basics of business shifted profoundly: Large production facilities were exported to the country to lower costs, improved transportation made manufacturing specialization possible, accounting
practices such as today's double-entry bookkeeping system were
instituted in business, and stock financing was first used to raise
capital for large-scale commercial ventures.

THE ORIGINS OF THE NEXT INFORMATION REVOLUTION

The first information revolution, based on Gutenberg's printing
press, was the precursor to capitalism, the foundation of modern commerce. The history of the last five centuries vividly recounts the huge
changes that occurred in business and society in the wake of that
revolution, changes that Gutenberg could scarcely have imagined.

The Industrial Revolution of the past two centuries was simply
the crescendo of the enormous changes in learning, exploration, and
production that began in the late 1400s. We are about to see the bold
beginning of the next 500-year cycle of change.

The transistor, which is the basis for today's computer and communications technologies, was invented almost exactly 500 years after
the printing press, in 1947. Future historians looking back at the
current age will describe equally astonishing changes in business and
society, changes that we can scarcely imagine now as three important
and highly predictable trends converge in the next decade:

- In America and most developed countries, the massive baby boom generation will move into its peak spending years from 1998 into the year 2009. The population of the world has almost quadrupled in the last century and is still expanding. The world economy has and will continue to grow at a rapid rate.
- The third world will continue to industrialize rapidly, bringing middle-class living standards to billions and creating a true world economy.
- In developed countries, powerful computer and software technologies will move mainstream to foster quick, convenient access to information, products, and services. This will create a new economy that can deliver custom-quality goods at mass consumer prices.

Today, there are powerful new technologies reshaping our world, including computers, electronic communications, jet and space travel, applied biotechnology, and atomic and natural power. We are about to witness the practical beginning of the second information revolution: the mass popularity of the Internet which will link literate individuals into a global network of communication, commerce, and learning. This revolution will be far bigger than anyone imagines. Mainstream Internet usage is not just an incremental step like the transition from the pony express to telegraph to telephones, or from steam engines to railroads to automobiles. It is a leap in technology, a full-scale information revolution as great or greater than the invention of the printing press.

THE IMPACT OF THE INTERNET

The Internet is to the coming economic boom of the Roaring 2000s what the moving assembly line was to the Roaring Twenties. It is the key productivity lever that will rapidly feed new technologies, products, and services into the mainstream economy. Widespread use of the Internet and allied technologies will fundamentally change the way we handle our business at home and at the office: the direct producer to consumer economy cited in Chapter 1. Whereas the assembly-line shift was fundamentally a production revolution, this will be a revolution in distribution and marketing. It will:

- Collapse many layers of administrative, marketing, and distribution functions to greatly reduce the cost and improve the efficient delivery of products and services to consumers.
- Allow companies to tailor products and services to individual needs at very low costs which will improve their quality and make customized luxury items more affordable.
- Initiate sweeping changes in management practices as successful companies radically eliminate, rather than streamline bureaucracy, evolving from a traditional top–down structure to a more consumer-oriented bottom–up structure, like the Internet.

We will understand the value of the Internet when we spend less time surfing through dreck and more time viewing the useful information and services that are delivered to us automatically. Powerful software that will search the Net based on our preferences is already beginning to hit the market. More focused, appliancelike computers will be easier to learn and operate than the PCs we tolerate today. Soon, we will have something akin to a personal butler or private secretary backed up by invisible software and server systems to make using the Net easy and convenient. Then, we can use our time efficiently by reading or listening to the information we need or teleconferencing with experts. Our routine purchases and chores will be tracked and automated. Everyday goods will be delivered by merchants when we need them. Our appliances will be coordinated around our daily schedules and even our spontaneous needs. The Internet will save us time to do the things that really count — just like powered machinery automated most of our physical functions at work and at home in the past decades.

After surviving a stressful era in which we had to work longer and harder just to keep up, creating time and having control over our time will be the status symbol of the next decade.

We need to broaden our view of the changes and opportunities coming our way in our work, our investments, and in our everyday lives. To prosper in this time of tumultuous change, we must understand the impact of these new technologies and the social changes they will inaugurate. The most important of these changes are predictable. Understanding them now will give us the time and resources to respond wisely to the random and chaotic changes we can't predict.

These opportunities depend on widespread computer literacy,

which is inevitable in the decades ahead, as more and more individuals grow up with computers. Don't wait for everyone else to jump on the bandwagon ahead of you. Become computer literate now and get ready for the next information revolution and the greatest economic boom in history, just ahead!

From One-Lane Roads to Highways

To help understand the history of the computer and the critical importance of the Internet, let's look at the history of the automobile. You'll quickly see the parallel between cars and computers, and the parallel between the vast network of roads and highways that criss-cross our country, and the Internet.

When the automobile was first introduced, car manufacturers first focused on making them available and affordable. Henry Ford, for example, standardized the design and parts of his Model T, used the first assembly line plant to mass produce the car, and then General Motors introduced installment financing to make the car affordable to the largest possible number of consumers. In subsequent years, automobile manufacturers continued developing new technologies to make cars easier to drive and more appealing to the average consumer. Electronic ignitions, balloon tires, power steering, power brakes, and automatic transmissions enhanced the basic design. All of this was phase one — applying new technologies to improve the product, an automobile.

Phase two focused on making the automobile more useful. Existing roads were paved and new roads were built to increase the driving range and speed of travel for car owners. Throughout this century, improvements in our transportation infrastructure — which includes the construction of highways, freeways, bridges, tunnels, and the use of traffic signs and signals — has never ceased. Today, most people consider their cars and trucks indispensable and use them far more than people did when the car first moved mainstream.

Phase one, building the automobile, was greatly leveraged by phase two, building a vast, complex network of roads and highways.

We can see a similar two-phase pattern in the development and marketing of the personal computer. In most businesses and in many homes, we now have the power of a mainframe computer of the early 1980s sitting on our desks. Innovative software manufacturers have made these personal computers a lot more personable, though they still have a long way to go. Graphical presentation of information and the use of point-and-click screen icons make computers easier to learn and use. They are powerful enough to handle sophisticated business needs, but they can also greatly simplify mundane household tasks like bookkeeping and letter writing. All of this is phase one.

We are just now seeing the practical beginning of phase two of the computer revolution: construction of the information highways that will let us easily and conveniently travel throughout a vast network of information. In the last five years alone, we have seen incredible innovation in the software needed to assist the flow of traffic, including faster switches and routers, web browsers and search engines, and traveling software called *Java,* used to facilitate interaction between end-user computers and host computers or servers. We also have seen innovations for piping more bandwidth through the direct wires and cables coming into our homes, and low-orbit satellites for rural and mobile access. In short, the Internet and growing bandwidth technologies are to the computer age what decades of road building were to the automobile. It will make the computer a personal, indispensable tool for work and at home.

Phase one, building the business and personal computer, will be greatly leveraged by phase two: building a vast, complex network of computer communications and the easy-to-use computer appliances to utilize it. Remember, cars were once as difficult to use and maintain as computers are today.

In the Roaring 2000s we will finally begin to see the real *computer information revolution:* more intuitive computing devices and powerful information servers working together. It's in this phase that consumers will drive the computer and communications industries to get exactly what they want, how they want it, and when. This will finally shift the power back to the individual and the consumer, keeping the promise that we all heard in the early stages of the personal computer revolution.

INTERACTION: THE KEY TO INCREASING WEALTH

If you think of economic progress throughout history, one thing becomes clear: The more we interact, the wealthier we become. Empires were built to facilitate trade and communication. Yet, the biggest stride towards greater human interaction hit as Americans moved from farms into the cities in massive numbers, starting only in the late 1800s. Productivity and living standards advanced more in the last century than at any time in history. For example, productivity rates averaged around 3 percent annually from 1900 into the 1960s, whereas 1 percent to 1.5 percent was the norm in the 1800s, despite the technological power of the Industrial Revolution. Why? Urban populations are far more interactive, innovative and specialized. Then, we expanded our large cities into surrounding suburbs to increase population density and interactivity beyond the finite limits of downtown areas.

Take a close look at a computer chip sometime. You'll notice that it resembles a dense city in miniature, perhaps symbolizing our move toward an ever-more-compact and interactive world. In the same way that microchips are increasing in power by providing more communication pathways, we are seeing the power of direct people-to-people communication, and the collapse of traditional bureaucratic hierarchies. This frees us to communicate in far more, and more profound, ways. For example, a century ago, few people traveled outside their own county. Today, some kids have more friends around the world that they've "met" via the Internet than they do in their local neighborhoods and schools. That's because they have grown up with technologies of interactive communication we never imagined.

Mainstream acceptance of the Internet will mark the second information revolution in five hundred years. It will allow us to meet with virtually anyone in the world without traveling. It will give us easy and immediate access to information, products, and services. And it will free up more of our time for those things we want to do by automating an enormous number of time-consuming business and household tasks.

For example, how would you like to live and work in a small resort town, conduct face-to-face meetings via a video-capable Internet, and travel only for important personal meetings and vacations? To get an idea of what you can expect to see very soon, here's a preview of some of the key technologies that will shape our ability to interact and learn.

Smart Cards — Our Personal Transaction Agents

The most personal computer technology that we will use will be the *smart card.* More portable than the wallet-sized computer forecast by Bill Gates, smart cards will ultimately hold all the data about ourselves needed to interact with the digital world, such as:

- Financial information, including banking and investment accounts, credit cards, credit limits, and credit history
- Medical information, including doctors, health history, hospitalizations, surgeries, the medications being taken, and allergies
- Insurance information and other legal documentation such as wills and power-of-attorney statements
- Preference information such as airlines, frequent-flyer account numbers, and other business and personal affiliations

We will be able to use one smart card to interact with any digital device anywhere, anytime, without our intervention. It will have the information and coding to communicate with other digital devices without requiring us to become digital. Best of all, smart cards will make information available to businesses in a convenient, efficient form, reducing the huge volume of complicated paperwork they need to deal with us. Less bureaucratic overhead will lower costs and improve service. Have you checked into a hospital lately?

For example, when we dial up an online travel agency, the information in our smart cards can help us choose the airline, make sure it has our frequent-flyer number, and select the best itinerary for our travel preferences and budget. Once we finalize the plans, our tickets would be loaded into our smart card, so that when we arrive at the airport, we simply swipe it through a card reader at the gate, board the plane, and drop our baggage off by the entry door on the jetway. There will be no need to stand in long lines for ticketing and check-in.

Even if we are unconscious on our way to the hospital, the smart card can be inserted into a reader to tell the paramedics who we are, what insurance coverage we have, how to notify our doctor, in-depth medical records, and what we need for proper care. The technology will simply provide the needed information on demand, automatically.

Because they will be used for virtually all transactions, using a smart card will be like having a personal accountant on call 24 hours a day. To find out where and how we spend our money, we'll simply download our transaction histories into a financial software program and get the answers we need.

Portable Smart Phones and Personal Computers — Mobile Access to People and Data

The automation of routine business and household tasks means that we are likely to become more active and mobile, yet we'll still need to stay in touch. One of the biggest trends in computing will be the popularity of portable smart phones and personal computers, soon to be voice-activated and even video-capable. They will be linked through analog cellular networks, personal communications systems (or PCS), digital cellular networks, and low-orbit satellites — providing greater access to vast quantities of information while we're on the go, anywhere, anytime, and anyplace.

Wireless communication, particularly voice- and e-mail, will become the most frequently used part of the information highway. Even today, it's easier to check the Federal Express web site for the status of your package than it is to make a phone call that routes you through a tedious options menu or a bureaucratic maze of operators and service personnel.

Ultimately, every person in your family will have a portable smart phone or computer that they carry with them as a matter of course. The only differences will be how fancy it is: some will want simple e-mail/voice/fax phones, and others will have video-capable color portable computers. But no matter which portable device we choose, we'll easily be able to stay in touch with business associates, family, or friends while on the move.

Computer Kiosks — Mobile Access to Even More Data

The popularity of portable computer devices for the average consumer will signal the success of this information revolution. Smart cards, smart phones, and portable computers are becoming more powerful and easier to use, and that's part of the story. The other key to their success is building the communications infrastructure that will make them useful. This includes smart stationary computers that can interface with the portable devices and communication links to quickly send and receive huge quantities of information.

When you're away from your home or office, stationary computers housed in convenient kiosks can provide the information you don't carry with you in your portable personal computer. Think of the ATM machine at your neighborhood bank. Now imagine it dispensing a huge variety of information and services, not simply ready cash or your current savings account balance. The next decades will see ATM-like machines evolve into powerful information access stations for workers and consumers on the go. You will be able to stop at such machines at a mall, in a convenience store, in the airport, at a hotel, or at an office complex, and pay a small fee to send or receive specialized information that can't be kept in your portable computer.

For example, while traveling you could download a color-graphic map and travel guide from a computer kiosk into your PC. Or, you could interact directly with an online company or catalog and have goods delivered to you. Or, you could transmit orders from your customers directly to your company's order entry and shipping systems. Such computer kiosks will provide information for people on the go when they can't access their powerful stationary computer at home or in the office.

Stationary Computers — Information, Business, and Entertainment Centers for Home and Office

The most powerful information systems will be the stationary computers at work and at home. These workhorses will handle the heavy information processing that businesses demand *and* the complex, video-intensive communications needed both at home and on the job.

In the home, desktop computers will become powerful entertainment and personal business centers with video on demand, fast Internet access, cable TV, e-mail, fax, games, educational software, and more. There will be few tasks that you can't do and little data or entertainment that you can't access from your home.

In business, powerful mainframes will store giant databases of complex information, while a subset of the data will be downloaded to *servers,* or specialized databases on mainframes, minicomputers, workstations, and PCs. They will be linked via the Internet so that information can be distributed throughout the network, available when and where it is most needed, and in a cost-effective manner.

For example, a small video server could store the movies that comprise, say, 80 percent of what customers in that neighborhood typically want to see. And, because it's local, the time and cost to deliver this 80 percent could be reduced dramatically. The other 20 percent would have to be accessed on demand at a higher cost from a centralized mainframe movie database. Or, traveling sales and service workers could store the most-needed customer data on their portable computers. Larger amounts of data could be stored on a workstation at the local sales office, and all the company's business information could be stored on the mainframe at the company's headquarters. As the power of portable computers grows, more data will be immediately available to improve the quality of customer service.

The falling cost of information that results from the rising power of semiconductor chips and higher communications bandwidth decentralizes information and constantly places more and more information out on the periphery, directly in the hands of front-line workers and consumers.

Not only will customer service improve, the cost of providing good service will go down. Since a personal computer is roughly 60 times more efficient than a mainframe, it pays to constantly move more and more information out to the end-users. The larger computers are there to store and route the information the most efficiently. As more companies see this competitive advantage, we anticipate that information traffic from local desktops and portable computers will heavily populate the information highway.

Advances in computer and communication technologies are not the only innovations that will make our world smaller in the coming decades. There's a new generation of jets and commercial spacecraft that, in the next few decades, will shrink the globe for those who rely on face-to-face communication.

SAY GOOD-BYE TO JET LAG

We've discussed the five-hundred-year gap between information revolutions—from the printing press in the 1450s to computers in the 1950s—and charted some of the results. Think of computers as customized, personalized, multimedia printing presses. But there is another, equally important, set of discoveries that occurred five hundred years apart.

The Age of Discovery in the 1400s was made possible by the adoption of celestial navigation and the large-scale production of sailing ships. In this century, 500 years later, we have seen our impetus for exploration extend beyond the boundaries of our own fragile planet as we reach for the stars not only with our eyes and our imagination, but with modern-day sailing ships. This new Age of Discovery, like the one 500 years ago, is based on two major innovations: radar navigation and the jet engine. Just as the mass use of the Internet will make virtual communication commonplace, jet and space travel will make face-to-face communication commonplace for a growing number of people. When that happens, we will be closer than ever to thinking of ourselves as *citizens of the world.*

There is a smaller cycle within this 500 year span that historians have noted, and that we need to pay particular attention to right now. Every 60 years or so, we see a major leap in transportation technology. The last such leap, in 1943, saw the introduction of the jet engine. In 1886, the internal-combustion engine made its appearance on the world's stage. The advent of railroads occurred in the 1820s and steam engines and steamboats were introduced beginning in the 1760s. Of all these innovations, jet-engine technology was adopted most quickly. In fact, jet planes largely replaced propeller planes in less than a decade. Ever since, jets have made the world a much smaller place, and more accessible to a huge number of travelers. Every day, people can and do travel across the country or across the world for vacation, while business people can attend a 9 A.M. meeting in New York and arrive in Los Angeles in time for another set of meetings later that same afternoon.

The next leap in transportation technology, due sometime in the next five years or so, calls for as much as a ten-fold increase in jet power from its original speed. That means air travel at 3,000 miles per hour or more. I have heard from a reliable source that there is such a jet in development, slated for prototype testing as early as 1998. The key innovation: a wing that allows it to accelerate at higher angles faster, with higher engine thrust and less noise impact. Such a jet would not only go from Los Angeles to Tokyo or Sydney in 2 or 3 hours but, unlike the expensive Concorde, it would cost approximately *20 percent less* than coach travel! That's because more expensive aircraft could be deployed on many more flights per day, better utilizing their very expensive fixed costs and crew. At this speed, it would be as easy to go on vacation in Sydney as it would to fly from New York to Disneyworld in Orlando. Business people who need to meet with others face-to-face could easily rocket from country to country, and return the next day if necessary.

The Internet will make the nonphysical world of information far smaller and more accessible. A 3,000-miles-per-hour-plus jet will make the physical world far smaller and more accessible on a human level. That means in the next decade or two we will truly begin to move into a global economy.

Here's another innovation already occurring that is just a matter of a decade or more from practical reality: A team of engineers from Boeing and McDonnell Douglas and astronaut Pete Conrad have formed a consortium. The project is called DC-X, and their goal is redesigning spacecraft for commercial travel. This aircraft would launch straight up to 500,000 feet off a small launch pad, fly anywhere on the planet in 45 minutes, and land on a site a little larger than a helipad. It would not require parachutes or heavy wings like the space shuttle does now, but would slow its descent by refiring its engines at around 10,000 feet to land more easily and reliably. All of the low-weight, high-strength materials, the engines, and the computer technologies exist today; the DC-X designers only need to continue to experiment to refine the designs. Nonetheless, they expect such an aircraft to be functional within a decade, perhaps two.

Obviously the first takers for such a venture will be NASA, then commercial cargo carriers, then business executives and overnight-delivery companies. Ultimately, the costs will come down to make the flights affordable to business executives and average consumers, with the cost equivalent to a first-class ticket on a conventional airline today.

Geometric increases in speed of travel will change how we conduct our lives and our businesses by greatly increasing interaction between far-flung cultures. Communication will truly become global and not just local—which will present us with new challenges and new rewards.

The computer information revolution, enabled by the next predictable leap in transportation technologies, will create radical changes in where and how we live, work, and play. It will fundamentally transform public institutions, private companies, social services, and the quality of life for ourselves and our families.

BIOTECH: THE ULTIMATE INFORMATION REVOLUTION

No discussion of technology would be complete without mentioning the largest potential revolution of our time: applied biotechnology.

Think of DNA simply as the human equivalent of the computer chip. It is the biological computer that stores the software to instruct our bodies how to grow, change, and respond to the highly complex world we live in. It is taking many more years to unravel the secrets of DNA than it did to program computer chips to automate many routine business tasks. That's because two human eyes have more information processing capacity than all the supercomputers in the world combined. Our nervous system has approximately 160 billion neurons, which are the human equivalent of the transistors on a computer chip. Even with the enormous power of microprocessors we anticipate in the next decade — the equivalent of 16 Cray supercomputers circa 1989 (more powerful than mainframes) on one chip — our computers will still only comprise 1 billion transistors, a small fraction of human capacity. Furthermore, the synapses or connections among these billions of neurons in our brains absolutely dwarf the number of switches and routers in our phone systems or on the Internet. The point: Since our biological systems are much more complex than computers, biotechnology research has taken much longer to produce useful, applicable information and technologies.

We should just start to see the beginning of the tangible payoffs from biotechnology research in the coming decade, including all types of new crops, foods, medicines, and preventative measures to contain or eradicate diseases. We should see health care that is customized to individuals' needs, which translates to a longer, higher-quality life span for most.

Perhaps most important is the real possibility that understanding how our bodies organize and use information will allow us to better design the high-tech tools and organizations we need to achieve personalized service and accelerated learning in our economy and society. Unquestionably, advances in computer technology are speeding up biotech research. But biotech research, which gives us insight into the complex adaptive system that is the human body, will also accelerate our understanding of how to construct complex, adaptive information systems for every kind of human activity and community.

Summary

Just because computer technologies have been slow to work their ways into our everyday lives in the past few decades, don't assume that will be the case in the coming decades. New technologies always move first into businesses, and then become user-friendly and affordable enough to move into our households. We are just about to transition from the business phase to the consumer phase. Chapter 4 will look at the eight critical technological trends that will thrust the Internet into the mainstream, and fuel the real information revolution, beginning in the next decade.

CHAPTER 4

The Eight Critical
Technology Trends
Changing How We Live and Work

THERE ARE EIGHT CRITICAL trends *already underway* in information technologies that will create the real consumer revolution and create unprecedented growth in productivity and personal wealth. They are:

Trend 1. Vastly expanded computer power
Trend 2. Mass adoption of portable and home PCs
Trend 3. Computers evolve into simple, inexpensive appliances
Trend 4. Microprocessor-embedded home appliances linked through the Internet
Trend 5. Consumers rapidly move online
Trend 6. Expansion of communications bandwidth
Trend 7. Object-oriented programming for customized software
Trend 8. Increased computer literacy, due to an aging population

These trends are the hallmarks of the second information revolution, the revolution that will usher in a whole new economy in the next decade and beyond. These are the trends that will drive the information revolution mainstream. As investors, entrepreneurs, business managers, and householders, we need to see and understand these trends because *how we live and work is about to change more than at any time in our history.*

111

TREND 1.
VASTLY EXPANDED COMPUTER POWER

The most powerful technology in history, the semiconductor chip, has been growing in power and declining in cost on a predictable path called Moore's Law. The power of these chips doubles approximately every 18 months while the cost decreases 30 percent every year. Inexpensive desktop and portable computers today have the power of yesterday's mainframe computers.

In the next decade, computers will grow in power at least 100 times. As I have stated, by the year 2009, we anticipate seeing the power of 16 Cray supercomputers (circa 1989) on one chip, and it will cost less than $100 to produce. We are likely to see the microprocessing chip merge into the memory chips, greatly increasing the efficiency and power in coming years. This will make sophisticated features such as voice activation and teleconferencing affordable to the average consumer and worker, making computers much more user-friendly.

As computers become standard conveniences for the home and office, they will facilitate direct communication between producers and consumers and foster business relationships that are nearly devoid of bureaucracy. Furthermore, the new generation of powerful computers will become more adept at handling many of the repetitive, left-brain functions that now require our time and effort at home and at work, freeing us to express our more human, creative, right-brain skills.

Computers are simply left-brain machines. In fact, the word *digital* literally derives from "left-brain circuitry." Picture a computer simply as the ultimate office worker with no emotional problems, who doesn't need a lunch break, a vacation, or health and retirement benefits! They can automate most of the routine, systematic, linear, left-brain functions performed at all levels of the organizational hierarchy in the same way that powered machinery has automated most physical work. By giving computers the routine left-brain work that they do so well, we will be able to focus on interesting tasks that require our more complex intuitive and relational skills.

In businesses of the future, human skills will be used for human endeavors. We will work as leaders, entrepreneurs, facilitators, mentors, designers, and service professionals. In our leisure time, we will similarly focus on the things that have human value and human rewards, and let the computers handle much of the tedious errands such as routine analysis, research, shopping, and paying bills.

Two technologies that require the vast power of the new semiconductor chips will make computers the simple, convenient, ubiquitous tools they can be: voice activation and teleconferencing.

Voice Activation

Until now, computer literacy has required typing skills, because we can't literally *tell* the computer what to do. But imagine doing just that — and no longer being tethered to a keyboard! This will give you some sense of the most important outcome of the growing power of computer chips: voice-activation technology. This innovation has been forecast and promised for years, but IBM, Microsoft, and other companies now have rudimentary software that can respond to voice commands. Voice activation is still under development, but we anticipate that it will become an affordable feature of most computer systems within 2 to 4 years. This does not mean that you will be able to carry on a casual human conversation with your computer. Software will only be able to deal with our voices in specific applications, like travel reservations where the vocabulary can be limited to something like 2,000 words and the contexts of meanings are also limited. There are many such applications that could simplify our lives and our interactions with computers. It does mean that you can increasingly have more of the world at the tip of your tongue, not at the touch of your keyboard.

Teleconferencing

A second major innovation that will become readily available on the new, more powerful computers is live-action video. With these new computers, and with the predicted increases in bandwidth — the volume of data that can be transmitted to and from your computer in a given amount of time — we will soon be able to *see and hear* the people we're dealing with. Imagine interacting directly with co-workers across the country without leaving your office! Imagine taking a real-life look at that vacation spot for your family from your living room! Consider the power of consulting with experts from around the world, face-to-face, when *you* need them, and at a radically reduced cost! With the new power of computers and increased bandwidth, we will see a video-capable, interactive Internet within the next decade that can *show* you who and what you want to see instead of just telling you about it. This is the real power of the Internet: not just linking information, but people; facilitating richer levels of human interaction. Many people have resisted Internet shopping because it's too hard to find things, and then there isn't the human help and interaction of real shopping. This will change, except for the products you literally have to touch or have demonstrated in the flesh. We buy lots of things today from mail-order catalogs. Don't tell me a video-interactive Internet wouldn't be far superior.

TREND 2.
MASS CONSUMPTION OF PORTABLE
AND HOME COMPUTERS

As we saw from the S-curve, products based on new technologies move into the marketplace in two phases. Only about 10 percent of the population will adopt an innovative product at first, so that product acceptance appears sluggish. But once the bulk of consumers begin to see its convenience and utility, the product rapidly goes mainstream in a flurry of popularity. This is exactly what happened to the automobile from 1914 to 1928, with television in the 1950s — and it's exactly what's happening now, with the Internet and home computers.

Looking at many S-curve histories, consumer products tend to fall into two groups: those that take 10 to 15 years to move mainstream and those that take 25 to 30 years. Like electricity and phones in the early 1900s, personal computers are on the slower path, as they are expensive compared to other appliances and hard to learn and maintain. Like cars, movies, radio, TV, and jet travel, the Internet falls in the faster group because it actually brings ease of use to computers and the conveniences we more easily embrace. Remember from Part I that the Internet and PCs are converging, like cars, electricity, and phones, to bring a mainstream consumer revolution in the next decade.

To understand this growth, let's review the personal-computer revolution and glimpse at where it's taking us next.

Phase One, 1977 to 1983:
The Innovation of the Personal Computer

From the first Altair 8800 and the beginning of Apple Computer, up until the introduction of the Macintosh, we saw the PC become a viable product, but personal computers primarily flourished among hackers and technical professionals. The average consumer saw little use for them despite all the hype and despite the genuine improvements in the technology. The PC was clearly a niche product, not even widely used in business.

Phase Two, 1984 to 1994:
PCs Become an Indispensable Business Tool

The second phase was the PC revolution, beginning with the Macintosh, which saw increasing numbers of people learning to use desktop and portable computers, mostly for business and professional purposes. Home-computer use was more an idea than a reality, largely due to the time and energy required to become adept with PCs. During this phase, however, important gains were made via the standardization of operating-system software and steady advances in raw computing power. Three of the biggest contributors were Apple and Microsoft, who popularized point-and-click graphical software, and Intel, who created powerful, standardized computer chips.

Phase Three, 1995 to 2001:
Connectivity Fuels Tremendous Gains in Business Productivity

We've all heard the phrase made popular by Scott McNealy at Sun Microsystems: "The network is the computer." By linking PCs in one vast communications system, we are seeing new ways to leverage their power. This is the third phase of the PC revolution, and it is happening right now, in the later 1990s. As businesses move quickly into intranets or powerful internal communications systems, consumers will just begin to start to use computers and the Internet. This will mean that the devices for consumers will need to be simple at this stage, and the server computers on the Internet will have to handle most of the complexity. Consumer use will remain primarily confined to casual information access and entertainment.

The most important innovation for this connectivity revolution is Java software by Sun Microsystems. These digital *applets,* or traveling software programs, can run on any computer and communicate with any operating system. This allows communication between powerful server computers and everyday personal computers. Java software, along with new Web browsers and search engines, will make it easier for everyday consumers to use the Internet to its full capacity because we won't need to handle the complexity of network communication: The server computers will. Java is also making it easier for businesses to install new computing systems that are compatible with their old ones.

These systems, a sophisticated integration of communications and data-processing hardware and software, will be the backbone of the Internet. These servers will provide on-demand access to huge databases, and deliver software when and where you need it so that you don't have to store it on your own hard drive or operating systems. By managing much of the heavy-duty data manipulation and storage tasks, such servers will stimulate innovation in simpler, more special-ized, computer appliances that will be easier to learn, operate, and maintain. The improvements to network technologies by businesses will pave the way for consumers to move onto the Internet in a serious way. Consumers will increasingly dabble with the Internet and some of the new, simpler, appliancelike computer innovations, but things like serious shopping will begin to emerge in the next stage.

Phase Four, 2002 to 2010:
Simple, Powerful Computer Appliances Coordinated with Sophisticated Information Servers Fuel the Consumer Revolution

This fourth phase of the PC revolution anticipated in the Roaring 2000s will feature the coordination of more powerful, customized, and intuitive computer appliances with the sophisticated networks of power-ful information servers built up in the last stage. Consumers won't really move in large numbers onto the information highway until this phase. Then, Internet commerce will become a practical reality.

New communications technology will eliminate traffic jams on the information highway, while sophisticated Web browsers and search engines will deliver select content, tailored to our interests, when and how we want it. We'll no longer need to search the Internet and *pull* information out of it. Instead, smart software that knows our needs and preferences will *push* the appropriate information to us. Computer power and connectivity will transform the Internet from an unwieldy behemoth into an efficient and dependable tool.

This will represent the real information revolution! This is when businesses will see strong payoffs from communicating more directly with consumers over the Internet. This will force more radical changes in corporate structures, and we will see companies and industries start literally operating from the customer back (instead of proclaiming it).

As consumers get used to using computers and become accustomed to higher levels of service and convenient access to products and information, huge numbers of people will trade up their equipment. We will purchase far more powerful computers and computer-driven appliances, and become much more sophisticated consumers of computer products. Computers, and computer literacy, will become indispensable.

There is an exponential rise in popular consumption when a product goes mainstream. Several indicators prove that this is underway for PCs and information devices now:

- Since the late 1980s, computers have moved from 10 to 45 percent of total households. In the next 7 to 10 years, they will penetrate 70 percent to 90 percent.
- Portable laptop computers are growing faster than desktop systems, emerging into the mainstream on an S-curve, recently passing the 10 percent mark.
- Cellular phones are moving mainstream rapidly, having passed 30 percent, while smart phones and digital assistants are just emerging as niche-market items and will probably begin moving past the 10 percent point into the mainstream within 2 to 4 years.
- The first low cost Internet devices hit the markets in late 1996, but the first applications are aimed more at reducing the costs of operating corporate information networks through intranets. This trend could catch on very quickly with consumers in a few years due to the popularity of the Internet, the low prices, and the potential ease of use.

When we factor in the tremendous power of 16 Cray computers on a chip, and the features this will support, we can see that personal computers and communications devices will continue to explode into mainstream consumer markets. Since 1997, Internet commerce has begun to catch on with a small minority of consumers.

TREND 3.
COMPUTERS EVOLVE INTO SIMPLE,
INEXPENSIVE APPLIANCES

David Kline, author of *Road Warriors* (Plume, 1996), compares the advent of computers to the advent of the electric motor. Such motors started out huge and unwieldy even for business, grew more compact and powerful, and eventually penetrated the home market. Electricity and electric motors were invented around 1886, but it wasn't until 1918 that Sears featured the first home motor, which weighed only 5 pounds and cost about $85 in today's dollars. This motor provided electric power for many of the first plug-in appliances such as beaters, fans, mixers, buffers, and grinders. Ever since, we have seen electric motors become ever smaller and more invisible. They have become embedded in a broad array of household appliances that require little skill on our part to operate. They have automated housework and simplified our lives in countless ways.

It is anticipated that computer and Internet technology will follow the same pattern. They will become consumer items, indispensable to the masses, by becoming easier to use, affordable, and by the complexity of such devices disappearing from our daily lives into the chips and software inside.

The prevalence of embedded microprocessors in standard home appliances such as washers and dryers proves that computer technology sells best when it is simple, focused, and *invisible.* Consumers don't want to spend weeks and months learning how to use a large, complex system. For the few routine tasks computers can handle for us — entertainment, information access, word processing, scheduling, messaging, or budget planning — we shouldn't have to.

A few innovative computer companies and many of the giants in the consumer electronics industry, such as Sony, have realized this. What we're seeing now is the beginning of a trend that will reach its peak in the next decade. This is the introduction of inexpensive devices designed to handle a very specific task, and as easy to use as standard home appliances. When you turn on the device, it will be ready to do the one thing it's designed for, and require little or no technical expertise to operate. For example, two of the new computing devices introduced in 1996 were WebTV and Palm Pilot.

WebTV, introduced by Sony, is a simple set-top box for your

television that allows easy Internet access for viewing Websites and exchanging e-mail. When you use WebTV's remote control, Web surfing is as easy as TV channel surfing. It has yet to explode in consumer popularity, but we think such a device will in the coming years, especially now that it has been acquired by Microsoft.

Pilot, the first focused digital assistant, doesn't surf the Web or fax documents or handle e-mail. It simply keeps you organized by scheduling appointments and maintaining phone and address lists, and interfaces wonderfully with the desktop system at your home or office to keep your information up to date. In comparison with the first digital assistants sold to consumers, Pilot has been a huge success.

In 1997 Brother introduced GeoBook for $599. It is a simple notebook computer for word processing and e-mail at the price of an organizer.

Trend 4.
Microprocessor-Embedded Home Appliances Linked Through the Internet

Many people aren't aware that only about one out of ten micro-processors are in personal computers. Nine out of ten are embedded transparently into everyday consumer products, from cars to VCRs, improving their performance. As a result, even today the average person uses *fifteen* computers, not *one.*

We predict that soon, the multitude of embedded computers in everyday products that are dedicated to specific tasks will become Internet-capable, due to the advent of Java software. Such devices will be able to communicate with each other and with us without technical know-how on our part. Mobile, automated software will connect our TVs, CD players, phones, heating systems, kitchen appliances, office equipment, PCs, and more, in a worldwide network. This will represent the practical impact of the Internet, a far more tangible benefit than global chat groups. Here are just a few basic examples of what it can do for us:

- A monitoring device checks all of your appliances and electrical devices for needed repairs, searches for the lowest cost service, and automatically orders and schedules such repairs.

- When you dial 9-1-1, push a button, or your heart monitor automatically senses a problem, a device automatically notifies you and the nearest hospital of your location.
- A mapping system in your car tells you where you are and how to get to where you want to go.
- Your home alarm system calls the police and your cellular phone in case of a break-in.
- Your alarm clock receives information on traffic and weather, and then determines the best time to awaken you for work.
- Your home appliances, from lighting to stereo to TV to stove, automatically turn on as your car approaches the house, or in response to your commands from the car.
- A global positioning system in your childrens' portable computers alerts you if they travel into certain danger zones or become lost.

TREND 5.
CONSUMERS RAPIDLY MOVE ONLINE

The S-curve shows us that consumers are moving online at a rapid pace, much more quickly than the rate at which they began to use personal computers. They will be drawn to the Internet by its growing popularity and the huge and growing variety of services that will become available to them, services that save them time and money.

Two converging trends, computer use in the home and burgeoning online services, will make the Internet an indispensable tool by the year 2002 or shortly thereafter. The Internet will allow businesses to easily and economically offer customized products and services directly to the consumer. When the Internet becomes a *direct producer-to-consumer distribution system,* it will signal an enormous change in retailing practices across the board.

From Mail Order to E-Mail Order

Think of the Internet as a huge online catalog, increasingly enhanced with interactivity, video, and 3-D graphics. It lets you access product information when and how you want it, not as it is provided by salespeople. Help commands will guide you through and alert you to ways of finding information of which you may not be aware. You will be able to summon such sales help, service, or expert advice when you need them. This will greatly improve customer service while eliminating the greatest expense for direct marketing companies: postage and printing. Competitive companies will pass these savings on to you, the customer.

Online Service Replaces Tedious Errands

Online banking is already becoming a reality for many of us, but it is just a hint of what's to come. The greatest innovation will be the online automation of our everyday shopping chores. A huge percentage of what we buy from grocery stores, for example, are repeat purchases. Each week your household probably uses a similar amount of basic commodities like milk, eggs, produce, and bread. With the powerful new smart card, discussed in Trend 2, our spending habits will be effortlessly analyzed, and a weekly shopping list will be printed to determine the optimum order sizes for different products depending on the quantity discounts available. Digital software will negotiate the best prices directly with cyberwarehouses and producers, and arrange for the delivery to our door while we're sleeping or working or playing. And who will deliver it? Probably UPS or Federal Express. After all, they won't be shipping many overnight packages when people can zip full-color animated documents to each other in seconds at almost no cost over the Internet!

Online shopping and delivery has already begun with services like Peapod, for groceries. Peapod handpicks items for you from existing grocery stores, and is therefore expensive. It represents a very small niche market for upscale consumers, nowhere near the 10 percent breakout point on the S-curve. It is closer to the tenth of 1 percent point. So, we'll have to watch the progress of basic online shopping over the coming years. But I expect it to begin moving mainstream at around 2002 to 2003.

Streamline, a more automated home shopping service in Boston, looks more like a viable concept. They come to your home and analyze your needs, then find the best prices on products and services through a highly automated warehouse.

Consider another innovation in online shopping: Firefly, an online music store. When you go to the Firefly Website, you can sample an infinite variety of music, then order what you want or download it immediately, online, at a price. Even more helpfully, Firefly can use a sophisticated database analysis program to compare your music selections with other people like you and suggest new titles you might enjoy. This is just one example of individualized service at its best in the new Internet world!

The online bookstore Amazon is another very successful retail venture on the Internet. From Amazon's Website, you can easily find and order over a million titles and have them shipped to you within days. Can you quickly find that many titles at your local bookstore? On the other hand, the recent success of bookstores like Borders and Barnes & Noble indicates that the best shopping experiences will not be replaced by retail Websites. These megastores are fun to visit. You can order an espresso, browse through books and magazines, listen to new music, and meet people. You're going to find some things you like and buy them, since you are there, things you might not notice on the Amazon Web site. But when you're short on time and know what you want, your best bet is to order it through the Internet. And now, Barnes & Noble is making a strong move onto direct sales over the Internet.

The point: Shopping in the Internet age means we will spend much less time on tedious errands and have more time to do the things we enjoy, things that require the touch and feel of direct human interaction. Shopping on the Internet will not replace traditional leisure activities, including shopping! Just the opposite. It will give us more time to go out to restaurants, concerts, parks, entertainment arenas, sports events, operas, symphonies, movie theaters — even all-star wrestling matches.

We will continue to shop for things that we need to see, feel, or experience, or products that need to be demonstrated in person. We'll shop where there is entertainment for our families. We'll want to go to a neighborhood specialty marketplace that has fresh produce, and specialty foods; all the things that make a difference. We'll go to a shoe store that measures our foot precisely and then has handcrafted shoes molded to our feet. But, of course, once you're on file, you can order the next pair through the Internet. In other words, we'll get consistently better service and have more fun when we do shop face to face!

Online Professional Help

When we go to our doctor for a general checkup, she will be able to directly access the finest experts in the world if there's a problem. We will be able to perform an even greater number of simple medical tests, and check in with our family doctor, right from our homes. This same convenient access will be available from a variety of professionals such as attorneys, financial planners, and accountants. Instead of making an appointment weeks ahead, traveling to their office, and possibly waiting for others to finish, we will be able to contact them face to face via the Internet.

In some cases, we may be able to minimize or eliminate our need for a professional service. For example, instead of driving around a neighborhood to look for real estate with an agent, we could easily dial up a real-estate Web site and find information on the latest houses for sale in the area. We could then preview many homes quickly, ultimately in 3-D presentation. By immediately deciding which ones don't really interest us, we give ourselves more time to look at the houses we really like and get a better human feel for them.

Here's another example: Have you ever traveled to a destination or hotel and found when you got there it really wasn't what you expected? With data and full-motion video delivered via the Internet, we can take some of the anxiety out of vacation planning. For example, we will be able to explore all the travel options ourselves or through a specialized travel agent. We will be able to customize a trip to meet our budget. We will be able to view color pictures and video clips of our destination, to help us plan our stay and "see" where we'll be going more realistically.

More people will start playing around on the Internet once an easy-to-use computer or set-top box is available for a few hundred dollars. Such devices will entice consumers to experiment with the Internet. And guess what? Once they're using it, they'll want more powerful computers, with faster access, to begin to truly benefit from the array of information and entertainment available to them. Furthermore, such devices will leverage the power of the Internet by communicating with each other and responding to remote commands from us when necessary. Thus the introduction of *computer appliances* will propel computer and Internet technology into the mainstream.

TREND 6.
EXPANSION OF COMMUNICATIONS BANDWIDTH

Now and in the coming decades, bandwidth will be the critical factor affecting the power and usability of computers — even more than the power of computer chips. We predict that increased demand for Internet access will stimulate investment in and development of two kinds of communications technologies: fiber optic and other cable options for dense urban and suburban areas, and satellite systems for rural areas. Since these technologies are still in their infancy, what we will see is a two-phase development of bandwidth, adequate to handle the huge volume of Internet traffic. In the first interim phase, lasting approximately 3 to 5 years, an assortment of technologies will be used to fill the gap. In the next, maturing, phase, technologies with much greater capacity will take the place of the stopgap measures.

In the Interim:
ISDN, ATM, Cable Modems, and Satellite Broadcast

In the interim phase, which is occurring now, several technologies will provide the greater connectivity we need to make our smart personal computing devices more useful, and to relieve some of the pressure on the Internet. These technologies include ISDN phone lines, ATM phone lines, cable modems, direct satellite broadcast, and wireless cable. Telecommunications and computer companies are scrambling to build this temporary infrastructure, meeting the current and growing demand for connectivity as best they can.

These solutions have substantial limitations, including that ISDN lines provide only marginal improvements but are still difficult to install. ATM phone lines look more attractive, but still have limited capacity for handling high volume or video applications. Cable modems have much higher capacity, but are more expensive and lack two-way, interactive communication capacity. Direct satellite allows low-cost downloading, but not two-way interactivity. And wireless cable can't broadcast through hills or buildings. Cable modems are starting to look the most promising of the alternatives.

We have seen a host of innovative startup companies look for creative ways to provide reliable, affordable access to television and movie programming and the Internet. For example, I've seen an argument that says that small, local phone companies could provide higher capacity, and more targeted Internet access, than the telecommunication giants by buying their excess capacity and combining it with powerful switches and modems.

There is one thing you can count on. Entrepreneurs and large corporations are going to find ways to circumvent the bandwidth problem precisely because it is the key limitation to the information revolution. Furthermore, the profit potential for adequate solutions is immense.

Like any new technology, the Internet will continue to face roadblocks in its dramatic growth. But it is a mistake to assume that such limitations will stop the Internet, any more than they have stopped any major technology revolution in history.

In the Near Future:
Fiber Optics and Low-Orbit Satellites

Telecommunication companies are also looking to the future, and beginning to build the highways that can manage the glut of Internet traffic they anticipate. They have realized that the mass acceptance of personal-computer devices makes expensive technologies like fiber optics and low-orbit satellites an exciting and worthwhile investment, and that these are the technologies that ultimately will make the Internet a truly global phenomenon.

Fiber optics, although potentially the ultimate two-way, interactive communications medium, have not materialized as anticipated. True, fiber can carry an immense quantity of data, but it is very expensive to install, and is installed in fixed locations. As we become more mobile at work and at home, and as more people move to areas outside of the major cities and suburbs that offer a lower-cost, higher-quality lifestyle, satellite-communication technologies look more promising. Satellites are even more expensive to launch. However, they have the flexibility to reach both fixed and mobile locations. This advantage will be especially important for the "wiring" of sparsely populated areas of developed countries, as well as the many third-world countries that are exploding in growth.

Over the next 5 to 12 years, communications between powerful stationary computers will be handled in two ways. In densely populated areas and in large corporate networks, these computers will be connected to the Internet via fiber-optic cabling. In less dense areas and for more mobile high-bandwidth users, very low orbit satellites will provide connectivity. This will meet the demand for high-bandwidth connectivity and make video-capable interactive Internet usage a reality for home and business, urban and rural. Figure 4.1 shows the four basic quadrants of the information highway.

- Fiber-optic cable will handle high bandwidth stationary and urban applications. As the cost of this technology comes down, fiber will begin to handle high-bandwidth stationary applications in broader suburban areas as well.

Figure 4.1: Four Dimensions of the Information Highway.

Figure 4.1 shows the four quadrants of the information highway and which technology pipelines are likely to dominate them increasingly over the next decade.

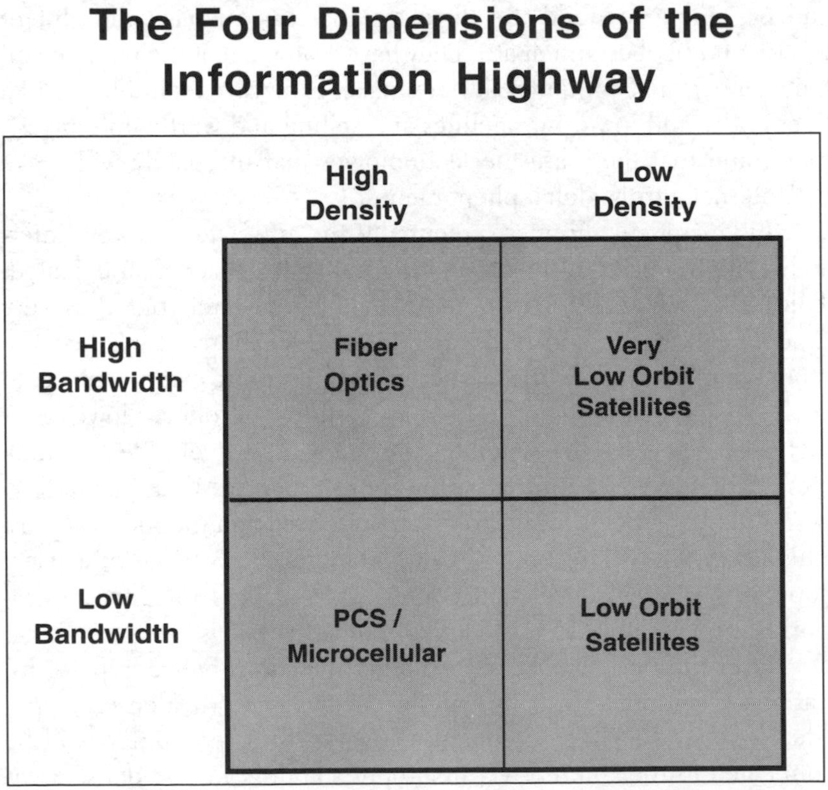

The Four Dimensions of the Information Highway

	High Density	Low Density
High Bandwidth	Fiber Optics	Very Low Orbit Satellites
Low Bandwidth	PCS / Microcellular	Low Orbit Satellites

- Very low orbit satellite systems, such as Teledisc, will handle high bandwidth mobile or less dense and rural applications.
- PCS wireless, microcellular, and, to a lesser degree, digital cellular towers will handle low-bandwidth mobile and urban applications.
- Low-orbit satellite systems, such as Iridium and Orbcomm, will handle low bandwidth rural and mobile applications.

PCS (personal communications systems) are simply smaller digital cellular transmission towers that are stationed close together. For this reason, they provide a higher quality transmission of voice and data at a lower cost than traditional cellular transmission towers. They also allow cellular phones and computers to be produced less expensively and to operate with a lower power requirement. The next wave about to hit is microcellular that leverages even smaller, more closely packed, transmission stations for even lower-cost systems in denser urban areas.

The dynamics of satellite systems are simple: The lower the orbit, the higher the bandwidth, because transmissions can move back and forth much faster in the same time frame. The lower the orbit, the more satellites it takes to simultaneously cover the earth due to the curvature of the globe. It would have been easier if the world were flat!

After Bill Gates wrote his book, *The Road Ahead* (Penguin, 1996), Craig McCaw, founder of McCaw Cellular, made a startling announcement. Between 2000 and 2002, he plans to launch 430 very-low-orbit satellites in conjuction with Boeing, which has invested $100 million in this plan. This new venture, called Teledisc, will bring high bandwidth access to the Internet to less dense areas and mobile users. Such an enormous breakthrough technology was not forecast by anyone, not even an insider like Bill Gates. But Gates, visionary technologist and businessman that he is, was one of the first to invest in Teledisc.

McCaw's plan for Teledisc is the kind of development destined to accelerate the speed and availability of the information highway. Most forecasters say that the Internet will take about 20 years to become a full-fledged, high-bandwidth information superhighway. I think it will happen to a significant degree in the next 10 years.

To create the high-bandwidth access needed for true two-way interactivity, McCaw's Teledisc system will require a large number of very low orbit satellites. And the risks of building and launching such a complex network of satellites is great. But don't discount Craig McCaw, Boeing or Bill Gates. If Teledisc is successful, and we ultimately believe it will be, it will greatly offset the costs of high-bandwidth access to the Internet outside urban areas and expensive corporate networks. This will make the information highway more easily available in these areas and allow many more people to live, shop, access information and education, and telecommute from smaller towns, resort areas, and third world countries. But, even if McCaw successfully launches his satellites, the initial estimated capacity of the system is 20,000 simultaneous users, which translates into millions of daily customers. That's probably enough for the near term, but other solutions will be required to meet the long-term demand.

More satellite systems like Teledisc will emerge and become the dominant communications technology for remote areas. That's because the cost of installing fiber-optic cable in these areas is too high to meet the demand economically. Satellite systems may become the most important lane of the information highway, as their costs decline over the coming decades. Companies have already launched satellites to provide cable and video service directly to homes in rural areas. For example, the Hughes Direct Satellite system has one very powerful satellite at an altitude high enough to reach all households, yet without sufficient bandwidth for two-way video interactivity. Orbcomm, a system of 23 satellites, can provide very low bandwidth communication anywhere in the world, which is ideal for simple paging services. Iridium, a system of 66 low-orbit satellites, will shortly be able to provide two-way phone service to anywhere in the world.

Trend 7.
Object-Oriented Programming
for Customized Software

There is a new approach to designing software that will make using computers easier and allow us to customize them to our individual needs at work and at home. It's called *object-oriented programming*. In object-oriented programming, teams of software designers build modules of code, called *objects*, that accomplish very specific functions, something like the point-and-click icons on the original Macintosh computer. Programmers are able to combine these objects to build custom applications, and easily recombine the objects to update the applications, add new features, and make them easier to use.

The benefit of object-oriented programming now is that it increases the rate at which software can be developed to bring us more powerful, customized applications for work and home. With the advent of Java — traveling *digital agents* that can access software programs and information according to current demands and leverage the network — these objects can be even more complex and mobile.

Largely due to the explosion of the Internet, changes in computer software and communications technology are happening so fast that companies have sought new ways to write software today that can be easily updated for tomorrow's needs. Whoever leads the way in object-oriented programming, this software innovation will be the key to creating a customized economy of commerce and communications that is directed by the consumers, not the producers.

The future of object-oriented programming suggests that we will increasingly be able to design our own powerful computers to accomplish specific tasks. Ultimately, personal computers will become more than personal. They'll be *personalized,* tailored to our individual needs. This is already beginning with new software like CyberDog, which allows you to program the news, sports, and weather statistics you want delivered to you every morning. Customization is the real trend in this information revolution, not merely low-cost, mass-produced technology. This means that companies such as Microsoft are likely to face more daunting challenges in the future, but it does not mean that Intel, for example, will see a decline in the demand for more powerful chips. Seeing the future of computer and communications technology requires a broad view of innovations in both software and hardware. That's why someone like Andy Grove of Intel has repositioned the company's strategy toward innovation in software and easy-to-use computing devices, not just more powerful semiconductors.

Trend 8.
Increased Computer Literacy, Due to an Aging Population

Younger people are more likely to use ATM machines, PCs, and to exchange e-mail with people around the globe, some of whom they may never have met face to face. Why? They've grown up with computers just like previous generations grew up with cars or TVs or coffee makers. In the next decade, we will have made the transition to a work force and consumer society that is almost entirely populated by *baby boomers* (those born between 1936 and 1961), *generation Xers* (those born from 1962 to 1975), and the new *echo baby boomers* or the millennial generation (born 1976 and later). Each of these succeeding generations is ever more computer-literate; there's no going back.

The Bob Hope generation that preceded baby boomers, on the other hand, is still largely computer-phobic. Although some do have the leisure time and the interest to learn how to use a personal computer and the Internet, they still resist computer use for one simple reason: They did not grow up using them. For example, when I was a consultant to the ATM industry in the late 1980s, I saw a marketing research study that pretty much said that the typical person over 50 wouldn't use an ATM machine if you put it in their bedroom, had it make coffee, and kiss them in the morning!

In the next decade, the majority of baby boomers will be reaching their forties while some will edge into their late fifties and early sixties. At the same time, those in generation X will be reaching their 30s, while the millennial generation will begin to enter the work force for the first time. This clearly means that virtually the entire work force will be composed of people ages 19 to 65, those who have grown up with computers. The overwhelming majority of people in their peak consuming years will be largely computer-literate. This means that the computer products and services spawned by the information revolution are certain to become mainstream consumer items. For example, you can soon expect to see these kinds of conveniences become readily available to a majority of consumers:

- Embedded microprocessors will handle many practical, everyday, physical tasks for us without our intervention. By adding intelligence to appliances and machines, they will become more responsive to our needs and commands, even from a remote location, and coordinate many routine household chores.
- Smart digital software agents will act as our personal butlers or secretaries. We will program these with our preferences and they will surf the Internet for us, bringing us the news and information

we need, and shopping for repeat purchase commodity goods and services. This will require little to no intervention on our part.

- When we need to make an informed decision we will use powerful browsers, search engines, and personal-preference filters on the Internet to get only the information we want. These tools help us quickly find products and services without leaving our homes or offices, directed by our needs for information, not by the advertiser's desire to sell.

When smart computing and communications devices handle our routine chores, they will expand the amount of time we have for genuinely enjoyable tasks that are best done with all our senses. We'll shop for fresh flowers and produce in an open-air market, browse through a bookstore while we sip an espresso, or run our fingertips over the smooth finish of finely made furniture. Or we will see powerful new human agents who will coordinate many product and service options into one-step integrated solutions to our needs, from investments to health care. We'll feel a net gain in the quality of our lives.

SUMMARY

The convergence of key technology trends with the aging of our population will cause the information revolution to accelerate and move mainstream in the next decade. This will create a broad-based productivity revolution, changing how we live and work more than any time in history. Add to this development the economic effect of the peak spending years of the baby-boom generation, occurring at precisely the same time, and we are almost certain to see the greatest boom in history. What was entirely predictable in the Roaring Twenties will happen on a much broader scale in the Roaring 2000s. Consider now how your personal, investment, and business strategies must change to leverage this new era of prosperity.

PART 3

The New Network Corporation

CHAPTER 5

Human Browser-Server Organizations That Operate from the Customer Back, Not the Top Down

WE HEAR CONSTANTLY that corporate re-engineering is creating unprecedented wealth for stockholders and equally unprecedented anxiety and chaos for the workers whose jobs may, or may not, be on the line. In the future, when we are able to look back at this time, we will see that re-engineering was a blessing in disguise for anxious employees, and a liability for corporate leaders lulled into complacency by their apparent success.

Re-engineering will force many workers out of companies that have outdated organizations with little future potential, into new companies offering superior growth and career opportunities. These are the companies that will usher in the greatest entrepreneurial era in history. These are the companies that will leave many of the re-engineered behemoths and their old-school corporate executives in the dust in the coming network economy.

The paradoxical problem with re-engineering is that it works! Re-engineering creates enough cost savings and incremental improvements in service and quality to make it hugely profitable. Such obvious results convince many business leaders that re-engineering is the answer, so they continue to streamline their bureaucracies and train employees to be more attentive to customers.

The danger in re-engineering, however, is that it merely reinforces the top–down, hierarchical, organizational model of the past century while masquerading as a revolutionary change. It isn't revolutionary, and it isn't the kind of change that will ultimately best serve these corporations. The real revolution began with the mainstream advent of the Internet in the mid-1990s. The stock market loves this trend. In recent years, average company earnings have been advancing at more than twice the rate of economic growth.

What we're about to see is a wholesale change in business organization, management, and philosophy that will make re-engineering look like the shortsighted tinkering that it is. In the 1990s, a huge number of companies have increasingly converted to client-server networks to manage their business-information needs. What they don't realize is that network systems are the technological precursor of the next successful model for human work and organization. Our investment in computer and information technologies is simply the first step needed to fundamentally restructure entire corporations — with profound implications for how we do business in the future.

The payoff for companies that organize their human resources along the network model will be immense. It is only network organizations that will be able to deliver customized products and personalized service to savvy consumers at affordable costs.

Our world is growing increasingly complex and interdependent. Consumers are becoming more individualistic, demanding choice and personalized service. Technologies are changing at an ever-faster pace. The companies that will be able to respond efficiently to these changes are those that literally run from the customer back, like the Internet. It is these companies that can handle the complex communications and rapid changes that customized service requires. They will make most decisions on the front lines, not from the back lines.

Companies organized as traditional, bureaucratic hierarchies simply can't respond quickly enough, no matter how their bureaucracy is streamlined. Networks don't have a sluggish bureaucracy. A premium is placed on delivering information at light speed, when and where it's needed, not in slowing everything down in heaps of red tape, petty power plays, and emotional problems. The new network model is a radical change in business structure and practice that changes the role of every person within the organization.

THE NEW NETWORK ORGANIZATION

The move to the network organizational model is the biggest single change that will result from the information revolution. As I mentioned in Chapter 1, this is the first such revolution since the invention of the printing press 500 years ago. Since these 500-year cycles always bring sweeping changes, don't expect this to be just another stage in the industrial revolution, because it won't be.

At the beginning of this century, the assembly line revolutionized the production of goods and services. At the end of this century, the network organization will begin to revolutionize product and service marketing and distribution. When the assembly line replaced the craftsman, production costs for most goods dropped dramatically. Now, about 20 percent of the purchase price covers the costs of production, while about 80 percent of the price goes for distribution, marketing, and administration. Now, for the first time since the invention of computers, widespread communications technology will support direct producer-to-consumer commerce, replacing the bureaucrat and middleman. This will fundamentally change the way we buy and sell products and services. In the decades to come, distribution costs will drop as dramatically as production costs have in the past century.

Let's put the essence of the new network organization in one sentence: The new network organization consists of leaders, guiding entrepreneurs, and self-managing teams in a chaotic, real-time process that is organized around the ever-changing needs of individual customers.

If this doesn't sound like the re-engineered companies you work for or deal with, guess what? It's not! Network organizations are fast, responsive, customizing, and entrepreneurial, where going with the flow is the only possible path. Hierarchical assembly-line organizations are just the opposite: slow, inflexible, standardizing, and highly managed, planned, and coordinated.

The main features of the network model for organizations are:

- Leadership at the center, not management at the top.
- Front-line human browser teams that customize solutions and represent the customers by connecting them directly to servers or specialized products and experts.

- The radical elimination of bureaucracy, not mere streamlining or improvements in a company's present systems.
- An internal, free marketplace that makes every front-line or back-line team as accountable to customer satisfaction and profit and loss as an outside business.

Leadership at the Center

Network organizations are concentric circles of influence whose center is the leadership team. Management does not run the corporation from the top of a hierarchy by dictating policy and procedure through thick layers of bureaucracy. They no longer make decisions except at the most central level. Instead, leaders establish the focus of the organization, an effective culture and network structure to support that focus, and rules for decision making within the network. In this way, they make it possible for others, particularly at the front lines, to make effective decisions.

Management in such an organization is like a self-regulating database at the center of a computer network. It maintains essential cultural principles and information, continuously seeks to improve how it organizes, and furnishes data to everyone who needs it (including the management team itself), and makes sure that such information is available in real time—where it's needed within the organization.

Front-Line Browser Teams Organized around Customers

Network organizations have a structure and philosophy that focuses on responding to the individual customer. I call this *operating from the customer back.* In this kind of organization, small, front-line teams focus on an individual segment of the customer population. They become expert at knowing and serving such customers, and make most of the key decisions right there, on the front lines. Most important, they represent the customer objectively, rather than just selling them what the company's back-line systems want to push out the door.

These front-line entrepreneurs are supported by back-line teams, or servers, within the company who provide specific products or specialized expertise on demand, rather than dictating decisions. In fact, the customers that the back-line teams are responsible for are their coworkers on the front lines! Think of it this way: The front-line teams put together the puzzle, the back-line teams provide the pieces. That's how a company can quickly and efficiently customize results to individual customers, and organize the company the way the customer would, responding to changing needs rapidly without bureaucracy.

The Radical Elimination of Bureaucracy

In a network organization, bureaucracy is not simply streamlined, it is eliminated altogether. Routine, repetitive, left-brain tasks are automated and assumed by sophisticated computer systems, which frees individuals at all levels of the organization to engage in more creative, right-brain customer-oriented work. The network computer systems provide the information that employees need to make timely business decisions, and also record the data needed to monitor employee performance.

Most re-engineering schemes are conducted by top management, back-line teams, and MIS (management information services) departments that don't have the objectivity to consider eliminating, automating, or outsourcing many aspects of their own functions and jobs. That's why they endlessly streamline their present systems, but retain the quality of bureaucracy and a top–down flow of decisions that can't possibly be driven totally by customers or front-line workers.

An Internal Free Marketplace

Every individual or team becomes a business with a clear idea of who their customers are, how to achieve customer satisfaction, and the bottom line on their own profitability to the organization. Individual contributions and accountability become more visible in a network organization. A network organization understands that its most valuable commodity is knowledge and information, and it therefore provides the communications infrastructure needed to wire together the front and back lines for real-time decision making. The information system simultaneously feeds key performance data to management to ensure that there is ongoing accountability for both qualitative and quantitative bottom-line results, from customer satisfaction to productivity to profitability.

This level of real-time information and microaccountability allows companies to operate on the same free-market principles as industries and the businesses within them do today. Hence, the need for management and bureaucratic coordination largely disappears as it does in broader industries, the Internet, or the financial markets, which are already examples of network or free-market principles discussed in Chapter 1.

Companies that adopt the network organizational model will enjoy unprecedented gains in productivity, even greater than the advent of the assembly line in the early 1900s. They will increase their earnings and their market share by efficiently delivering the highest quality of customized goods and services, or by delivering commodity products at radically lower costs. We, as consumers, will see a precipitous rise in service and in our standards of living, while having more say over our work. We will become entrepreneurs and businesses, not just employees and work teams.

THE WHALE *versus* THE SCHOOL OF MINNOWS

I use a metaphor to describe the enormous differences between the old organizational paradigm and the new one: a whale versus a school of minnows.

Whales represent the old structure of business. They are massive, powerful organizations, vertically integrated and designed to do one thing well: produce standardized products or services at a very low cost. Such organizations are successful when employees follow the game plan devised at the top and passed down through intricate layers of bureaucracy.

Such organizations are successful when the standardized items they produce can be sold to consumers who are convinced of their worth by mass advertising and strong sales techniques. In such organizations, analysis of the process — how to do better what they are already doing — becomes far more important than customer responsiveness, innovation, or ingenuity.

Who needs that much innovation when customers keep buying the same thing from you? Furthermore, the layers of bureaucracy insulate so many of the workers from actual customers and, often, from the finished product itself, that they don't really know whose interests or needs they serve. Except those of the internal bureaucracy of the whale, of course. That's where politics arise.

The new network organizational model operates like a school of minnows, not a whale. It is comprised of individuals and self-managing teams who share critical information in real time for fast, informed decision making. Each one is wired directly into large-scale production, specialized experts, and information systems, guided by centralized leadership that establishes the company's strategic focus and agrees on its core competencies. This allows individuals to move together in specific directions in a strategic manner, but not in a linear, calculated, planned way. As a result, such organizations can have the mass of a whale but, like a school of minnows, can turn, change, and respond instantly—exactly what's needed for our world of fast-changing technologies and individualistic consumers.

Whales Can't Dance

Most larger and more established companies talk about listening to their customers and customizing their products and services. I deal with these companies just as you do, and I've found that most of them are just whales in disguise. The top–down nature of their organizations, no matter how streamlined, simply doesn't support the personalized service customers want. It also doesn't provide the entrepreneurial environment that the most creative and productive workers want.

Network organizations combine the innovation and responsiveness of small entrepreneurial structures with the economies of scale of large corporations: in other words, the best of both worlds. They run from the customer back, not from the top down, to maximize flow and responsiveness. That is a radical difference in organizational behavior, and the next revolution in business.

BEYOND RE-ENGINEERING: THE NETWORK REVOLUTION IN BUSINESS

We can see the future if we observe the innovators who are always ahead of their time. Henry Ford was successfully producing cars on a moving assembly line in 1914. In the first year of operation alone, he cut the price of a Model T in half, while doubling the wages of the workers in the plant. He wasn't re-engineering and streamlining old business practices. He was doing something radically different. As a result, the very nature of work and business management changed.

Ford was an innovator, blazing a new economic trail for almost all businesses and institutions that followed in the decades afterwards. Ford even predicted many of the recent innovations in manufacturing, such as just-in-time inventory, partly because he so thoroughly understood the hierarchical, sequential, left-brain logic of the assembly-line system. Like Henry Ford, we, too, can see the future organization of our society and economy by understanding the right-brain, intuitive, random-access logic of the emerging network world.

DIRECT PRODUCER-TO-CONSUMER DISTRIBUTION SYSTEMS — THREE NEW BUSINESS MODELS

To summarize our discussion so far: We are witnessing the network or right-brain revolution — the real information revolution — that began in the mid-1990s and will blossom into the next century. This revolution will have two components: the increasing automation of repetitive, left-brain tasks, and the linking of all consumers, workers, and organizations into one real-time communications system through network and Internet technologies. These changes will allow us to move increasingly into a direct producer-to-consumer, or *network* distribution system. The first companies to reorganize will be the first to profit, as Henry Ford did 80 years ago. There are three new business models emerging for the Internet age. Which is most appropriate for your business?

Direct Producer-to-Consumer — Dell Computer

For larger-ticket products and services that are commodities or easily customizable to individual needs, Dell Computer is the model. The customer calls Dell directly or dials into their Internet site. If the customer knows what he or she wants, he places the order. If the customer is not sure, the sales consultant will bring him through a simple series of questions that will identify the right computer configuration for that customer. Dell will then custom produce a computer the same day to those specs and ship it out the next day with clear instructions for setting it up, as well as help over the phone or Internet if needed.

By doing business directly with the customer, Dell cuts out the retail store, distributors, warehouses, inventory, and most of the bureaucratic and information-processing costs. And the buyer doesn't have to leave home or office. This custom-produced service can be delivered at lower costs and higher convenience than purchasing a computer in a store.

Direct Warehouse-to-Consumer — Streamline

We wouldn't want to order a can of soup directly from Campbell's. When there are many lower-ticket, repeat purchase items, like most of what we tend to buy from grocery stores, drugstores, franchises, and discount superstores, then the direct-warehouse-to-consumer model will tend to emerge.

Streamline is a new company in Boston that surveys the buying habits of our households and then operates a significant warehouse and buying system to purchase everyday goods at the lowest prices and deliver them regularly to your front door. Streamline is more highly automated than other home grocery services like Peapod and hence has the potential to become mass affordable as they grow. They also offer everyday products and services beyond groceries. Ultimately, I predict home delivery of most of the repeat purchase items we buy will become cheaper than shopping in stores, with incredible time-saving convenience to the customer.

By eliminating costly retail stores and dealing directly from the warehouse, costs will be lower. Most commodity retail and franchise concepts will be replaced in the coming decade by direct warehouse home and office delivery. Our computers and smart cards will ultimately be able to measure our repeat purchase needs and preferences and automatically order and negotiate prices and deliver without any time or effort on our parts.

Front-Line Consumer Customization — Financial Planners

The greatest impact of the network revolution will be the advent of a new front-line service level that I call the human browser. For higher value or more complex products or services that require significant customization to individual customers, we will see new retailers, consultants, sales and service entities. This new emerging model of business will be described extensively in this chapter and this section.

In a complex world of nearly infinite choices, customers increasingly need a new middleperson to fit a broad array of products and/or services into a customized solution. The only way to accomplish this affordably is to have highly specialized front-line stores, individual agents, or self-managing teams that focus on a narrow niche of customers. By knowing their needs intimately they, the browsers, go out to the servers, or teams or units of people who specialize in producing a more limited line of products or services.

The front-line browser teams find just the right pieces from the servers to put together the puzzle, or solution, for the customer. They represent the customer, not the producers. They simplify a complex world and add value for customers who don't have the time or expertise to go directly to producers.

Financial planners and advisers are emerging in the investment industry to coordinate a one-stop financial and investment system for individuals. They, the browsers, integrate mutual funds, variable annuities, life insurance, mortgages, and cash-management accounts from a broad array of specialists to customize financial plans. For busy professionals who have little time and less complex investment needs, 1-800-mutuals can customize a mutual fund portfolio over the phone — more like what Dell computer does at lower prices. Specialty mail-order catalogs and specialty stores represent this browser/server model. They select a narrow range of products that are targeted to niche markets of consumers.

The real impact of the information revolution will begin in the next decade as consumers move online in mass numbers for the first time. This will dramatically shift the market advantage to companies who adopt the network model. They will lead the way in eliminating bureaucracy within businesses, and unnecessary distribution channels within industries. The result will be the greatest productivity revolution we have yet seen. Businesses will start to see the real profits from doing business directly with customers once the majority of us are online. I predict this will occur most dramatically around 2002, or shortly thereafter.

The result of this information revolution will be that we will increasingly enjoy customized products and services at affordable prices. As computers efficiently handle more of the routine tasks, we will gravitate towards creative, right-brain, relational work as entrepreneurs, leaders, designers, and facilitators.

The End of Office Work as We Know It

The biggest impact of new technologies throughout history has been to automate many current jobs and change the roles workers play in the production of goods and services. The introduction of the network organizational model into businesses today does not merely streamline bureaucracy, it eliminates it altogether. It shifts the burden of repetitive, left-brain work to sophisticated computer systems, while workers become increasingly involved with the human aspects of the job that require our more intuitive judgement and ingenuity. Ultimately, there will be no visible bureaucracy in the network corporation. Computers will become the new bureaucrats.

You may wonder how this is possible. After all, computers today are used as tools by office workers, but they certainly don't replace bureaucracy! The answer lies in the development of the technology itself. With the predictable progress of Moore's Law, computer chips have doubled in power every 18 months and dropped in cost 30 percent every year.

When a single chip has enormous power, and a typical desktop computer offers features such as voice-activation and full-motion video, computers really will become the ultimate office workers, with no emotional problems! Computers don't need vacations, sick leave, or coffee breaks. They don't need retirement and health benefits. And they don't sue you for wrongful termination or sexual harassment! Instead, the new computers will assume the routine clerical functions that are a burden to all employees, whether they work in the mailroom or the boardroom.

We have no hope of competing with such powerful computers in routine, left-brain work, just as humans in the last century could not compete with the powered machinery that assumed most of the physical work. A quick look at the statistics is compelling:

- Farm work comprised 70 percent of the jobs in our economy in 1820, dropped to 43 percent by 1890, and now comprises a mere 1.9 percent.
- Factory work comprised about 50 percent of our economy and 40 percent of our workforce in the 1940s and is now at 15 percent and falling.

- Managerial, professional, technical, service, and clerical work comprised only 4 percent of the jobs in 1850, 13 percent of the jobs in 1900, and now make up the overwhelming majority of the jobs in the American economy.

Many aspects of this last category of jobs — managerial, professional, technical, service, and clerical work — revolve largely around linear, systematic, left-brain skills. As computer power and sophistication grows, and computers become easier to work with, they will continue to assume larger portions of these jobs. As a result, the key human skills in the future will be the intuitive, right-brain, creative, entrepreneurial, and relational abilities. It shouldn't come as any surprise that these are the very skills that make work interesting, meaningful, and rewarding — and that computers are miserable at!

Remember that two human eyes have more information processing capacity than all of the supercomputers in the world put together. The best supercomputers today can't perform the simplest common-sense tasks a 2-year-old can. We are not here to compete with computers, but to use them as tools to amplify our human ingenuity.

One obvious problem with the re-engineering revolution is that it sets out to improve the present systems of delivery, albeit often using radical methods. Why spend most of our time streamlining and improving left-brain, repetitive work when we could focus on identifying the key creative human skills that will be essential to our long-term success, and focus computers on leveraging those skills? Why think of better ways to do clerical work when we can concentrate on delivering unprecedented levels of high-quality, customized service and products? Why build a better bureaucracy that our customers never see — and don't care to see — when we can build better direct producer-to-consumer relationships directly with those customers? The only way to dramatically improve customer service is to eliminate bureaucracy, not streamline it!

Let the computers do the accounting. Let the computers allocate fixed and variable costs to each individual or to small teams of employees. Let the computers purvey rules and policies for making decisions and technical logic directly to front-line workers. Let the computers connect the front-line workers directly to the back-line specialists when they need their expertise to solve a customer's problem. Let the computers help diagnose a patient's symptoms in the hospital emergency room.

In other words, let the computers do the work they are designed for so that human employees are free to do what computers cannot: soothe the anxious relatives at the hospital, converse with customers to find out what they really need, develop original and inventive product ideas, brainstorm on improvements in product quality and service, and keep their finger on the pulse of the organization to sense where it's going, and come up with ingenious solutions to get there.

THE AUTOMATION OF MANAGEMENT

The most far-reaching impact of the network organizational model is not how it will change the lives of everyday workers, but how it will change the role of management. We can get some idea of this by referring to the two broad-scale examples of network organizations in Chapter 1: The Internet and the New York Stock Exchange.

The Internet and the stock exchanges run themselves with a set of rules and some very sophisticated real-time information systems. As network organizations, they have something akin to invisible direction at the center, not visible management at the top. It's not that management, with its goals, systems, procedures, policies, and evaluation, isn't absolutely necessary to run a company efficiently. It's that a great many of these tasks can be automatically incorporated into a company's powerful, left-brain, information systems. They will only become the new model of business organization, however, if the executive staff understands that its job is to facilitate this transition. The executives must identify which aspects of their jobs can be programmed into software, freeing them to become leaders and facilitators instead of corporate cops.

These networks with no apparent management are the epitome of the new right-brain communications and organizational systems that will dominate the new economy. I have worked with many leading-edge companies that have already successfully used this network organizational model to deliver everyday products and services. It is not a theoretical possibility. It works, and it is working now in a variety of industries. But these companies are in the very small minority, like Henry Ford in 1914. The network model is our future, as real as the moving assembly line was to Henry Ford in the early 1900s.

Just as Ford discovered, the first companies to embrace a new model will be the few visionaries courageous enough to break with the weight of tradition. It is these companies that will reap the rewards first, before the network organizational model becomes the choice of the many. These companies will force the rest of us to move rapidly into the network economy, or face the consequences of losing market share more rapidly.

The End of Sales

The most important part of this revolution for consumers is that network companies will focus far less on selling us the goods they want us to buy. The front-line sales and service people will become consultants who represent our interests, help us clarify our needs, and find the best product from many available choices. This is the epitome of the human browser-server model that I discuss later in this chapter. But what a relief! Instead of *being closed,* sales jargon that sounds a lot like getting caught or cornered into a purchase, we as consumers will be consulted. Our need for service, in addition to their specialized expertise, will drive the system.

HUMAN BROWSERS AND SERVERS IN THE NETWORK ORGANIZATION

Our left-brain computer systems used in business have already evolved into a clear network model of organizational success. Figure 5.1 shows the typical organization of large data-processing and data-dissemination systems. As personal computers grow in power, more computer tasks are being pushed out to the front-line portables in the field and the desktop systems in the local offices. These computers can access huge data servers, as necessary, to get the information that can't be stored or analyzed on a PC.

This distribution of data across an array of computer systems, each targeted to handle what it does best and most efficiently, is perhaps the greatest organizational change driving the acceleration of corporate earnings in the mid-1990s. Computer networks, which coordinate access to this distributed data, have made it possible to achieve economies of scale in the processing of information, the most valuable commodity in the world today. It's called the *client-server model,* or in today's Intranet jargon, the *browser-server model.*

Computer Network Organization

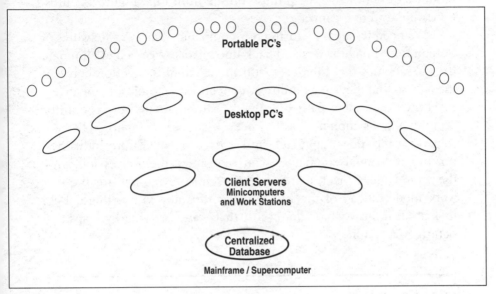

Figure 5.1: Computer Network Organization.

Figure 5.1 shows the organization of a computer network. The fundamental idea behind networked systems is to push as much information as possible to the periphery so that PC users have the information they need at their fingertips. More specialized information that's used less often is kept on the larger computers, where it remains close at hand.

In the browser-server model, end-users can directly access, or *browse,* for specialized information that is available on demand from powerful *server* computers. Browser software provides the user-friendly interface for navigating the network. In fact, it was sophisticated browser software, as well as traveling software (Java) that can easily connect end-user computers and servers, that helped launch the Internet as a popular, mainstream service for business and, ultimately, for the home.

Our human organizations need to evolve in this same way. Instead of the typical top–down organizational charts that still govern most companies today, we must adopt the network organizational model. Employees on the front lines, in the field, drive the organization by making the critical decisions that serve their customers' needs.

Employees on the back line, who specialize in particular kinds of products or knowledge, help those on the front line. Figure 5-2 illustrates this kind of organization.

We need to begin picturing our companies simply as networks of human front-line browsers and back-line servers. We need to eliminate the bureaucracy that interferes with the efficient interaction between the two, so that they, in a nonlinear concert, can rapidly and creatively meet their customers' particular needs. Running a network is not like "conducting a symphony," as has been used as a metaphor. That still suggests a top–down approach and a fixed result. Entire industries, not just individual companies, can reorganize themselves following the same logic. In fact, many industries are moving towards the network model ahead of the individual companies within them. Let's look at an industry that's doing just that—and growing by leaps and bounds as a result.

Figure 5.2: Human Network Organization.

Figure 5.2 illustrates what a human organization modeled on a computer network looks like.

Human Network Organization

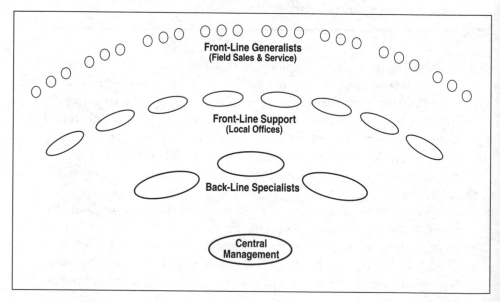

Mail-Order Companies Lead the Way

Would you believe that companies competing with one another share their most vital, strategically important information? That's how radically different network structures are!

Through a company called Abacus Direct, over 600 of the largest direct-mail catalog companies anonymously share their client information. This gives all of them a much broader picture of the purchasing behavior of their own clients, and of virtually all households in the U.S. The Abacus database can tell its subscribers what products individual households tend to buy through mail order, how they buy them, and even when. Abacus can pinpoint whether people buy in spring or fall or March or December, and, ultimately, on Mondays or Fridays. This helps the companies target their promotions, which in turn can reduce mailing costs and improve customer satisfaction and retention.

Why is this important? The direct-mail industry competes with retail stores, telemarketers, infomercials, and other marketing and distribution channels. By pooling information and sharing their expertise, each individual company improves their market share and profits while at the same time elevating the competitiveness and attractiveness of the direct-mail industry as a whole. In fact, direct-mail companies have far more in-depth product and customer data than the typical retail outlet. However, each individual company simply couldn't afford to acquire and maintain their own internal database with the wealth of information Abacus offers. Software and services provided by Abacus allow its clients to cooperate, shaping and updating the database continually to meet their needs. It fills an important need by collecting and serving them the information that will help the browserlike companies find new markets or consolidate their position in existing markets.

True, some of the direct-mail companies compete. Most don't, however, because they are so focused on product categories and customer types. That's what makes them browsers. They know the unique needs of a narrow band of customers. It's not called *direct marketing* for nothing. Remember, that's the essence of the network economy. Producers sell their specialized products directly to interested customers, without extra layers of distribution or the need for retail stores.

Abacus and other direct-mail experts aren't the only servers in the industry. Many product specialists also act as servers. These specialty producers focus on specific products and try to attract the attention of the specialty catalog companies (and other retailers) who are focused on a niche market of customers. These browser companies must select the right products and use the expertise of their suppliers to best meet their clients' needs. The suppliers that don't meet those needs lose the business fast.

The direct-mail catalog business has blossomed in the last few decades because consumers, faced with a bewildering array of products and services, need help sorting through it all. Many products are more convenient or cheaper to purchase through the mail. The success of direct mail is largely due to the fact that it operates on the browser-server model, just like our computer networks. Individual catalog companies are like browsers that help a group of like-minded consumers to find servers, or the specialized products that most interest them. They do this with little or no bureaucracy, and they know their customers intimately and change rapidly as their needs change.

Using direct-mail catalogues for commodity shopping is a lot like tuning in to Siskel and Ebert when you want help choosing a movie. Siskel and Ebert watch all the movies for you. They summarize them, categorize them, and rate them; with this information, you can make a more informed decision. Don't most of us quickly decide which reviewer, Siskel or Ebert, we agree with most? Isn't this what mail-order companies like Hammacher-Schlemmer do?

THE TRANSFORMATION OF
FINANCIAL SERVICE COMPANIES

Let's return to the financial services industry which will move quickly into the network model. Because it is such an information-intensive industry, computers are already widely used. They have automated most of what brokers did in the last century: executing trades and providing performance and price data.

In response to this change, brokers are becoming financial planners or advisors. Often, such brokers develop a *niche market* in the same way direct-mail catalogues appeal to a specific segment of the population. For example, an advisor may build a clientele of small-business owners with a high net worth, or women who have recently received substantial divorce settlements, or senior corporate executives with complex compensation schemes, or young professional couples with high incomes and low net worths.

Let's consider just one such niche market: the small-business owner. Most owners are so busy running their businesses that they don't have the time to manage their investments, let alone do the research to choose a balanced portfolio. Did you know, for instance, that there are currently 8,000 mutual funds available? It's also likely that small-business owners have a large part of their net worth tied up in one fragile nest egg, so they often need to find a tax-deferred means of diversifying their wealth. They face unique challenges in income- and estate-tax planning and, for instance, need to know what their businesses would be worth if they were sold.

Small-business owners don't simply want a salesperson for certain funds, insurance products, or other investment commodities. They want someone who is both objective and expert at handling their kind of account. The advisor should be able to educate them about financial planning, create a workable system that suits their goals within their tolerance of risk, and maintain an overall view of investments, insurance, and tax considerations to meet long-term goals. They must also be able to coordinate with the other professional experts they work with in their business, like accountants and lawyers. In fact, they may be the financial advisor's competition.

A financial planner who intimately understands the needs of this segment of investors becomes a human browser. The advisor anticipates most, if not all, of the client's questions and concerns, supplies key information, and devises customized financial solutions. He or she is an expert filter, giving clients the few, excellent choices that meet their needs, while shielding them from the overwhelming volume of options that aren't suitable. Clearly, it is the clientele who testify to the advisor's credibility. If the best small-business owners in your area tend to go to a certain advisor, wouldn't you be confident that this is the advisor for you?

The financial advisor's job is to simplify a complex world and customize solutions for busy clients who don't have the time or the desire to become financial-investment experts themselves.

Adapting the organizational principles of the network model that includes browsers and servers is ideal for the financial services professionals and companies. A large number of such professionals can share the economies of scale and specialized expertise through becoming a school of minnows as a brokerage firm or a network of independent financial planners. The larger brokerage firms are moving to convert their brokers to financial advisors who can leverage their incredible networks of research and brand recognition. At the same time, many independent financial planners are networking around new companies that act as servers to them, or around more established companies like Charles Schwab or Jack White, that provide marketing referrals and low-cost trade executions and reporting systems.

When we apply this model to the industry as a whole, we can compare financial service companies, not just individual advisors, to network browsers. Investment analysts, insurance policies, mutual funds, tax experts, and economic forecasters become the servers. That is, they offer an array of financial options that the browsers can select. In fact, it will be increasingly difficult for financial-service companies to sell their own investment funds. Clients will perceive this as biased service, and will look to other advisors who consider every pertinent option in an objective manner. In other words, clients will look for browsers who truly represent their needs, not those of the producers or servers, and who operate with the client's interest uppermost in their minds. Such firms will need back-line specialists to help in the analysis of such producers and services.

Using the Network Model in a Financial Services Company

What would we see if we applied the network model within a financial services company? Business would be organized around the client's needs, with a centralized management team that focuses on strategic objectives and places decision making at the periphery, where the front-line financial advisors deal with clients directly. Each of these front-line teams would concentrate on portfolio planning for a different market segment. In short, they would act as browsers for a specific type of clientele. When customers beyond that clientele approach them, they would be referred (with appropriate rewards) to an advisor in the firm or network that specialized in their needs.

The front-line team of financial advisors would be continually backed up by expert teams that, like computer servers, are the specialized information or product sources. These back-line teams would supply the front lines with all the specialized expertise and products they need to keep the customer satisfied, without unnecessary bureaucratic overhead and inflexibility. For example, the back-line teams, or servers, would conduct mutual-fund performance analysis, asset allocation research, tax and estate planning, economic forecasting, political risk analysis, and provide information on other pertinent topics such as the best insurance options and mortgage loans.

Specific investment funds or insurance options would be sourced from outside firms. In-house funds would be spun off as outside providers and compared with outside investment options to maintain absolute objectivity for the customer. However, by focusing on narrow segments of customers, small, niche firms or individual financial advisors would tend to represent a narrow range of funds and experts that best met the needs of their narrow band of customers. In this way, they could track the quality and consistency of those funds and experts for their clients.

BROWSERS AND SERVERS IN EDUCATION

Let's take a brief look at how the network organizational model could change our educational system. How might schools teach our children in the future?

In a network organization, the teacher isn't a teacher. He or she becomes a human browser or child psychologist who understands how children develop, how they learn, and what motivates them. Teachers must have the emotional intelligence to cultivate a relationship with each individual student. They must determine exactly where each child is in the development process and their specific strengths and weaknesses in learning. They must give each child the individual attention he or she needs to feel valued as a human being, which generates self-esteem and motivation.

By establishing a personal relationship with each child, the teacher can determine which subjects and skills need emphasis at each stage of education. They can protect children from the often-cruel criticism of others by not putting them into classes and learning experiences for which they aren't yet ready. They can push or challenge a pupil to go to the next level just when they need it. In other words, teachers in the network organizational model become expert at delivering customized education. They don't apply the same standardized teaching and testing methods to every student in the classroom, regardless of individual differences.

Teachers at the front line facing a room full of students every day are supported by a back line of experts or servers. They can consult with this host of specialists, the best anywhere in the world, via the Internet and many other sources. They can put each child in special study courses — self-help or online and interactive. If a large enough group of students will benefit, there can be live presentations by local or traveling specialists, either within or beyond the school. And, of course, there will be regular courses that almost all students take, but at the right time.

By adopting the network organizational model, the school becomes wired into the wider community. The community can provide supplementary funding, vocational education suitable to the business interests of the community, and guest lectures by expert retirees. With Internet-capable computers in the classroom, the teacher can rely on an assortment of online programs, videotapes, audiotapes, workbooks, and manuals as teaching aids. Parents, too, can become more involved in stimulating extracurricular education and activities in the home that will augment the school programs.

Our top–down, left-brain, mass educational system cannot provide the individualized education that our children need to develop their unique creativity and the right-brain skills of the future. One expert says that merely by entering our school system, the average child loses 90 percent of her creative skills between the ages of 5 and 7. Part of this is natural, as the development process moves beyond the raw creative disposition of children. But, do we need them to lose their creative skills almost entirely as logical and linear thinking skills progress?

Just as management's fixation with command-and-control hierarchy prevents them from seeing the obvious benefits of the network model and stifles innovation, so does the tenure system and the longing for the good old days of authoritarian teaching methods keep many educators and parents from considering the radical changes in education that we desperately need. Many teachers and administrators tell me that it is the parents who are blocking new, interactive, and creative approaches to learning. Parents insist that the schools return to the tried and tested methods of the past, they say.

My advice: If you're a parent, and you want your children to only learn the linear, left-brain skills that will one day pit them against computers, that would be a good approach. If not, perhaps you should consider the wisdom of the network organizational model, and begin demanding real change in our educational system rather than a simpleminded return to outdated tradition.

BROWSERS AND SERVERS IN HEALTH CARE

Today's HMO (health-maintenance organization) trend is just like the Wal-Mart innovation in retailing. It is merely a re-engineering of the top–down, standardized health-care and hospital-centered system of the last century. The real revolution will occur when our medical institutions adopt the network organizational model, and become a customer-oriented industry.

This can only occur through the transformation of the health care system into service-oriented human browsers and servers. This would automate the routine tasks that create crushing bureaucracy. More important, it would create the time required to address the patients' individual needs and feelings with respect. Why should a routine visit to the doctor or a few stitches take half a day?

The health-care industry clearly has one of the poorest track records in customer orientation. This simply means that there are incredible opportunities for companies that radically change the way they do business. Oxford Medical, for example, was one of the fastest growing health-care plans. It's not because they cut costs more than the competition. It's because they deliver a higher level of personalized service and offer and insure a number of alternative treatment options, something more and more people are seeking. But their lack of successful systems design caused a recent crisis despite their marketing success.

As you can guess from our previous examples, general practitioners in a network organization become human browsers, monitoring health and providing information about preventive care and treatment options. Many will become practitioners for a specialized clientele such as the elderly, or young families, or high-stress professionals and so on. As a result, they'll be able to answer most questions and foresee most problems. But, when an extraordinary situation does arise, your doctor will bring in experts from anywhere in the hospital, the city, or the world to address it, all via the Internet when necessary. Your doctor will be able to instantly and automatically send all pertinent files and test results to that expert for the consultation. In other words, your doctor will browse the medical system, the servers, to get you the best possible diagnosis or care.

You should only have to enter personal and medical information once with your primary-care physician. After that, any specialist can access it instantly from a computer. The bureaucratic overhead that is such a nightmare in most modern hospitals and doctors' offices will simply cease to exist. Soon, every patient will have a personal smart card — a computer-readable card that contains your entire medical history, insurance coverage data, and so on. A computer system will be able to read the card's data and check you into a hospital or outpatient clinic with no paperwork. Even if you were being rushed to the hospital unconscious, your smart card would tell the paramedics everything they need to know to deliver you safely.

Many people will have a practitioner for each of the three main areas of health care — general physical health, dental health, and mental health. Some clinics will combine all three areas of expertise under one roof and specialize in a specific clientele. It's likely that insurance will be issued by the doctor or general clinic you join, something like a personalized HMO. Then they will truly be accountable for the quality of service and the costs.

Hospital and professional-care firms' computers will constantly analyze the demands for different types of services and adjust their capacity to meet your needs. With these kinds of analytical tools available, you won't have to wait 5 hours to get a wound stitched in 3 minutes. To further improve the efficient use of medical facilities, many specialized services will be handled by quick outpatient clinics. More simple diagnostic devices will make it possible to administer medical tests and monitor your own health right at home. The professional expertise will be built into the device itself.

SUMMARY

The network organizational model represents the only means that we have for regaining the personalized level of service and craftsmanship of the past, without sacrificing the incredible cost efficiencies we gained in the assembly-line revolution. We can't get there by endlessly streamlining our old top–down organizations. Nor can we get there by holding on to the jobs and roles that suited such organizations. Everyone, not simply management, must reevaluate their careers, skills, business practices, and beliefs with an eye toward what the network model can teach.

CHAPTER 6

The New Look of Work:
Everyone a Business

SINCE ONE PAIR of human eyes has more information processing power than all of the computers in the world put together, the entire thrust of the information revolution is to leverage this power — the eyes of every consumer and every worker — at all levels of every organization. After this revolution, every customer will be a market and every employee will be a business, making decisions in their own sphere of influence, as executives have always done. Rewarding everyone for making more and better-informed decisions is what will motivate the new generation of workers and fuel the great productivity gains in the coming decades.

Within a company organized according to the network model, every individual or team of employees will work in one of two places: at the front line, specializing in a narrow group of customer's needs, or at the back line, specializing in a narrow area of expertise to support the front line. That is, the front-line workers will be like browsers, while the back-line workers will be like servers. There will be no more bureaucrats. It's that simple! Each individual or small team will become a specialist or a business. Each one will have real customers with real accountability to those customers — even for the bottom-line profit.

159

A NETWORK ORGANIZATION AT WORK

Let's look at one practical example of how a network organization might handle a typical business transaction through a front-line human browser. I'll use a phone-sales transaction from my book, *The Great Jobs Ahead.*

A mail-order catalog customer is calling. While the phone is ringing, a computer is at work behind the scenes analyzing the number to decide if it is a previous customer. If so, the computer will access the customer's record to find out vital commercial statistics such as age, income, past buying history, credit approvals, ages and birthdates of family members, comments about past preferences and experiences, credit card numbers, and so on. The file and the call will be routed to the sales representative who last spoke with this customer, so that she can handle the transaction.

If the call isn't from a past customer, the computer will determine the exact address of the number, or at least the area code from the phone number, and access an online marketing database to pull up a likely income, age and life-style profiler, including propensity to buy and product preferences. All of this will be done in milliseconds, before the sales representative can even pick up the phone to say:

"Hello, this is Customers 'R' Us. How can I help you?"

"Well, I'm interested in ordering a jacket from your catalog."

"Oh, is this Mr. Kearny? Hi, this is Linda. I helped you last year when you called in. Is your wife's birthday coming up on June 24th? I remember that you ordered the leather pants and vest outfit last year. How did she like it?"

"She loved it. But how did you remember all that?"

"We like to keep track of our customers—kind of like one big family!"

"Hmmm. Well, I was looking at that red coat on page 25, the one with the rhinestone buttons."

"Mr. Kearny, you picked one of our most popular items. These coats are just running out of the warehouse, and I'm sorry to say that I

won't have any more in stock until June 25th. That'll be too late for your wife's birthday."

"Darn," says Mr. Kearny, *"I should have called sooner."*

"Well, let's see what I can do for you. We may have some other options here."

Linda quickly refers to the past purchases file, and notices that Mr. Kearny's wife tends to buy higher-quality brands than does her husband. She also notes the leather ensemble bought last year for her birthday. Linda quickly accesses another file that lists new items on sale and locates a red leather jacket.

"Mr. Kearny, I think I've got a solution for you. We have a beautiful red leather jacket on sale that would go with the leather pants and vest you purchased last year, and it's only $200 more than the rhinestone coat. I bet your wife would love it!"

"Do you really think it will work? It's just two weeks to her birthday and I really want to get something nice this year. Maybe she wouldn't like the rhinestone coat anyway. She always says I have incurably tacky tastes."

"Well, this just may change her mind. How about this: I'll ship the coat to you overnight, no charge" —Linda is allowed to authorize such a shipment if she thinks it will help close a deal or if the dollar sales are high enough — *"and you can look it over, perhaps even consult one of your wife's friends. If you decide you don't like the coat, just call me back tomorrow and I'll have it picked up, no charge, and we can try another option."*

Mr. Kearny is deeply impressed and relieved. *"That sounds great."*

"Good," says Linda, genuinely pleased to help her customer. *"Shall I put it on your VISA card like last time?*

"Sure," says Mr. Kearny.

"Okay. I'll handle all of the paperwork from here, Mr. Kearny. Next time you need anything, or have any questions, ask for me and I'll be glad to help you."

"Thanks, Linda, I will. You've been a big help."

The advantages to someone like Mr. Kearny are obvious: He gets personalized attention from someone who, with a little help from the computer, remembers what he likes and the dates of important family occasions. He doesn't have to go on an exhausting and bewildering shopping expedition. Instead, because the company has information about other purchases for his wife, Mr. Kearney can have a gift she'll enjoy delivered right to his doorstep.

The advantages for Linda are equally significant. She enjoys the opportunity to use her people skills and the information on hand — thanks to the speed and efficiency of the computer network — to truly help someone and make them happy. She earns much more money today than she did as an accounts-payable clerk in the past. Furthermore, Linda is trusted with important decisions, such as shipping the item at no cost if she judges that it will help make the sale. Finally, since her employer has found that home phone salespeople are 28 percent more productive, she saves the two hours per day in commuting time, and can spend more time on her own or with her family.

But most important, Linda is her own business. She is measured by the computers on her net profit to the company after allocation for all of her variable and fixed costs. She gets a percentage of those profits as a primary component of her compensation, and can choose how much of it to allocate to the benefits she most values. Linda feels she could never do this well in her own business. She has a real network of support behind her: She's been trained, she is backed by an established brand name company, and she has the help of a powerful computer network to give her the information she needs to provide a high level of customized service.

LEADERSHIP MEANS HELPING EMPLOYEES TO BECOME BUSINESSES

The real information revolution isn't about highly creative entrepreneurs starting software companies out of their garages. That was the beginning, years ago, and we all have benefited from their courage and vision. The real information revolution, the one that's beginning to happen now, is about companies that use computer, telephone, and Internet technologies in a network organization. It's about companies that have the vision to make everyday workers into stellar producers by placing them in a structure that supports and rewards individual productivity and customer results. Such a company gives their employees instant access to critical information, authority to make decisions in their arena, and clear accountability for performance and results.

Sound like an entrepreneurial model? It is! The organization of the future will be a network of browsers and servers translated into human terms. Doesn't creating a two-tiered organization like this sound a lot simpler than the endlessly complex iterations of reengineering in business today?

Let's take a look at the more obvious career implications for intrapreneurs within companies or entrepreneurs outside.

In the new network economy, there won't be jobs, only businesses. We will all become entrepreneurs, either on the front lines as human browsers or consultants or on the back lines as human servers or consultants to the front lines. Thus, it will be the front-line personnel who run network organizations. The back-line personnel, like management, will be responsible for supplying the organization with the direction, power, and expertise it needs to accomplish its overall objectives efficiently.

Unlike command-and-control hierarchical organizations modeled on the assembly line, network organizations have a center, not a top. The role of management in such organizations will look completely different, but it will retain its crucial importance. That's because in any business, industry, or marketplace, central management will coordinate the information needed for strategic and financial planning, basic product research and innovation, brand name creation, market assessment, and promotion.

The many individuals and small-business teams within an organization will also benefit from a set of common rules and decision logic as much as they benefit from access to centralized company databases. After all, the nonlinear, random-access, right-brain, grass-roots nature of the Internet itself wouldn't be possible without commonly used protocols. It is these few rules and structures that form the foundation upon which the enormous innovations in Internet commerce and communications are being built. Such standards become the center, the *raison d'etre,* for any network. Management or leadership in the new network organization simply becomes the steward of those standards and the vision and direction they support.

Network organizations give consumers the power to mold the system to their individual needs at very low costs and with very responsive service. Thus, the individuals who deal directly with the consumer are critical. They are where loyalty in employment and customer retention intersect. Everyone else within the organization, from central management to back-line experts, exists to serve the front lines, and their roles will be more flexible and temporary as needed.

THE FRONT-LINE CAREER PATH: BROWSERS IN ACTION

Companies that adopt the network organizational model will design their business around the customers and the front-line employees who deal directly with those customers. The front lines will be composed of individuals or small teams that focus only on the unique needs of a specific group of customers. Customer specialization is the new focus, not the functional specialization of the past.

Front-line positions will be the first and fastest-growing career path within network organizations for the coming decade. Just like a small, niche business, these front-line employees must be entrepreneurs — creative generalists with cross-functional skills that can focus on and solve the unique needs of a distinct segment of customers. Since the smallest teams can be the most focused, innovative, and responsive, people in such front-line browser functions must have general knowledge, and the ingenuity to apply it in unique ways. Furthermore, they must easily adapt to new situations and learn as they go. I call these people *specialized generalists.* Their specialty is customer knowledge, but they are generalists by being flexible in their skills.

The goal of the organization when creating the front lines is to bring together the smallest number of people who have the cross-functional skills to solve most customer problems with little or no back-line intervention. Many customer solutions require a team of individuals who have areas of specialized skills, but can generalize and expand those skills to the broader team's needs, and even take on the functions of other team members temporarily when necessary.

The people who work best as specialized generalists in this new front-line career path:

- Are relational, service-oriented, and like dealing with people.
- Have a natural interest and experience in the arena of customer interests they will serve.
- Enjoy creative problem solving using a variety of generalized and changing skills and knowledge.
- Are action-oriented and experiential by nature, and tend to thrive in small, fast-changing environments.
- Are looking for long-term employment, and want to be rewarded for the increasing relationships they build with ongoing customers over time.
- Have excellent communications skills and work well with customers and teammates.

Front-line people must like the responsibility of making decisions and learning from their mistakes. The stories they tell of their career path probably include a rich assortment of real-world experiences and the lessons they have gleaned from confronting new situations, and often from failing in the attempt.

But, of course, such front-line teams will need members to do the organizing, recordkeeping, and computer-equipment maintenance. As a result, there are plenty of opportunities for workers traditionally found in a support role, but who prefer to be out on the front lines serving real customers and making decisions. As more and more routine support jobs are automated, many of these workers will move into front-line teams that serve customers. Such a worker can't remain in one specialized role, such as an accounts-payable clerk. Instead, their challenge will be to broaden their skills, becoming more like small-business controllers or MIS directors.

Large companies merely have to study the structures of very small businesses to see how they work. Out of necessity, small companies have already perfected the concept of cross-functional teams, because no other model better serves the needs of their fast-moving, competitive environment.

The Back-Line Career Path: Servers in Action

The other important career path in network organizations will be the expert employees who support the front-line workers. The back-line experts will have the specialized information, products, and services that front-line workers must have to solve their customers' unique and changing needs. The requirement for these experts is to provide expertise on demand, much like computer servers provide information to the browser software.

Just as the front-line employees have responsibility to their customers, the back-line employees have responsibility to their customers, who are their coworkers on the front lines. The back-line specialists either provide expertise and products useful to such front-line teams or they go out of business!

The back-line employees must focus on specialized areas of expertise or products rather than on one segment of customers. I call them *generalized specialists,* the opposite of the specialized generalists, or front-line professionals. They master a specific area of expertise or products (that's why they're specialists) that can be applied generally to many kinds of customers and applications.

I was speaking with a top executive at Hewlett-Packard recently about this kind of organizational change. The company had restructured its strategic-planning department into an in-house consulting firm that was responsible for helping the various business units to identify business opportunities. The strategic planners were forced to market themselves to these business units. They had to demonstrate their value to internal customers, the business units, who were now free to use them or not. In short, the strategic planners became servers and the business units browsers in the kind of network organizational model I've been describing.

At first, this was a difficult change for the strategic planners. They were accustomed to having top management's backing to enforce their authority and position within the organization. The rules of a free-market economy did *not* apply. Once they reorganized, they ended up generating more business and more revenue (which were now measured) than before. In turn, this meant higher salaries and more career opportunity. The key result was that these strategic planners felt better about themselves. Their value to the company, and their impact on the organization, was both greater and more obvious than ever before. I'm sure that the business units were even more pleased to have people serving them, rather than dictating policies to them.

Some examples of generalized specialists are advertising experts, accountants, estate tax lawyers, strategic planners, economic forecasters, Website designers, and industrial psychologists. The people who work best as generalized specialists in this new back-line career path:

- Will have in-depth expertise in one functional area.
- Will be more left-brain in skills, but more creative in applying them to front-line teams and workers.
- Will be more loyal to their profession, more technical than people-oriented.
- Will tend to constantly move in and out of project teams with other specialists to solve specific problems, and then move on to new clients and projects.
- Will have to compete with outside specialists as a benchmark of efficiency and effectiveness, or risk being outsourced.
- Will focus on continuing education to keep abreast of their ever-changing fields, or risk having their very specialized skills become obsolete.

These back-line specialist functions have emerged over the past century into full professional and technical career paths. With the advent of network organizations, they will further specialize in their area of expertise and focus on meeting the needs of the front-line employees and customers. Note how different or, to be more precise, opposite, these skills are from the front-line professions. It's best to choose one career direction or the other within your fields of interest, and stick with it.

A key difference in the network organization is who the back line specialized generalists truly serve. In the past, such experts were responsible to the top management and acted to support their need for decision and control. Now these experts will increasingly be acting in support of nontechnical, front-line individuals and teams that need immediate, simple, and personalized customer service.

The challenge facing traditionally left-brain specialist employees will be to distill the essence of their expertise into a form that is accessible to the front-line generalists. That means identifying what specialized knowledge can be automated and placed in the information systems of front-line teams. The reason? Automating as much of the expert knowledge as possible reduces the number of times that a front-line entrepreneur has to request in-person backup from the experts. It helps the company implement the *80-20 Rule*—making the 20 percent of your expertise that has 80 percent of the customer impact automatically available to the front lines.

Above all, it means taking the jargon out! Specialists who have been accustomed to working in hierarchical organizations will have to discard their professional terminology and orient their language and focus to the customer and the market. Their major responsibility will be to transmit their knowledge in the most effective way possible to the front-line teams. In the new front-line-driven organization, such experts will go out of business if they can't serve the front lines, and their specialized functions will be outsourced to consulting firms or eliminated. This will create a strong market for professional, service, and specialty firms who do have the customer focus that companies need and want.

SUMMARY

In the network organizational model, there are many great opportunities for employment. Companies will need professional and technical specialists, as well as people-oriented service professionals interested in different products and markets. We can step out of the employee role and chart our own destiny and reward in the career path of our choosing in one of two ways: either independently, as self-employed professionals, or as an independent business unit within a network organization.

We can do this by starting our own business in a niche market that requires specialist expertise, or as a generalized browser who sees a need that other companies have overlooked. Or, we can work for a company that wants to help specialists and customer-oriented individuals become businesses within the organization. This way, we'll have international brand names, economies of scale, and specialized expertise to back us up and help us be successful. Don't tell me the old jobs were better! We just have to be willing to embrace change as willingly as our best companies must.

The next chapter will look at how companies can effectively adopt the network organizational model. Though simple in concept, the network organization can present complex implementation problems for one simple reason: Human beings resist radical change, even when it is in their best interests.

CHAPTER 7

The Secret
to Changing Companies

MANY COMPANIES facing tough economic times try to re-engineer the organization, focus its priorities, and campaign for a participatory, proactive *zeitgeist* that emphasizes customer satisfaction. However, here's what I see happen most of the time:

The top executives make sincere proclamations about being "a customer-oriented company" and repeatedly say that "our most valuable asset is our employees." They talk about rising competition and the faster pace of change. They advocate listening to customers, offering customer solutions, and describe how individuals can spot opportunities to make a difference. This makes the executives feel good, and often makes the employees feel good, too. The executives believe that they are preaching a radical revolution and implementing all the key ideas in the latest Tom Peters book.

The employees, on the other hand, are convinced that they know more about what's really going on than anyone at the top does. Moreover, they see lots of things that could be changed to improve and streamline the operation of their department and increase customer satisfaction. This knowledge and the executives' invitation to use it gives employees hope: Somehow things will change, someone will alleviate the tedium of their routine bureaucratic jobs, and, one day, the endless trivial company politics will cease. Best of all, they

170

think they can enjoy all of these long-overdue changes without having to sacrifice their job security, pensions, and automatic pay raises.

Employees want more of a say, and it's certainly true that they have valuable input for management—but many don't want the responsibility of becoming more accountable. They don't want to endure the transitional aches and pains that are part of significant change. The truth is that in many traditional companies, neither the executives nor the employees want real change. If they did, they would already be working in a more entrepreneurial environment. Why? Simple human nature. The great majority of people prefer the status quo because it is more familiar and less risky.

The fact is, DNA research has shown that 70 percent of the human population has a risk-averse gene. Furthermore, there is at least one piece of significant evidence to corroborate this finding: Growth companies in this country can't find enough good people to work in their fast-paced, demanding environments. Most applicants do not proactively embrace change and are not willing to learn new skills and new ways of working.

Human nature makes the secret of change very simple and obvious: Most people will only change when an emergency or a radical change in the structure of their living or working circumstance forces them. In a crisis, everyday people become heroes, but only then. Most people resist change, period!

Even with the best of intentions, corporate executives and employees will never accomplish meaningful change unless there is a crisis that threatens their very existence, or unless management makes a unilateral decision to radically change the structure of work and its rewards. Speaking about radical change while remaining in a traditional structure does little or no good. The system rewards conformity, not risk. It watches the subtle maneuvering of hierarchical politics, not the needs and priorities of customers. And it has implemented a secure system of steadily rising pay scales and promotions that are viewed as entitlements rather than as recognition for individual results and productivity.

When every process is broken down into many specialized functions, coordinated by people who never see the customer, who knows who is responsible? Most employees in hierarchical, bureaucratic organizations just do as they're told, play politics with the right people, and then blame another department or the management when something goes wrong.

What I typically observe is that management blames employees for not wanting to take responsibility and accountability. Employees blame managers for not really leading change, not meaning what they say, not walking the talk. In most cases, they are both right, and this is the way they both avoid making genuine changes!

All of the talk, all of the motivational seminars, and all of the profit-sharing plans that give minor rewards across the board if the company achieves certain goals will never change the basic behavior of most of the employees in such a system. Why? People won't become decision makers and hold themselves accountable for two reasons. One, they would rather continue playing the old game and manipulate the old, familiar system than experiment with a new one that may sound good but is not proven. Two, management has asked for a behavioral change without changing the organizational structure, demonstrably and clearly communicating the new structure they are planning to implement. I have found that structure determines behavior. Changing the structure of an organization, including measurements and rewards, is the only way to establish genuinely new behavior.

The secret to corporate change is that you must shake up the old system and create a new structure first.

THE TWO WAYS TO APPROACH RADICAL CHANGE

Real structural change can be accomplished broadly and urgently in an organization only during a period of real crisis, bordering on business failure. Such an across-the-board, radical change is necessary if the business or industry is suddenly threatened by major competitors, radical changes in technologies, or significant changes in the marketplace. Occasionally, a long, cancerlike complacency may suddenly become terminal, providing the necessary impetus to change.

Whatever the cause, urgency works to eliminate the natural human resistance to change. It is a true luxury for a change-oriented leader or project team, because most people will face reality more directly, react less selfishly, and exhibit heroic efforts when faced with a truly urgent situation. You can leverage such an urgent situation to make rapid changes in a matter of months that, in a relatively success-ful and stable organization, might take years.

When your company is not in crisis, there is a better way to implement radical organizational change: the pilot-project approach. Begin by introducing the new structure to a small group within the company—a project team or division, for example—that appears ready to embrace change. Involve your best and most progressive customers, the ones demanding a higher level of service and response from your company. Work out the difficult bugs and chaotic experi-mentation with this prototype group.

Use their energy and ingenuity while protecting them from the rest of the organization. Nurture their process of change where you can, and give them visible, tangible rewards and recognition for taking this risk. Then, when you can hold this successful prototype up as an example, implement the new structure in other areas of the organiza-tion. This will tend to eliminate much of the natural human resistance to change, because people largely fear the unknown, not the known. When they see that the new model is workable and attractive, they'll be more likely to give it a genuine try.

In either method, shaking up the whole company or just part of it, the only effective way to change basic behavior is to create a new structure, a new system of accountability and new rewards.

NEEDED: THE ADVANTAGES OF BIG AND SMALL

Now, let's examine a simple insight I have learned from dealing with huge organizational changes in businesses both large and small: Most of the problems that large corporations have to face right now are not the problems plaguing small businesses. Similarly, small busi-nesses face problems that larger companies don't.

For example, a large company has the hardest time breaking the organization into self-managing teams because it has existed in an overly specialized, unaccountable bureaucratic environment for so long. One re-engineering project leader told me that his company was excited about a new idea: having the members on each team set each others' salaries. This is absolutely absurd! No small business would even consider such a thing. Every small business, or small busi-ness team, has a leader to make such decisions. Why burden the team with a task that will only end up pitting the members against one another?

Employees in large companies also have the hardest time learning to take initiative and to be accountable for their own decisions. Yet, initiative and accountability are inherent in small businesses because they don't have layers of insulating bureaucracies, overspecialized employees, and reams of policies and procedures to protect those who aren't pulling their weight. In a small company, it's obvious to everyone who the performers are.

Small companies don't have to get employees to listen to customers because their size dictates such intimacy and focus. The customers are always highly visible. This customer focus is often reflected in the company's structure and in priorities. Most small businesses can go under in a short period of time if they don't satisfy the needs of customers—and every employee knows it.

Every employee of a small business must know who their customers are and what they need, demonstrate concern for productivity and the bottom line, and acknowledge their own individual accountability to the company.

However, small businesses typically cannot benefit from economies of scale as do larger corporations. Furthermore, they lack the specialized expertise to guide them in making better strategic decisions. In other words, smaller businesses tend to be excellent browsers, that is, good at customer focus, but they lack the power of the servers, the vast sources of expertise, and economies of scale that large corporations enjoy. As a result, in niche markets, smaller companies tend to have the edge. In huge commodity markets, larger companies have the clear edge.

The ultimate beauty of the network organizational model is that it allows a business to combine the best of both worlds, just as we do within industries. Network organizations can benefit from the economies of scale of large commodity production systems and specialization in expertise, while paying attention to the individual and changing needs of their customers.

Such a network model starts not with computer systems design, not with the MIS department, or any such top–down approach, but with a clear understanding of customers' needs and the areas where the company can sustain a competitive advantage over other companies in meeting such needs.

The secret of change is to start with the customer and redesign your company from the bottom up, the way your customers and front-line employees would.

What does your company do better than anyone else for a certain segment of customers? How are the customers that you serve best different from others? How can you create effective small teams comprised of individuals who have the cross-functional skills to meet the needs of each group of customers? How can you organize your company or institution from the customer back, not from the top down? How can you transfer as much decision-making responsibility as possible to the front lines, where the customers are, and not to the back lines or to central management? How do you eliminate or automate bureaucratic functions rather than improving and streamlining them? How do you make every individual or team as accountable as a small business? How do you link everyone in your organization in a dynamic real-time information system so that they can learn faster as a collective and respond rapidly individually to changes?

HANDLING JOB SHOCK AMONG EMPLOYEES

These are just the basic questions we need to answer to success-fully move our companies into the new economy of network organizations. First, managers and business owners have to become more sensitive to the shock many workers feel due to the rapid, overwhelming changes that are already upon us. Our employees are not only apprehensive of change in general, they simply don't understand the changes they see. They aren't in control of downsizing and re-engineering. They just feel the effects.

The real point is that our employees should be the ones re-engineering our companies. They need to form the small, entrepreneurial business teams that understand the customers and redesign the operation around customer needs. This won't occur unless we radically change the structure of our organization, employee accountability, and the rewards.

Employees, on the other hand, must see that this revolution in organization and communication is an ultimately positive one that will both increase the competitiveness of the company and enrich their work environment and their financial rewards. Employees must see that they are the ones who will re-engineer the company around the core strategic directives of management. They must take on more responsibility and voluntarily improve their skills. They must be in charge of the needs of their customers, whether they are the end customer or an internal customer within the company. They must be in charge of their own careers. They must either become front-line browsers focusing on a small segment of customers' needs or become back-line servers who provide specialized expertise or products to the front lines.

In other words, as executives, we must involve our employees in the process of organizational change, and help them to become more focused and accountable for their contribution and their success. We must explain clearly to them why these changes are necessary and how they will help the company to grow and compete. We also must describe what types of skills and attitudes the company is going to ask of them, and how the employees will benefit from these changes. We must make it clear that individuals and small teams of employees will be evaluated and rewarded for entrepreneurship and that as small businesses within the organization, they will have more control over, and more accountability for the results they produce.

Above all, we must create a clear and compelling vision of the network organizational model and the mission and values of the company so that everyone can see how things will look once the transition is complete. We must stay in constant communication with everyone in the organization: listening, asking questions, and coaching them through the messy, confusing, and anxious process of change.

If your company is simply streamlining functions and departments and expecting people to perform the same jobs faster and for longer hours, or combining two jobs into one, then you are not re-engineering your company. You are just adding stress to an already stressful situation. If, on the other hand, you are truly interested in adopting the network organizational model that will help your company be creative and competitive in the next decades, you will work towards making fundamental changes.

First, you will cultivate individual and small-team initiative so that more of the important product and service decisions are made on the front lines. Second, you will reward employees for solution-oriented thinking that creates ways to tailor products and services to the needs of each customer at a low cost. Third, you will radically eliminate the expensive miasma of a multilevel bureaucracy. And fourth, you will continually support a proactive, entrepreneurial, results-oriented, corporate culture with every decision and action.

A NEW LOGIC FOR TRANSFORMING YOUR COMPANY

There are four principles that I have observed in the best small-to medium-sized companies that have already pioneered the shift to this network organization. Briefly, these principles are:

1. Clarify your company's strategic focus.
2. Organize from your customers back.
3. Make every individual or team a real business.
4. Create real-time information systems to wire the organization together.

There is also a logic or progression to the process, because these principles tend to build on one another. Therefore, though some principles may be addressed simultaneously, in general you should follow them in order, trying to clarify the implementation and results of one principle before jumping fully into the next. For example, you don't want to waste time and money organizing around your customers (Principle 2) when you haven't clearly defined your strategic focus (Principle 1), which helps you to understand what you do best, and which customers you should focus on to create a sustainable competitive advantage. Similarly, why make huge investments in real-time information systems (Principle 4) if your people aren't trained to use such information, or aren't held accountable (Principle 3) for the cost of the information and services they use?

Here, then, are the four principles in greater detail.

Principle 1.
Clarify the Company's Strategic Focus

In this age of fast-changing markets and extreme specialization, no one can do everything well and compete successfully. So, your first task is to clarify what it is that your company does best, and what has the most strategic value for your customers. Once you have done so, your next step is to subcontract nonstrategic functions to a network of outside partners.

To institute this principle, ask yourself these questions:

- Looking at our company's history, what have we consistently done well? What specific function or role do we play for our most satisfied customers? Would they agree or disagree with our assessment?
- Of all the things we do for our direct customers, which create the most value for them? For what product or service that we provide will they pay the most and be the least concerned about price? What do they value more highly that our direct or indirect competitors do well?
- Is there another company, either within our industry or outside it, that can or would be able to perform better in the areas of our strategic focus, because of greater economies of scale, a broader base of shared expertise, or better customer relations?
- Are there other customers we can serve who could benefit from our proven strength, and whose business would help us to build a more dominant position in this market?
- Who are the outside vendors with whom we are willing to build strategic alliances, with whom we want to have a close, long term relationship, and who produce a quality product or service at a low cost that our customers cannot get from us?

As you approach the end of this list of considerations, you should be very clear about what your company does best and who its best customers are. When you apply the next principle, you will organize around the needs of these very customers and not around the needs of the company's internal bureaucracy.

Principle 2.
Organize from Your Customers Back

Once you have begun to clarify your company's strategic focus, you can look toward organizing the company around the customer segments that you have determined to be strategically important to you. This is where the network approach diverges so sharply from typical re-engineering approaches. You do not analyze your present systems and processes and merely focus on streamlining their speed and costs. You literally design the company from scratch, the way your customers and front-line service people would. The most important result of applying this principle will be the elimination of your company's bureaucracy. By the time you complete this, the structure of your organization should look entirely different.

To formulate the structure of your front-line and back-line teams, ask yourself these questions:

- What people, skills, information, training systems, and equipment are required to meet the needs of each customer segment that we have determined to be strategically important?
- What is the minimum number of multifunctional people we need for each front-line team to maximize their flexibility and minimize the bureaucracy and cost?
- What specialist expertise should not be placed on the front lines, because it is too complex or needs to be shared across many front-line teams to achieve economies of scale?

Your purpose as you apply this principle is to move the bulk of decision-making responsibility to the company's front lines. That is why one of the most persistent questions a leader should ask in building a network organization structure is this: *Why can't this be done on the front lines?* Keep asking this question over time, as advancing technologies may soon make functions not practical on the front lines today possible tomorrow.

To help you in this process, address the following five questions, in order, to every back-line function:

- Can we eliminate this function? For example, do we need to check credit on all our customers, or can we safely narrow our inquiries to the high-risk 5 percent?
- Can we automate this function? Many routine, left-brain tasks can be performed more quickly and cheaply by computers. For example, let your front-line salesperson run a credit check with a simple formula programmed into his or her personal computer.
- Can we move this function to the front lines and simplify it? For example, have your salesperson or their assistant check the credit, whether or not it can be done automatically, instead of asking the accounting or credit department to check.

- Can we outsource this function? Finding outside vendors that can do the job better or more efficiently than you can will help you eliminate weighty bureaucracy and maintain your company's strategic focus when a function is too complex to automate or move to the front lines.
- Can we assign this function to an in-house support team that is just as responsive as an outside consulting firm? This may be necessary as a last resort when outsourcing isn't economically feasible due to transaction costs, time requirements, the need for corporate secrecy, or if the function is considered part of the company's core competence.

As you are completing the process described in Principle 2, you should have clearly delineated which individuals and teams are front-line browsers, each responsible for a clear segment of customers, and which in-house and outside teams are back-line servers, positioned to support the front line on demand. Such outside servers must obviously become a focused and intimate part of your network to be effective. That's what is meant by partnering with suppliers. The result will be a radically decentralized organization, wholly different from the command-and-control hierarchy of traditional corporations. When you apply the next principle, you will introduce clear business accountability to every team or individual within the company.

Principle 3.
Make Every Individual or Team a Real Business

The purpose of applying this principle is to create a corporate environment in which the smallest efficient teams have the urgency and opportunity to be proactive, creative, and accountable. To accomplish this, constantly strive to make every process that your company performs the single responsibility of one individual or self-managed team. To be successful, every team that you create must have:

- A clear idea of who comprises their external or internal customers.
- Quantitative and qualitative accountability for customer satisfaction.
- A solid understanding of what productivity means for this team and how their productivity will be measured.

- Responsibility for bottom-line financial performance, with a P&L for each team.

The teams you create at both the back and front lines cannot be truly self-managing if they are not responsible for their revenues, costs, customer satisfaction, and productivity. This will require an investment in software to allocate goals, customer satisfaction, productivity measures, fixed and variable costs, and a fair share of revenue to all teams, even to non-value-added departments like accounting. These measurements need to be reflective through your information systems without significant delays, or you risk losing timely information and feedback. If the teams lack this sense of accountability, they will tend to make bad business decisions and tradeoffs. Your job is to teach them how to be managers of their own businesses within the company, instead of making decisions for them.

As you complete the recommendations in Principle 3, you should have a network of browser and server teams that are accountable for results, and for the cost of their information and operations. In the next step, you will link them into a fast-paced, decision-making network. This step comes last in the process as it will tend to be the largest investment your company will make.

Principle 4.
Real-Time Information Systems to Wire the Organization Together

The purpose of implementing a network organizational model is to give self-managed teams more decision-making power, and eliminate bureaucratic overhead to provide quality, customized products and services for your customers. The spiderweblike structure that holds all these teams of entrepreneurs together is real-time information systems. Such systems give employees the information and recommendations they need as quickly as possible so that they can make good decisions in a timely manner.

The most critical aspects of real-time information systems are the vertical and horizontal links that wire the entire organization together.

Vertical, or *process links,* connect all small teams and outside vendors who ultimately make up a larger process or end-customer results online, so that they can stay in communication and coordinate with each others' efforts as they simultaneously move toward meeting customer needs. They also link the front-line teams who are dealing directly with customers to the back-line teams of experts, whose specialized input can assist them in the decision-making process.

Horizontal, or *peer links,* connect similar people in other teams and in other geographic locations who share similar experiences and can learn from one other. This fosters the dynamic learning organizations that many futurists have stressed. These kinds of links must necessarily be fostered by social functions and face-to-face networking events.

Once you have fully applied all four principles, you should have a company that is modeled on network principles, and ready to meet the challenges of the twenty-first century. Your company will be making most decisions on the front lines, rapidly responding to customers' needs with virtually no bureaucratic costs or delays. You are one of the innovators who will lead the way to the customized business practices of the future.

SUMMARY

Transforming your company into a network organization is an arduous, confusing, and chaotic process. Sticking to very simple, fundamental principles helps to keep you on the path. Communicating this simple vision will keep your employees and your industry allies clear about your direction, even during periods of chaotic, disruptive change. The end result is that your company and its strategic partners will have the collective intelligence and responsiveness of a school of minnows, not the slow-moving mass of a cumbersome whale. You will have access to the ingenuity and expertise of proactive employees and you will achieve economies of scale in information — the most important commodity your company trades. Furthermore, your company will be able to turn on a dime, while remaining focused and competitive in a world that is rapidly changing.

The network organization will be the key to sustaining your competitive edge in the race to dominate the new growth segments in all industries. The companies that adopt this model today will be prepared to take advantage of the enormous technological changes that are underway in our society and economy. So don't waste time merely re-engineering your company.

These times demand revolutionary change, not simple evolution. The executives who have the courage and foresight to lead the way will reap the lion's share of the reward. Are you going to be one of them?

Such dynamic organizations are fueled by leaders at all levels that can attract the best talent, and motivate them to higher levels of performance instead of merely following the rules of the past era. We must create attractive causes and learning environments that draw the best people and cultivate their inner spirit for growth and success. Are you willing to become such a leader or proactive professional?

CHAPTER 8
The Right-Brain Revolution

THE BEST-SELLING BUSINESS BOOK of all time is Stephen Covey's *The Seven Habits of Highly Effective People* (Simon and Schuster, 1989). Covey points out that companies are looking for leaders, not managers; facilitators, not supervisors; self-managing teams and workers, not employees; entrepreneurs, not bureaucrats. Covey and many others declare that people will only follow organizations that inspire in them a sense of purpose and meaning. The most successful people today model such principles and behaviors, inspiring others to perform at higher levels of creativity, productivity, and satisfaction.

Paychecks and other traditional incentives, though still important, are no longer sufficient. People need to develop their own internal principles and standards, their own ability to spot opportunities proactively, and to make decisions that make a difference. This is especially important now that change is occurring so rapidly that corporations and institutions can no longer manage change for us. Executives play an important role in easing the transition from the follower mentality so useful in the assembly-line era of top–down management to the responsible, proactive mentality demanded in the best businesses today.

Is this just an organizational fad, or is it the sign of meaningful changes to come? If we look objectively at the evolution of human intelligence, we can see clearly that we are poised for the next leap in human consciousness. We are about to enter the nonlinear or right-brain era. It's not just that our technologies and businesses are changing. We are changing, and we will be the ones to fundamentally change the structures of our society. We can't do this without learning new skills and adopting new behaviors.

Let's recall a simple point I discussed in previous chapters. Computers will automate most of our left-brain office jobs, just as electrical power and powered machinery automated most of our physical work, on the job and at home, in the last century. Yet, we might naively assume that it is technology alone that is fueling this transformation. That's only part of the story, and perhaps not the greatest part. In fact, there is a simple principle that we must grasp to fully appreciate the changes that are imminent in our work and institutions: It is not only new technologies that drive human progress. The evolution of human consciousness drives technological, organizational, and social progress.

THE REALITY OF HUMAN DEVELOPMENT IN HISTORY

We tend to look at history and assume that people who lived centuries ago were just like us. The only difference, this argument goes, is that they developed different technologies like the wheel or the plow or the printing press or the steam engine, and that these technologies shaped their lives; but this is not an accurate picture of history at all.

For nearly all of human history, from the original caveman to the farmer plowing his field in the 1800s, the consciousness of the average human has changed profoundly. The fact is, in most important respects our ancestors were not like us. Sure, extraordinary individuals may have enjoyed our average life span, living into their seventies, eighties, and even into their nineties. The elite had the leisure time to pursue their interests, which often included conquering other nations, or at best developing new philosophies, art forms, or mathematical formulas. However, most people's level of intelligence, and their consciousness of a personal self and their relationship to the world, was simply not what it is today.

The advances in the last century have been phenomenal when

compared to the very slow pace of evolution for millennia before that. Would the average person in the United States today submit to being slaves or serfs, or believe in the mythical Greek gods, or worship the sun? Remember that up until the 1500s it was commonly accepted that the earth was the center of the universe and that the sun revolved around it. And, of course, the world was flat! Were ancient civilizations really ecologically aware? Or did they just lack the technologies with the vast power to destroy the planet that we possess today? Was living on a farm in the 1800s really the idyllic life, or have our romantic notions colored the truth? Did the noisy, bustling, new cities offer nothing of value to the average person? If so, why did most people voluntarily flee the farms and rush to the cities in the late 1800s and early 1900s?

We take today's standard of living and our level of consciousness for granted. If we were transported back to the past we would experience more culture shock than nostalgic relief. Life may have been simpler in the past, but it was more brutally primitive. Most of us can't even handle a weekend camping trip!

Maslow's Hierarchy of Needs

Before we look more closely at human evolution, let's review a very simple concept introduced in the early 1900s by Abraham Maslow, one of the founding fathers of modern psychology. It's called *the hierarchy of human needs.* He developed a scheme for classifying levels of human development that is very easy to understand and apply. Figure 8-1 will make the discussion of our evolution much easier to follow.

Maslow points out that our first need, and first priority, is survival. Until people are able to meet their most basic needs for food and shelter, they can't concern themselves with personal development, or any other higher needs. People dealing with survival issues tend to be very egocentric and even violent when their survival is at stake. In one sense, very young children deal primarily with survival. Most impoverished people in the United States, approximately 10 to 20 percent of our society today, are living at or near survival levels long past their childhood. Basic survival needs shape the existence of the greatest proportions of people in developing countries. For billions, starvation is a daily reality.

Maslow's Hierarchy of Human Needs

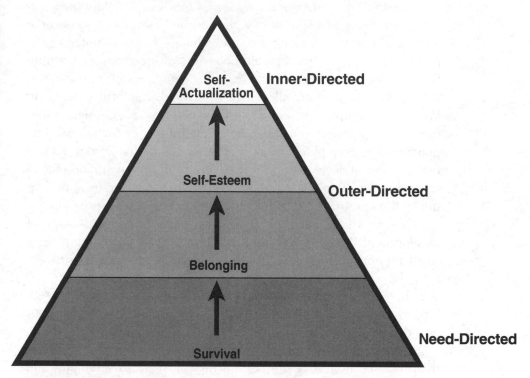

Figure 8.1: Maslow's Hierarchy of Human Needs.

Figure 8.1 illustrates the four stages of Abraham Maslow's hierarchy of human needs. It illustrates how we tend to develop as our standard of living advances.

The second stage of human development identified by Maslow is belonging. Once basic survival needs are met, people focus on belonging to a group, a family, a community, a tribe, a country. This is the first step towards socializing, building relationships to others that don't exclusively serve survival needs, and learning to follow rules of behavior. The group or community becomes everything, and everything outside the community is foreign and therefore suspect. Children from 6 to 12 years old tend to concern themselves primarily with belonging. So has the typical middle-class factory and clerical worker. This group dominated our society increasingly over the past century.

They still comprise approximately 60 percent of our society today, although this number is rapidly dwindling.

Maslow's third stage is self-esteem. Once people attain the security of belonging to a community, they aspire to stand out, to become achievers. This is an urge towards individuality, but it is limited by the prevailing values and acceptable behaviors of the group or community. Teenagers, for instance, increasingly compete with one another, yet maintain their group allegiance with highly conformist behavior. What they compete in, and how they perform, largely determines their career interests and self-esteem for the rest of their lives. The upper-middle class of technical, professional, and managerial workers fits this stage of development. Self-esteem is of primary importance to approximately 20 to 30 percent of our society today. But this number, unlike the number of second-stage individuals, is rapidly expanding.

Maslow's fourth stage is self-actualization, the highest stage of development that he observed and named. Even today, there are a small number of individuals at this stage of development—realistically, between one-half percent at the low end and at the greatest stretch, 4 percent at the high end. These people have achieved self-esteem and material success, and, therefore, choose to shape their own destinies. Conforming is not the path of these people. By developing two skills, first critical thinking in the self-esteem stage, and then introspection, they understand their own needs, strengths, and weaknesses. As a result, they become capable of setting their own direction for life and of managing their own path of development and learning. These people represent the rare leaders and visionaries who produce the most important innovations in our society. The most mature people typically develop these qualities in their twenties and early thirties. This is when they are most likely to clarify their career and lifestyle preferences.

In the last century, massive numbers of people moved from the survival to the belonging stages in developed countries like the United States. At the same time, a substantial minority moved from the belonging to the self-esteem stage. This all happened more rapidly than at any time in history. It was the result of the unprecedented advance in our standard of living due to the emergence of new technologies during the assembly-line era.

Today, and into the beginning of the next century, the network revolution in business will advance our standard of living even more rapidly. As computers automate our routine tasks and consumers demand, and get, faster, better service and customized products, a leap in the standard of living is inevitable. Remember the lesson from Chapter 6: Every customer becomes a market, every employee becomes a business! But remember, too, that this technology revolution did not occur in a vacuum. It was created by a huge, educated, and creative generation, a generation that had the highest proportion of individuals in Maslow's self-actualizing and self-esteem stages of development in history. This generation, which will soon enter their mature power years, will shape our organizations and institutions to an even greater degree in the decades to come.

Massive Shifts into the Higher Maslow Stages

Everyday workers in offices and factories are increasingly being redirected into self-managing teams that make their own decisions in their own areas of expertise. They have their own internal or external customers to whom they're accountable. They seek out the information they need to make independent decisions, rather than expecting guidance or asking for permission from a supervisor. These workers are developing self-esteem instead of simply belonging and conforming to the system.

More of the managerial staff are becoming leaders and facilitators to guide these new self-managing workers—because you can't tell them what to do! An even smaller percentage is moving out of corporate structures altogether, or they're moving to elite teams as entrepreneurs who innovate and pioneer new products or new markets. These people have to become more self-actualizing, creative, and visionary, simply because there are no fixed rules when pioneering radical changes and creating new approaches.

Billions of people in developing countries, who are enjoying middle-class living standards for the first time, are now moving into the belonging stage. They will industrialize faster than we did, benefiting from our technologies, capital, and management experience. This may mean that they will move to the self-esteem stage of development more rapidly, too. The elite in these countries are already doing so.

Clearly, we are witnessing the most massive advance in human psychology and development in history, but not without chaos and confusion. How could it be otherwise?

The most important changes in our society are clear. For the first time in history, massive numbers of people are moving into Maslow's self-esteem stage of development, while a strong minority is moving toward the self-actualization stage. To attract the best people at the highest stages of consciousness, companies will have to offer more than just monetary rewards. Meaning and purpose are far more powerful incentives for people who already have mastered the basics of survival and belonging. They are the prime incentives for the self-actualizers who direct their lives according to higher inner principles, and who take on a greater responsibility for their impact on others and the world.

CAUSE AND EFFECT

If effect, or effectiveness, motivates employees concerned with belonging and self-esteem, then cause, or purpose, motivates individuals concerned with self-esteem and self-actualizing in the new network world. Sophisticated computer networks make these individuals effective by handling the administration of goals and procedures, the coordination of people and ideas, and the measurements and distribution of rewards. Proactive, self-actualizing people give the system its cause — its direction and focus, consistent with the objectives of the organization as a whole — through constant innovation, communication, and creative decision making.

People throughout the organization must be trusted to make good decisions and must be rewarded for taking risks. They need the skills, expertise, and information to choose intelligently. But, most important, they must understand the organization's vision. That's why our companies and institutions need good leaders at the center who can communicate the direction of the company and tap their employees' ingenuity to figure out how to get there. These leaders must be among the tiny percentage of the population that are self-actualizers, because it is they, in turn, who will guide their companies towards becoming self-actualized organizations.

A BRIEF HISTORY OF HUMAN EVOLUTION
AND DEVELOPMENT

Two new books do an extraordinary job of clarifying the course of human development, and even help us to see the incredible stage just ahead. The first book is *A Brief History of Everything* by Ken Wilbur (Shambhala, 1996). Wilbur is an extremely astute and realistic scholar of developmental psychology, human evolution, and spiritual traditions. He offers the broadest and most complete understanding of human evolution I have come across, and even documents the role played by technology and economics in our history.

Wilbur makes a very factual and convincing argument that the concepts of developmental psychology, which traditionally address the individual over a lifetime, can be applied to collectives; for instance, to the human species as a whole over great expanses of history and evolution. Just as we can track the stages of development in a child, noting when he or she gains different kinds of intelligence and capabilities, so, too, can we track the development of an entire culture or civilization.

Both the individual and the collective pass through distinct stages of development. Despite the fact that, as individuals, most of us clearly mature into adults over the course of a single life, humanity in a broader sense has remained at a more childlike, immature stage of psychology and spirituality. We can look to our religious beliefs, for example, to gain insight into our collective psychology. While there are many religions in the world today, there is a clear common denominator among them. Most people in developed countries worship a parental god that authoritatively sets rules of behavior and metes out rewards and punishments. In a recent survey, 70 percent of young people stated that they believe in a judging god that monitors their lives. In a broader survey in the United States, 80 percent believe in a heaven and hell, and almost half of those believe that heaven is outfitted with winged angels and melodious harps.

In a similar fashion, most people have looked to institutions as parental figures that will take care of them. The corporation has provided them with lifelong jobs, health care, and subsidized their retirement. The government provides them with welfare benefits, Medicare, and social security. On the job, most people are told what to do, and when and how to do it. They follow the rules and roles established by their superiors who run their lives and reward them, or withhold reward, just like a parent.

If anyone can persuade me that this is not a childish view of life, I would like to hear it. We look in disbelief at how people in ancient Greece could have believed in Zeus and Aphrodite, or that tribal cultures today believe in gods that blow out the volcanoes and create bountiful crops. Future generations will see our belief in a father god who takes care of us and punishes us when we're bad in much the same way.

Without going further into the sensitive area of religion, here's the critical point. Our beliefs do not signify that something is wrong with our society. They do signify a certain natural and useful stage in our evolution. We create and rely on belief structures and ethical standards that are consistent with our stage of development. Our psychological (or as some would call it, spiritual) development clearly evolves. Furthermore, expectations about behavior coincide with these developmental stages. For example, we don't expect children to stop believing in Santa Claus, or to make sophisticated judgments, or to take personal responsibility for their actions, or even to support themselves until they're old enough.

Periods of radical technological and social change like this one tend to force leaps in evolution that move us into new stages of human growth. Part of the process of moving to a new stage of development is becoming more aware of the stage we are leaving. This awareness needn't be accompanied by judgment or condemnation, but it would help to have a clear picture of where we are now and where we are going.

THE ADOLESCENT ERA OF HUMAN EVOLUTION

The powerful, new, industrial technologies developed at the beginning of the twentieth century, and the two World Wars that used them, perhaps marked the very beginning of our society's transition from later childhood to adolescence. The widespread political and social rebellion against authority by the massive baby-boom generation boldly committed us to the struggles of adolescence. Yet, at the same time, five billion people in developing countries around the world are beginning to move into the industrial era we are just leaving, making the transition from the first-stage concern for survival to the second-stage, preadolescent concern for belonging.

Any parent could describe the basic stages of a child's early life that have been documented in detail by developmental psychologists. Children start out in the first year with no sense of their physical differentiation from the world. Everything is just one big soup to them. By about age one, they attain a basic sense of physical autonomy and identity, but emotional differentiation doesn't begin until around 18 months to 2 years. That's when children enter the terrible twos, and assert their separate egos and feelings.

To such a child, the world seems magical, as it did to our ancestors and does to many tribal cultures today. Things simply happen according to their needs and wishes instead of as a result of their own actions and efforts. From this state of consciousness, a mythical, magical, and Disneylike cartoon world is the basic level of reality; it's what they can manage. Their relational capacities arise from their own dependencies and needs, not from an ability to understand and empathize with the needs of others. Children at this age demand emotional recognition and push the limits of their power. Everything is "me, me, me . . . mine, mine, mine." They must learn that they are not the center of the universe and that their parents are in charge. That's why it's so difficult, even terrible at times, for everyone involved!

If we look at classical history between the writing of the *Iliad* and the *Odyssey,* we can see the collective consciousness of humans going through the same basic transition. Wilbur shows through a close analysis of how consciousness before the flowering of Greek culture was collectively like that of a 1-year-old. People had no real sense of individual self. That's why there was no sense of individual rights. Then, in the age of Greece, consciousness of a personal self developed to the point that the idea of citizenship in a democratic structure, and the concept of individual rights, became possible. Though the Greek idea of democracy was very elitist compared to our idea of democracy today, the concept itself simply did not exist previously. This fact is evidence of a remarkable growth in consciousness, not unlike the difference between a 1-year-old and a 2-year-old.

Let's skip about 2,300 years of human evolution, and look at the level of human consciousness and intelligence just a century ago. To do this, we'll review some of the data from Chapter 1. Did you know that the average person today has a standard of living nine times better, adjusted for inflation, than the average person living 120 years ago? This person does left-brain work instead of hard physical labor, works fewer hours per week in an air-conditioned office or factory, and enjoys pension plans and health benefits.

In the 1890s, 43 percent of our population worked on farms. About 1 to 2 percent had college educations and only 10 to 14 percent had high-school educations. The average person could expect to live to their mid-forties. We didn't have cars, electricity, indoor plumbing, anesthesia, aspirin, frozen foods, canned foods, radios, TVs, movies, cameras, elevators, skyscrapers, home appliances, electric lighting, air conditioning, and on and on. It was a different world. Again, it wasn't just a different era with respect to technology and education, it was a different era of human consciousness.

Kids growing up in the early to mid-1900s, the retired Bob Hope generation of today, experienced a very authoritarian upbringing. Their Henry Ford–generation parents set the rules and the kids followed them without question; they were physically punished when they didn't. Kids simply did what they were told, even went to the bathroom when they were supposed to—tied to the toilet if necessary. Our entire industrial and assembly line system just continued such an authoritarian or top–down structure of living and work. The last two generations, the Henry Ford and the Bob Hope, were perfectly prepared for such a system.

If we look at the prevailing cultural values of the last century, it closely resembles what Wilbur calls the "rules-and-roles" stage of child development that occurs between the ages of about 6 and 12. Children at this age think in literal or concrete terms, which represents the beginnings of linear, left-brain, conceptual thinking. They learn to follow the rules set by their parents, and achieve more autonomy in the process. They learn to take the role of the other for the first time in their lives, seeing beyond their own egocentric needs.

Rules and roles are important in a world that is structured by hierarchical relationships. They are critical, if belonging to a specific world is extremely important, because they define what the group will and won't tolerate. Rules and roles were essential to the development of the linear, clockwork world first pioneered by geniuses like Newton.

The Bob Hope generation was the last to be comfortable *en masse* with obeying clear rules and taking on clear roles. Being dutiful and conformist was their creed. Law and order was their highest value. They conformed rather than stood out as individuals, the epitome of the late-childhood stage of development. They mastered the stage of rules and roles more than any generation in history — so much so that they paved the way for the next stage of evolution.

The baby boomers were the first of many adolescent generations to come. They were brought up in an era of affluence and permissiveness shaped by the new authority on parenting, Dr. Spock. Baby boomers learned that they were special. They had a higher level of self-esteem, and naturally assumed that they should trust their own independent judgment at an early age. Like adolescents, they were people who questioned authority, broke all the rules, experimented with new things, and felt more allegiance to their peers than respect for their parents.

Adolescence is when kids break out of the rules-and-roles stage and begin to develop their own personality and self-esteem. And it is quite a struggle. They begin to think critically — about rules, and roles, and themselves and others, and the world they inhabit. This stage moves beyond concrete thinking into complex abstract thought. This is when an individual develops a sense of self-esteem through making his own judgments and decisions, and begins to become his or her own person. As maturing adolescents approach college age, they increasingly develop the capacity for relativistic thinking or the ability to see many points of view, instead of just one. This is the maturing stage of self-esteem, or it could be seen as the transition to self-actualizing behavior.

The achievement of self-esteem is a difficult and risky undertaking. People who experiment with their own authority will naturally make many painful mistakes. Life is obviously simpler and more concrete when you just follow the rules laid out by someone else, but thinking critically and reflectively allows individuals to see multiple points of view, rather than just fixed rules and roles. This gives them the freedom to leave their peers and seek out other individuals and groups. This is a more mature stage of consciousness, and it is where many people in our society are headed today.

We will never be like people in the 1800s or 1900s, any more than they were like people in renaissance Europe or ancient Greece. The chaotic adolescence of our culture is a difficult stage to endure, just like adolescence is the most difficult, frightening, and confusing of stages for an individual. It is a necessary step to move into adult-hood, and to have the capacity to function autonomously in an increasingly self-actualizing mode of behavior. What most of the Bob Hope generation views as signs of immaturity are actually signs of evolution. It's just that the transition, for an individual or for a culture, is never smooth or easy.

DEVELOPING HUMAN CAPACITIES, ONE STAGE AT A TIME

This brings me to the second book I want to discuss: *The Stages of Life* by Clifford Anderson (Atlantic Monthly Press, 1995). Like Ken Wilbur, Clifford Anderson has mapped the developmental stages that unfold as a healthy individual ages. These basic capacities begin with the most basic functions, which gather information by way of the five senses. This is Stage 1, ages 1 to 5, and is what he calls *prelinear.* The next capacity to develop is linear, abstract, or conceptual skills (more left-brain). This is Stage 2, ages 6 to 26. He breaks this stage into three basic steps of development: concrete (ages 6 to 12), abstract (ages 13 to 18), and relativistic thinking skills (ages 19 to 26). The last capacity to develop is nonlinear, intuitive thinking (more right-brain). This is Stage 3, ages 26 to 33. I like to make a rough comparison between these stages and skills in the workplace. I equate concrete and basic clerical skills, abstract and higher clerical, supervisory and technical, relativistic and professional/managerial, and intuitive and leadership/ visionary skills. Our educational levels would also correspond similarly: concrete with elementary school, abstract with high school and technical schools/junior colleges, college and graduate school with relativistic, and postcollege with intuitive (most people in this stage have to go outside our school systems to foster these skills). Simply going to school at any of these stages does not mean that someone achieves that level of skills or profession. I am referring to the higher range of achievement in each education and life stage.

Anderson points out that each capacity is stage-specific. Also, it's necessary to master the capacities of one stage before moving on to the next. The insight Anderson offers is simple: If individuals are properly nurtured and challenged as they grow up, their basic capacities and intelligence will unfold in a natural and predictable sequence. If their development is blocked at some point along the way, or if their learning is disrupted, for instance, by the need to go to work full-time or support a family, their basic capacities do not develop properly or any further.

Anderson also differentiates between these fundamental learning capacities which he calls Type 1 skills, which represent the capacity to learn basic types of skills. Then there are specific and application-oriented skills, like geometry, within a Type 1 capacity range, like abstract thinking. For example, some people simply have a hard time learning complex, abstract, professional skills, like basic accounting, because they never progressed to that point of basic human development growing up. Without psychological maturing into this stage of development, efforts to teach Type 2 skills will not be very fruitful. This is something our school system does not generally recognize.

Anderson explains that it is only during the last century that the average person in our society has developed the most basic capacity for concrete, linear thinking (again, which is typical of the most basic clerical jobs), while the higher levels developed abstract and relativistic thinking capacities in greater numbers (technical and professional jobs). This is a point I emphasize in my seminars and in my book *The Great Jobs Ahead.* In the last century, we have moved from an economy based primarily on physical labor to an economy run primarily by linear, left-brain, thinking skills. This transition is due to two revolutions: the technology revolution at the end of the nineteenth century and the assembly line revolution in work and management in the first decades of the twentieth.

Anderson's stages of life and Wilbur's analysis show that the capacity for left-brain, conceptual–linear thinking only fully emerges during adolescence, when the individual passes the stage of concrete and literal thinking. If adolescence is interrupted, development stops. This was precisely what happened to the average person at the turn of the last century. They typically went *directly* from childhood into adulthood! At puberty many went straight to work on the farm, and perhaps even got married and had to start raising a family. Most never had an adolescence that the typical person today endures, because a hundred years ago nearly 90 percent of the population didn't attend high school. No wonder many parents want to return to the good old days of the little house on the prairie. No adolescent crises, no teenage rebellion, and the kids start earning their keep at puberty!

This omission of the adolescent years explains why so few people at the beginning of the twentieth century had developed the more basic capacity for higher abstract learning and critical, left-brain thinking. It also explains why few jobs could require such capacities. In fact, the assembly-line revolution worked because it was able to profitably employ nonskilled, nonabstract-thinking people, which describes the bulk of the labor market at the turn of the last century. Employees were told precisely what to do and were rewarded for performing simple, repetitive, physical tasks — not something most of us would accept or be challenged by today.

As more people were needed to coordinate and control the assembly-line organization, they had to develop more left-brain skills, clerical, mathematical, statistical, technical, scientific, professional, and managerial skills, and, of course, better verbal and communications skills. A person simply had to be able to read and write for most of the jobs that emerged in the last century.

To fill this need, more schooling was required. Along with extended schooling, and the time to be adolescent for the first time in history, came the development of Stage 2 linear, abstract capacities that develop only during adolescence. Over the course of one hundred years, it is the capacity for abstract learning and left-brain thinking that we have most emphasized and developed. It is these skills that have increasingly dominated our school systems, our institutions, and our business organizations. Today, the bulk of our educated workforce depends upon concrete thinking (following rules and procedures), abstract thinking (technical skills), and relativistic thinking (complex professional knowledge and judgment). These are all linear and left-brain–dominant skills that we use to earn our living in most factory and farm work, not just office jobs.

The first standardized intelligence tests — the SATs, which primarily measure left-brain math and verbal skills — were not officially developed until 1926. This followed the advent of the assembly-line system and the rapid automation of physical work which made left-brain skills more critical in our economy. The origin of the SATs was in World War I, when the need to test for such basic intelligence was accelerated by the war effort. The IQ or intelligence tests that followed allowed us to determine, at age 7, which children had the highest left-brain intelligence. This way, the school systems could favor those who scored well, and groom them for professional occupations that would earn the best incomes.

The last century saw the massive expansion of left-brain intelligence in the most developed Western nations. Now, the Eastern nations are quickly challenging the West with success in assembly-line manufacturing industries and SAT scores that often top those in the West. We must understand that the leading edge of Western societies are moving into the beginnings of a nonlinear or more right-brain era where intuitive, relational, and creative skills will increasingly dominate. That's why the West dominates new, emerging industries, ranging from computer software to entertainment to biotech, that require more creative reasoning, with almost no competition from other countries . . . yet!

The Advent of the Nonlinear, Right-Brain World

Clifford Anderson points out that we are moving into a more complex and fast-changing world, where nonlinear and intuitive thinking become increasingly required and more common. This is occurring now because the period in which we learn and prepare for life is longer than it ever has been. New basic capacities for learning and function emerge during this even more extended time of development before entering the workforce. In the early adult years, intuitive, nonlinear, more right brain–dominant thinking begins to emerge. This level of consciousness is referred to by Wilbur as vision-logic. Anderson is quick to point out that it is more than our standard definition of creative. Such nonlinear thinking does not fully develop in a healthy, mature individual until the late twenties or early thirties.

The greatest progression in the past decades has come in relativistic thinking—the ability to analyze thinking, or what many call *critical thinking*. Anderson and other leading-edge developmental psychologists have therefore added another stage of learning and development to their model to account for this. They call it *youth*.

This new stage of development became apparent in the 1960s and 1970s, and spawned the greatest social revolution in our history. It occurred just when the baby boomers began to enter college, the first generation in history to do so in large numbers. Again, these are the years during which relativistic thinking starts to emerge. Today, nearly half of the population (46 percent) enters college, or seeks an advanced education. About 25 percent actually earn a four-year college degree, while approximately ten percent go on to earn a master's degree or higher. College-educated baby boomers are more creative, entrepreneurial, and inner-directed than their parents, simply as a result of a longer development period that allows these basic capacities to emerge. They see the world from new and broader perspectives because they have developed a greater capacity for developing judgment or professional expertise. They can understand many different points of view, not just a concrete set of rules, or an abstract view that sees one way of doing something.

Members of the Bob Hope generation, who think in more concrete and abstract, black-and-white terms, may never understand this revolution. This also explains why they are convinced of their own moral values — and equally convinced that the baby-boom generation has none.

As generation X, or the baby-bust generation, comes of age, they are even more oriented towards relativistic thinking. If individuality, the beginning of relativistic thinking, was the baby boomers' creed, diversity is theirs. Top–down, hierarchical corporate structures just don't make much sense to them, just as our left-brain, assembly-line school structures make little sense to the young, more interactive, and technologically literate kids today (the next generation, called the *millennial generation* or *echo baby boom*). The Bob Hope generation tends to view individuality and self-actualization as self-indulgence and narcissism. In their era, the prevailing ethic was conformity, or being outer-directed. The more advanced baby boomers and generation X view self-actualization as a new level of freedom, *and a higher level of personal responsibility.*

As our life expectancies increase, and as our education and human development stretches later into life, we develop higher capacities for complex consciousness. Wilbur emphasizes that "the world looks different" at each stage of development, because each level of consciousness offers a different view of it. That's why we must stop trying to recreate the past. There is no going back in the evolution of consciousness, intelligence, and the educational systems that cultivate them. Instead, we must go forward to the next stage, and start bringing new principles into our institutions and business organizations.

Longer learning cycles for youth, continuous learning throughout adulthood, and multiple-career cycles are on the rise. If we can, we should remain in a learning mode throughout life, trying different jobs and functions instead of getting locked into a single career path, putting off having kids until we gain more wisdom and maturity (so more of us can develop the higher levels of right-brain capacity). And why not? We continue to live longer. What better way to use those years than to take longer to educate ourselves, and prepare for varied and interesting careers, and acquire more complex skills and organizational systems (networks)? Better yet, there is no age at which it's too late to learn. You can develop these more right-brain capacities at any time, providing you have already developed the basic left-brain capacities that precede them.

Today, human maturity means developing the intuitive capacities to recognize your own needs, your own values, and your own purpose. It requires granting yourself permission to pursue your particular path, via your own learning process. This is what Maslow calls *self-actualization* in his hierarchy of human needs. This occurs increasingly between the relativistic and nonlinear stages of development. That is where the leading edge of people are moving, at this point in time. The most leading-edge nonlinear thinkers are the visionaries and entrepreneurs who are leading us into this new era, and are setting new moral values consistent with a new economy and new stage of consciousness.

The new paradigm of the right-brain revolution is the individual who determines, through introspection and personal evaluation, how he or she best fits into society. The new organizational paradigm is a school of minnows instead of a whale—a network of vertical and horizontal intelligence and learning that depends on individual creativity and accountability. Since the new organization runs from the customer back, not the top down, such organizations require inner-directed people who, at a minimum, make decisions and are operating in the self-esteem stage, and even better leaders and entrepreneurs who are primarily in the self-actualization stage.

In others words, we need entrepreneurs, not bureaucrats. We need more leaders and fewer followers. This is what people like Stephen Covey and Anthony Robbins mean by *proactive* behavior. Where it concerns human behavior, and not merely the technologies we employ, this represents the real revolution. New technologies that assume our existing jobs and perform our routine tasks simply force most of us to move into higher levels of consciousness.

One of the most brilliant insights Clifford Anderson gave to me was this: the baby-boom and baby-bust generations' higher divorce rate and greater career experimentation was merely the result of their need to grow and experiment into this new youth stage. They tried getting married and getting set in careers like the generation before them, but their need to learn and grow into the relativistic and intuitive skills necessary for this era was inconsistent with that model of growing up and becoming an adult. Many found that they weren't ready to make such decisions at those ages; this led to high divorce rates and frequent career changes, with people often moving into more creative work environments, and experimentation with extended travel and learning experiences and more entrepreneurial career paths. I have already explained how an accelerated rate of change contributes to the instability of family and institutional structures, but I think Anderson is on to the more fundamental cause of the disconcerting statistics of the past decades. We should see the benefits of this difficult transition in the decades ahead.

It certainly doesn't mean that marriage and families or fruitful careers are a thing of the past. These are still important values for the new generations, especially as the baby boom is maturing into its thirties, forties, and fifties. Most of the more successful of the new generations simply hit a greater degree of maturity and clarity in their late twenties and early to mid-thirties. That's when Anderson feels that people are prepared to make such longer-term commitments to marriages and careers. My experience and many others I have witnessed testify to that.

This means parents should reconsider pushing their kids into marriage and career formation too early. It means our whole view of education and careers must change. Ongoing learning and multiple careers will be the norm in the new economy, as will alternative education and many other concepts like alternative health care.

SUMMARY

The most critical changes coming in the next decade and beyond will affect where and how we work and live. We are about to establish a new network-driven society that will elevate relativistic and nonlinear, right-brain skills that are necessary to build new organizational structures based on the network model. Returning to the values and principles of the past is not the answer. Instead, we need to move forward, to the next stage of human consciousness, intelligence, work, and responsibility.

Computers are the powerful linear, left-brain machines that are going to assume most of the managerial, professional, technical, and clerical job functions of today, just as powered machinery assumed most of our physical farm and factory jobs of the past. Nonlinear, more right-brain skills are the key to the new economy. The new network structure for management and communications will increasingly dominate in the coming decades, just as the assembly line and linear, left brain–oriented skills did after 1914.

This right-brain revolution does not ignore or disregard left-brain skills. Human development is best understood as adding new skills on top of previous ones. The Information Revolution allows a much greater quantity of linear, left-brain input, managed by computers and the Internet, to feed our intuitive and more creative right-brain processes. Therefore, we need school and business-management approaches that build both kinds of capacities and coordinate them in new and creative ways. Whereas we once exported assembly-line business practices to our educational institutions to meet the economy's demand for left-brain skills, now we must bring the network model to our schools to stimulate the development of creative, right-brain skills that will be required in the twenty-first century.

We need to take the best, most enduring values from the past and move on into this exciting and challenging new era. Such transitions have always been difficult, especially in the early stages. This is what we have endured in the past two decades. No matter how much we long for a return to simplicity, we simply cannot go back to "The Little House on the Prairie" or even to the "Leave It to Beaver" and Lawrence Welk world of the 1950s and 1960s. If we take the time to look at the best examples of our new companies and institutions, and the most innovative and responsible members of the new generation, I think we'll see something worthy of our highest aspirations.

Be sure of this: The baby-boom generation will become the most moral generation in our history. Precisely because they experimented to such an extreme degree, they have learned the benefits of new approaches to life and the consequences of violating values that should endure. The next 30 years will see the baby boomers establish the new direction for cultural and moral values that will demand conscious intelligence and responsibility. It will be generation X and the next civic-minded, millennial generation that will shape and refine these values and structures for many decades to follow. The millennial generation, children in our primary schools today, may be the first nonlinear thinking generation in substantial numbers in history (having grown up with interactive games and technologies).

This is just the powerful beginning of the network organizational structure and the right-brain era of creative, self-actualizing behavior. These new structures and skills will dominate the next decade and continue to unfold until the middle of the twenty-first century, just as left-brain assembly line consciousness dominated the Roaring Twenties and most of this century. Then we will be poised for the next leap in human evolution — but that's another story.

PART 4

The Next Great Population Shift and Real-Estate Boom

CHAPTER 9

The New American Dream: Big-City Incomes, Small-Town Living

IMAGINE A COUPLE at midlife, exhausted from the years of hard work needed to raise their kids in a stable family environment and send them off to college. This couple, in their early forties, Ellen and John, are equally exhausted from the struggle to succeed in their own careers. John has been working overtime to install computer networks for a large telecommunications company. He's been doing it for so long that the word *overtime* has lost all meaning. Eleven hours a day is simply business as usual. Ellen has dedicated years to changing her career by going to medical school and has just recently earned her degree. Talk about stress! She's one of the few who made it all the way through the program!

Now, Ellen and John are in debt from her medical training and they've still got to support their kids through college. So, while they've got more time on their hands without the kids at home, they still need a high income. John sees little chance for further promotion and a bigger paycheck. The starting salary for Ellen's medical specialty is half what it was before she started medical school, thanks to the HMO trend. John has reached his limit of endurance, but the salary Ellen can expect won't support the family and all of their debts — at least not in California.

John and Ellen start looking around to see if there are other cities   **207** where Ellen's specialty can command a higher salary. Both Seattle and Dallas are excellent prospects. Before they make the final choice, and much to their surprise, Ellen gets a call from a physician's clinic in a small town in Texas that had gotten her name from one of the Dallas clinics. The clinic needs a specialist in her field to join the practice. It is willing to offer her the salary level she first anticipated before going to medical school. Furthermore, if things work out, she can become a partner within two years — a brief span of time unheard of in most places.

This opportunity is too good to be true, but it gets even better! When John and Ellen visit the clinic, meet the people, and take a look around at the area, it suddenly dawns on them how much less it will cost to live in this lovely, small Texas town. Suddenly, the dream of big-city incomes and small-town living becomes a tangible reality. The only hitch is that John doesn't have a job offer there. They go for it anyway, because Ellen's new salary can now support the family. A few months later, John finds a better job in his industry. He'll have to travel more because he simply can't do that many computer-network installations in a town this size, but he'll work less overtime and get a higher salary. For Ellen, who lives just minutes from the clinic, there's no commute at all.

Big-city incomes, small-town living? A lot more of us are going to consider options like this in the future. Why? Changing technologies and a new shift in where we live will create opportunities in new-growth towns and cities.

LIVING SMARTER, NOT WORKING HARDER

Most professionals today live with the daily stress of trying to handle two imperatives: being a success at work and creating a comfortable home. For many of us, this has meant buying a house in the suburbs where we could raise our families safely and affordably — and paying for it every day with an exhausting commute. The price of having both has been steep indeed.

We are about to see the next great population migration in our country, which will be the force driving real-estate appreciation in the next decade. An enormous number of people will escape over-crowded, expensive suburbs and move to a variety of attractive small towns, new-growth cities, *exurban* areas beyond the suburbs, and even back to trendy urban areas. Whether you're looking for a new home or a new investment, you can be among those to reap the huge profits.

This next migration is not merely about financial profit, it is more fundamentally a lifestyle opportunity. It reflects the unprecedented range of lifestyle choices we now enjoy. Simply put, we now have the flexibility to choose a geographic area that supports both our personal and our professional goals. We are no longer bound by the commute between home and office.

We've tried working harder. We've also tried working longer. We've tried cutting expenses and debt to lower our need to work so much. Most people, though, haven't considered *living* smarter — moving their home and work to an area that doesn't continually cost more for a decreasing quality of life. And wouldn't business costs be lower for companies? In short, we don't consider relocating to higher-quality, affordable towns outside of the congested suburbs. That's largely because we are just now beginning to see the possibilities offered by the network revolution in business: communication technologies that will foster radical changes in how and where we work and, as a result, give us more choices about where we live.

THE IMPACT OF KEY TECHNOLOGIES

It should come as no surprise that certain key technologies, in fact the most basic ones, fundamentally change the way we live. We could not live in the suburbs that most of us inhabit today if it hadn't been for the invention and commercialization of cars, phones, and electricity. These key technologies were invented at about the same time, in the 1870s and 1880s. As we saw in Chapter 1, their widespread consumer popularity didn't occur until 30 to 40 years later, during the Roaring Twenties. By the height of that economic boom in 1929, approximately 90 percent of urban households had electricity, phones, and an automobile.

Migration from the crowded cities to the suburbs, which accelerated after the Roaring Twenties, happened for one simple reason: because we could! Cars, phones, and distributed electricity made it possible to live at a distance from where we worked. We could move without sacrificing the conveniences that made modern urban homes so attractive. The more of us that moved, the more phone lines, electricity, and roads could be affordably extended. These basic technologies gave us more choice. We no longer needed close proximity to large factories, power plants, or to a telegraph or railroad station. Furthermore, since land was much cheaper outside the cities, businesses, too, could profit from moving. Since the 1930s, moving to the suburbs was the solution to expensive, overcrowded, unsafe, and hurried city life.

Naturally, as more and more people and businesses moved to the suburbs between the 1930s and the 1980s, they began showing all the signs of urban decay, along with a few unique problems of their own. As the density of population increased, suburban real-estate prices skyrocketed as high as millions of dollars per acre. Eventually, it became *less* affordable for most businesses and consumers. Suburban crime rates are rising, yet there is little sense of community to comfort the victims or seek a common solution. Pollution and traffic congestion — since virtually all suburbs were never constructed with a view toward good, affordable, public transportation — are commonplace. The smooth streets, clean sidewalks, beautiful parks, and pristine schools that once made suburbs attractive to families are in desperate need of capital improvements. The dream of suburbia has failed precisely because of its very growth and success.

We are on the brink of the next major population migration, fueled by the same incentive that drove us to the suburbs: an affordable, high-quality lifestyle. Furthermore, this migration is fueled by innovations in the same three areas of technology: communication, transportation, and energy. We are going to see at least 20 percent of the population of North America, or approximately 70 million people, migrate to exurban areas, small towns, and new-growth cities in the next three decades. This will create an enormous opportunity for consumers interested in a better quality of life, for real-estate investors interested in predictable profit, and businesses interested in reaching new consumers with less competition.

PREDICTING THE PATTERN OF MIGRATION

The secret to building your net wealth through real estate, the largest portion of most peoples' net worth, is predicting where large numbers of people and businesses will move next. When you understand the basic technological innovations in three key areas that underlie all migrations—communication, transportation, and energy—this becomes entirely possible.

We can see how we have moved from the farms to the cities and from the cities to the suburbs in a very predictable pattern. These migration trends, illustrated in Figure 9.1, occur in an S-curve fashion. That means the movement is more a trickle than a flood for about 30 years, then, suddenly, an enormous number of people migrate over

---

Figure 9.1: Three Migration Waves

Figure 9.1 shows the three waves of migration in which large-scale movements of the population fit the familiar S-curve of social, technological, and product acceptance trends. In the first wave, we moved from the farms to the cities; the rapid growth phase occurred from around 1875 to 1905. In the second wave, we moved from the cities to the suburbs; the rapid growth phase occurred from the mid-1930s to the mid-1960s. The third wave of migration, which is imminent, will see a mass exodus from the suburbs to lower density exurban and rural areas. The rapid growth of this migration is just ahead, from the mid-1990s to the mid-2020s.

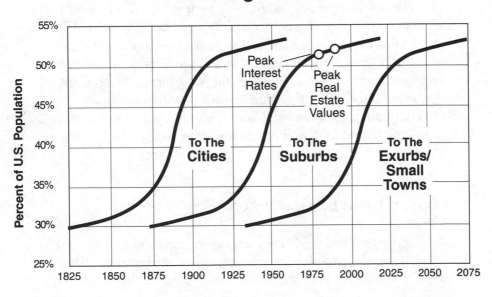

the same span of time, about 30 years. When such migrations become a mainstream phenomenon, demographers begin calling them *population shifts.*

That's exactly what's about to take place. Over the next 30 years, a huge number of people are going to migrate from the suburbs to what would have been considered, until just recently, rural areas or small towns. These areas will continue to grow over the next 60 years until they peak at around the year 2050.

In Figure 9.1, we can see the first migration pattern, from the farms to the cities. The most marked population shift occurred during the rapid growth phase of this S-curve, from approximately 1875 to 1905. The popular availability of railroads, telegraphs, and large-scale power plants made cities the attractive, economical place to live and work. These were *centralizing* technologies. Consumers simply couldn't get cheap power at the farm, nor was it economical to string telegraph wires or lay railroad track between farm and city. Also, the cities offered a different place to live, plentiful entertainment, innovative products and services, and new, higher-paying factory jobs.

In the second wave of migration shown in Figure 9-1, from the mid-1930s to the mid-1960s, there was a mass exodus from cities to suburbs. This movement was made possible by the rapid proliferation of cars, phones, and electricity. These were *decentralizing* technologies. They allowed us to travel to and communicate with the cities for business, yet live in uncrowded, affordable suburbs.

The third major population migration shown in Figure 9-1 will begin its growth phase from the mid-1990s and last into the mid-2020s. During this migration, we will return to smaller towns, called *penturbia,* and to more remote suburbs, called the *exurbs.* A study of past migration trends by Jack Lessinger at Washington State University —who coined the term *penturbia*—suggests that approximately 20 percent of the population will make this shift. That means as many as 70 million people in North America will be on the move in the next 30 years!

60-YEAR BASIC INNOVATION CYCLES

Consumers and businesses migrate *en masse* to new geographic locations to take advantage of low-cost real estate, better lifestyles, and better jobs. Such migrations are made possible by major breakthroughs in communication and transportation technologies and by the discovery of new energy sources. Breakthroughs in these three key areas — communication, transportation, and energy use — predictably occur every 60 years. Because these key areas are so fundamental to how and where we live and work, they are called *basic innovations.* Let's examine this 60-year basic innovation cycle in more depth, to see exactly what drives it and why the next major population migration is just ahead.

About every 55 to 60 years we can see peaks in the cycles of basic innovations that are broadly usable. Don't ask me why this occurs, but we can document clearly that it does. (These cycles in basic innovations are different from the 40-year cycles covered in previous chapters that reflect innovation in business management, work, products, and services.) These basic innovation cycles change how we work and live at the most fundamental level. There are several examples from history that will clarify just how fundamental these innovations are:

- The invention of the steam engine, steamships, and stagecoaches from the 1760s to the 1780s on, and the construction of canals that laid the foundation for the Industrial Revolution. Energy use increased; wood was the primary source of fuel.
- The railroad, power plant, and telegraph that were invented from the 1820s through the 1840s greatly furthered the spread of industrialization and allowed the population to travel and to relay messages at unprecedented speeds. Coal started becoming the principle energy resource.
- Automobiles, telephones, AC/DC electricity, airplanes, and the electric motor, inventions that clustered betwen the late 1870s and the early 1900s, made speedy transportation and communication much more convenient and readily available. Oil started becoming the principle energy resource.
- Transistors, the building block of digital computers, television, atomic energy, radar, and the jet engine, inventions and discoveries that all occurred between the mid-1930s to the mid-1950s, again increased the speed and availability of transportation and communication, and provided us with new forms of energy.

If we take a single type of basic innovation and use it as a lens through which to view history, these 60-year basic-innovation cycles become obvious. In transportation technology, major developments occurred about every 60 years: Steamboats were developed in the 1770s, railroads in the 1820s to 1830s, automobiles in the 1880s, and jet airplanes in the 1940s. In technologies of energy use, we have moved from wood to coal to oil from 1760 to 1940. The next phase will probably see not just increasing contributions from nuclear, fusion, solar, and wind energy, but the hydrogen and fuel cell revolution which will dominate in the coming decades. In communication technologies, we see the same 60-year cycles: horse couriers were used from the 1780s, the telegraph from the 1840s, telephones from the 1900s on, and finally television and digital computers from the 1950s/1960s. If you are a serious economist, you'll recognize that the basis for this basic innovation cycle is the Kondratieff Wave.

THE NEXT MIGRATION: OUT OF THE SUBURBS

The accelerated consumption of personal computers for household use and the radical decentralization of business decision making due to advances in network technologies will transform what is now a fringe trend into a mainstream one. Many of us will soon work out of the home, part-time or full-time, instead of commuting, or more likely will work in satellite offices closer to our homes. The advantage of satellite offices are greater technology connections and more social interaction. Working at a distance from centralized corporate offices will become an increasingly popular alternative for all kinds of business people, not just for the writers, consultants, salespeople, and entrepreneurs who enjoy this freedom now. As a result, many of us in the coming decades are going to consider moving out of the suburbs or cities to a small town or exurb. Why? Because the suburbs aren't going to get better. They're going to get worse.

Within the next 30 years, a new social ethic will reshape the American Dream, and new technology will make it possible. We are about to witness the resurgence of this country's venerable ideal of individualism and simple community living while our sophisticated communications technology will give us ready access to most of the information, education, and entertainment we need.

The strongest incentive for the return to small towns is the deteriorating condition in the suburbs. Now suburbs, like the urban areas 60 years ago, are feeling the effects of a rising crime rate. They simply aren't the safe havens they once were, especially for the elderly and for families with young children. The fact is, inner-city crime doesn't pay as well as it used to. Urban dwellers are increasingly streetwise. As a result, smart criminals are moving out to the suburbs where the prey —and that means you—are naive and vulnerable.

Though the rising crime rate is the most significant factor causing suburban flight, there are other problems as well. Traffic congestion and pollution are becoming commonplace, the cost of real estate has skyrocketed, and the once-pristine infrastructure, including roads, commercial buildings, malls, and schools, is badly deteriorating. What makes matters worse is that suburbs generally lack the business and industrial tax base to finance the much-needed repairs.

We can't expect these trends to stop any time soon. Crime is not going to stop moving into the suburbs, pollution is not going to disappear, most schools won't turn the corner for a long time, and traffic will certainly get worse. In fact, the only viable solution for these pernicious social problems is suburban flight. This will relieve the population pressure that contributes to the problem. In the coming decades, that's exactly what is going to occur, but on a scale far greater than most people expect.

This exodus from the suburbs will guarantee that there will be only a modest appreciation in home values, despite a booming economy. This will put an even greater strain on the tax base in suburban areas, which threatens the quality of life or makes the suburbs an increasingly expensive place to live. Suburban dwellers need to consider whether staying put is the best choice, even if the population pressure is relieved.

On the other hand, the impending suburban exodus does not mean that existing suburbs will shrink in size. History teaches us that the locales left behind during these population shifts often continue to grow. For example, almost all cities have a larger population in their downtown areas now than they did when the suburbs took off decades ago. The difference is that suburban real estate will grow and appreciate at a much more modest rate than it did in the 1970s and 1980s. The real growth—and the opportunity for real financial gain—will occur in the new areas: exurbs, small towns, new growth cities, and downtown areas.

The New American Dream: Big-City Incomes, Small-Town Living

Wouldn't you like to live in a safe town where you know your neighbors, where crime is almost unheard of, where taxes are low, where you can have an impact on the local politics and school system, where you can get a home for half the price you're paying in a big suburb, or less?

Americans have endured and enjoyed two decades of social experimentation and technological innovation. College-educated baby boomers have experimented with everything in the search for new values and new lifestyles — from hippies to yuppies, from cocaine to Rogaine! The baby boomers are now feeling the effects of *their* midlife crisis. We are reconsidering the wisdom of the middle road, one that includes the best of both worlds.

The baby boomers have started a massive social revolution that will affect our country for decades to come. All revolutions begin with a fervent rejection of tradition. We throw out the baby with the bathwater. During the next phase, consolidation, we consider what we have mistakenly thrown away and take the baby back by conserving the best aspects of the old and combining them with the best aspects of the new. The baby boomers rejected the lifestyle of their parents: suburbia, conformity, contentment with standardized products and services, and a lack of passion for life. What the baby boomers still want is the opportunity to express their individualism, but without sacrificing the community ethics that make for good families, good friends, and good neighborhoods.

Many baby boomers long to restore a balance between our material desires and a rich inner life that is sustained by simple community living and a slower, more reflective pace. In essence, this dream combines the hippie values of back-to-basics living with the material affluence that yuppies enjoy. For the first time in our history, we have the technology to make that happen. In the last two decades, the enormous changes in communications technology alone make it possible to return to simple small-town living, yet stay in touch with the urban professional world.

As stated in Chapter 3, by 2002 Craig McCaw and Boeing plan to put up 430 low-orbit satellites that will bring fiber-optic bandwidth and information capacity to rural areas. Other satellite systems are bringing mobile phones, pagers, and inexpensive cable TV to rural areas. There will be nothing you can access on the Internet or TV or phones in the largest cities that you can't get in a small town, albeit often at a slightly higher price. When you factor in what you can save on a home and the commute by living and working in a small town, this added expense becomes virtually meaningless.

Satellite communications will allow many people to take their professional work with them to the exurbs. Others will see opportunities for starting new small businesses in these booming towns. They can maintain the high income levels they earned in the cities, while greatly reducing the costs of living. The only real sacrifice in moving to a smaller town is more limited access to urban entertainment such as theater, symphony, and fine dining. Thus, people in these smaller towns will tend to vacation and take frequent weekend trips to the big cities instead of going to some quaint town or resort. The most affluent will have a resort home and a downtown apartment, getting the best of both worlds, but with their taxable residence in the smaller town. The tax savings alone can often pay for the downtown condo. Many will look for community living in renovated urban areas where work, entertainment, and shopping are reintegrated into urban villages.

THE ULTIMATE TREND: CUSTOMIZED-LIFESTYLE COMMUNITIES

The real impact of the information revolution is this: We are moving inexorably from a standardized economy to a customized economy, as we discussed in Chapter 2. The sprawling suburban developments with their lookalike houses on small rectangular lots devoid of trees, streams, or other interesting natural geography represent the epitome of the old economy. They were uninspiring to begin with, and now that they're heavily populated, they're even worse. High costs, rising crime rates, soaring taxes, crippling congestion, stifling pollution, and deteriorating schools and public services have turned what used to be a safe, affordable haven into a nightmare for more and more households.

We simply can't change most of our present suburban developments: Their standardized design and absence of natural beauty is already fixed. As a result, even in the best suburban neighborhoods that are minimally affected by problems of crime and congestion, the rate of appreciation will decline steadily in the coming decades.

The new customized economy means we will be looking for unique homes and interesting communities rather than the sterile, featureless tract housing of the past. We will see the emergence of innovative housing developments that will require new settings in growing small towns, exurbs, and new-growth cities.

What does the new community look like? Not like the standardized suburban neighborhood. The first principle to understand is that there will be many kinds of communities to fit the many new lifestyles that are emerging in our increasingly customized economy. The sophisticated psychographic or life-style models we've already mentioned—from Claritas' *Prizm* to CACI's *Acorn* to Donnelly's *Lifestyle* —have segmented American households into anywhere from forty to seventy distinctly different lifestyles despite commonalities in traditional demographic categories such as income, age, and ethnicity.

My favorite model is Claritas' because of its clever, clustering logic and evocative descriptions. I hardly have to describe lifestyles such as "Blue Blood Estates" or "Shotguns and Pickups." Not only do we get a quick feeling for them just by the names, we know almost instantly if they are our kind of lifestyle. Each of these models has their advantages. The CACI Acorn model focuses on the type of housing people choose, which makes it useful for real-estate developers and investors. The Donnelly Lifestyles model is the best at pinpointing lifestyle characteristics all the way down to individual households, not just zip codes or neighborhoods.

We will seek housing developments, communities and neighborhoods that increasingly reflect our individualistic lifestyles. New, more attractive communities that cater to our taste for unique, customized homes will appreciate dramatically.

The basis for psychographic marketing models is that birds of a feather *do* tend to flock together. Where we live reflects our lifestyle preferences. The options for such lifestyles are going to expand dramatically in the coming decades, due to advances in information technologies that will revolutionize the way we work. By determining which lifestyle or lifestyle combinations suit you, you can buy inexpensive reports from companies like Claritas, which screen towns that aren't suitable and save you a lot of time. You can then focus on evaluating a select group of towns that you are most likely to enjoy.

Six Winning Characteristics of the Best Communities

There are six characteristics shared by the most successful communities that you should look for: a new look that includes intelligent town planning for increased human interaction and abundant open space; flexibility in home design; planning for safety; shared facilities; and a high-tech communications infrastructure.

Village Designs that Maximize Human Interaction

First, there will be a new look to these communities that accords with one of the major consumer trends of this era. To give you an idea of this look, consider what vacation spots people choose when they take their families on a vacation. Generally, they go to clean, well-designed theme and amusement parks such as Disney World. These have a small-town feel and offer an attractive aura of humanness and activity, a quaint or nostalgic quality, and are constructed to take advantage of the natural geography.

Intelligent, creative town planning is one of the principal reasons that vacationers flock to places like Whistler (British Columbia) and Aspen, and why the real-estate values remain consistently high. Like these award-winning towns, the layout of the best new communities will take on a new look that's a takeoff on the old. We will see the downtown areas designed to have all of the quaint charm and nostalgia of turn-of-the-century towns — areas designed before the advent of the automobile that are safe and convenient for slower-paced pedestrian traffic — with fresh ideas for entertainment and retail business, places where you can live, work, and shop. Most of the houses or apartments will cluster near the downtown area to provide easy access to the village of services.

This is a radical departure from the suburbs. It brings back the interactivity and excitement of the city, but combines it with the quaint charm of a small town. It minimizes the need for cars and all of the accompanying congestion, parking problems, danger to pedestrians, and pollution. This village feel, in fact, is exactly what's drawing many people back to the cities, where small urban villages are springing up. Village life in the city? It sounds paradoxical, but it isn't. It is just one expression of the longing many of us feel to live in genuine communities.

Disney has recently designed and built its first residential community, Celebration, just outside Disney World. Perhaps this is just the beginning of their venture into real-estate development. It is certainly an example of successful design and is selling very well. Other similarly designed communities include Seaside in Florida; MacKenzie Town in Calgary, Alberta; and Clover Valley Station in Surrey, Vancouver.

Abundant Open Space for the Public

Second, the best developments will be designed to maximize open community space. This will include land left in its wild, natural state as well as parks and recreation areas that have clean, attractive facilities. These open spaces will allow nature to thrive and people to get away from it all — to enjoy a quiet walk in the woods, sit on a bench alongside a stream, or to watch children scampering around a playground. Homes and facilities will be designed to blend in with the natural environment more. Large cities are likewise creating more parks, and setting aside more open space outside to stave off suburban sprawl.

Flexibility in Home Design

Third, within an acceptable overall design scheme, buyers will be offered maximum flexibility in the layout to meet their individual needs. For example, buyers might choose the number of bedrooms, the space and wiring for home offices, the layout of family and recreation rooms, ceiling height and shape, and options such as skylights, fireplaces, pools, and spas.

Planning for Safety

Fourth, safety will be an important part of these new communities. The history of humanity shows that most of us increasingly insulate ourselves from the dangerous natural environment that once greatly reduced life expectancy. We will continue to want the best features of life without the worst, even if it means taking some of the real-life natural environment out of our more immediate living circumstances. That's why even though white-water rafting offers plenty of excitement, it is far too risky for most people. Or, though going out in the wild to see animals is surely exciting and a great way to learn, the best zoos today display animals in habitats that are as natural as possible and that keep both animal and human at a safe distance from one another. Here's yet another example: Scores of people who love the Earthquake ride at Universal Studios haven't the slightest desire to endure a real earthquake.

The best new communities will give residents this feeling of safety. For example, parks and recreational areas will be well-designed and well-lighted. Downtown retail areas will be developed with an eye towards safe pedestrian traffic, perhaps by creating attractive mall areas that are closed to vehicles, so that people and families will be able to stroll safely and enjoy the slower, meandering pace that is a hallmark of village life. This sort of planning for safety isn't restricted to small towns. Santa Barbara is a great example of a large city that has a retail shopping village right in the middle of downtown. This beautiful area attracts a huge number of shoppers, both locals and visitors.

Shared Facilities

Fifth, such communities will share large-scale facilities that are essential to the lifestyle they offer. For an affluent and professional population, a golf course will be essential. For communities with a high percentage of home-based businesses, a central business center will be required. Homeowners with young children will demand day care facilities. Most communities will want recreation centers with pools, gyms, tennis courts, and so on.

Communications Infrastructure

Sixth and finally, the best new communities will share the high-tech communications infrastructure that makes it possible to bring electronic entertainment, learning, and business to the area. This kind of development — the real boon of the information revolution — is necessary to offset as much as possible the disadvantages of living in more remote areas.

The most attractive housing developments for lifestyle quality and financial appreciation will be planned communities in growing new cities, towns, and exurbs. The smart investment move is to review your plans for relocating your home or expanding your business with an eye toward buying in the areas that will appreciate in the next great real-estate boom. You should place boomtowns that cater to baby boomers looking for vacation property, and rental housing for echo baby boomers at the top of your list. These planned communities offer

Disneylike qualities such as quaint design, cleanliness, and safety. They provide centralized facilities that the community values and can share affordably. They offer high-tech communications facilities that bring the world of electronic entertainment, learning, and business directly into the home.

Chances are you don't currently live in such a place. Maybe it's time you started looking for a town or community that fits your values and lifestyle, and helps you almost effortlessly achieve those important life goals for your family. It may be the most important decision you make affecting the quality of your life and it may have the biggest impact on your net worth decades from now. For serious real estate investors, using the guidelines in this book can only steer you towards huge profit.

CONSIDER CHANGING YOUR LIFE, RIGHT NOW!

For just a moment, I want you to throw away your preconceived notions of where you *could* live given your work and family obligations. Then simply ask yourself this question: If I could choose to live any place in the world, where would it be?

This doesn't mean you should drop all of your obligations, leave family and friends, and move to Bora Bora this weekend. However, everyone should allow themselves to fully consider their ideal living environment — especially right now! The massive changes in communications technologies we're beginning to see will make it more possible than ever before to live where you want to, and do the work you love. With creativity and persistence, you can enjoy your ideal home and have your ideal job.

The simplest way to answer the question "Where do I want to live?" is to reflect on your travels. Where did you feel best? What place made you feel most alive and content? The answer to this question will be different for everyone. Some people love the beaches and tropical climate of Maui; others love the ski slopes in Aspen; or the college town of Bloomington, Indiana; or the sunny and calm desert in Tucson, the red rocks in Sedona, Arizona; the country-music mecca in Branston, Missouri; the golf and tennis paradise in Hilton Head; the gentle mountains and fall colors around Stowe, Vermont; the year-round Shakespearean theater and fine restaurants of Ashland,

Oregon; the tranquil lake cottage in Northern Minnesota; or the old-fashioned town square and lush vineyards in Healdsburg, California.

Really allow yourself to feel where you felt most at home, and where you most desire to return on your next vacation, not as another new place to explore but the place you would return to again and again. This will then bring up the question: Why shouldn't I live there, either now or in the near future? Why wait for retirement, when many people will have increasingly limited physical capacity? Why not do so in the prime of life, especially if the kids are leaving the nest? Once you decide where you imagine living if there were no constraints, then, and only then, should you consider the constraints and get creative about dealing with them. The vision comes first. The strategy second.

If you use your creativity and don't assume too many limitations, you may just find yourself coming up with a strategy to live where you have always wanted to without paying for this luxury with a reduced income.

Here's a quick example. You live in a large city like San Francisco, and your children are still in junior high. You enjoy the California culture, your kids like the schools and their friends, but the crime rate is rising and the drug trafficking at your childrens' school is becoming worse. Your most cherished friends have moved away, so the nice suburban neighborhood doesn't have the same appeal it had years ago. When you add up all your taxes — from sales taxes to state income taxes to car registration to property taxes — the sum is staggering. This cost only makes the steep price tag on a nice, basic three-bedroom middle class home (about $400,000) even more ridiculous. Furthermore, both you and your spouse spend an hour or two per day commuting to work, instead of enjoying the home you work so hard to pay for.

You've just been reading this book or that article about people moving back to small towns. You have envisioned yourself in Colorado or Utah or Idaho, where there is a strong community of people like you and, of course, plenty of convenient skiing, which is your favorite pastime. Then you consider the constraints: You are a stockbroker with clients in San Francisco. How would you make a living in Park City, Utah, or Aspen, Colorado? Would your children be able to make the transition to Aspen or Park City? Would the small town eventually bore you?

Before you talk with your children, which is likely to be your first priority, take them to Park City and Aspen for extended vacations of a week or more at a time. Do they meet people they like? Do they enjoy the trip as much as you do? Are the schools there good? If your children like it, then you have an opening to consider such a move.

If they have no interest, then you have many more options. Maybe this town is the place for you, and your children would be better off in a private boarding school anyway. They're expensive, but the move would finance it: There would be tremendous capital gains from the sale of your urban home and extra income from lower taxes. Or perhaps there's another area that has a great school system and offers the lifestyle you want, such as Stowe or Waterbury, both in Vermont.

If you can't imagine doing this research on your own, finding a suitable place for the family, and starting a new business without some security, there's help at hand. For example, the brokerage firm Edward Jones focuses on starting investment-brokerage companies in small towns, exactly the sort of place you're considering for relocation. Perhaps they need a broker in one of the towns that interests you. With their assistance, you might be able to start a business there quickly — if the children are willing to move now.

It may be that you simply have to wait until your children are out of high school to move to one of these towns. If so, what's to keep you from buying a house or condo there now, using it for vacations, and renting it out when you're not there? This way, you'll get to know the town better before you move, avoid paying a much higher price later, and expand your net worth in the interim.

In terms of moving your business as a stockbroker and maintaining your income, why not open a part-time office in your new hometown while maintaining a presence in San Francisco? It would give you more reason to vacation and work there, with great tax write-offs, too. After all, you can have an assistant and answering machine in both locations and telecommute with clients from either location by phone or computer. Isn't a town like Aspen exactly where you might find the wealthy clientele that need your services?

Such a plan may provide the perfect transition while the children finish high school. Furthermore, you could eventually shift your entire brokerage operation there and sell your San Francisco business to another broker. This would give you an even larger down payment to build your dream home, make it possible to work part time, or to provide you with a nest egg to insure a comfortable, secure retirement.

You may be thinking that not everyone is in an information-intensive business that's fairly easy to move, like stock brokerage or consulting or writing or research. So let's take another example. You may work for a manufacturing business like a steel company or, say, a bicycle company and since your work is tied to the physical plant, you can't just open up a branch office in a new town. You may think that all of the large firms like yours operate in larger cities or suburbs, and you can't get a job like that in a smaller town.

Stop! Look at some of the faster-growing, more niche-oriented companies in your industry, like minimills in steel or mountain-bike manufacturers. Next thing you know, you will discover that there are more options than you thought. You'll realize that there is a growing bicycle company with even better career advancement opportunities that has just opened a plant in Durango, Colorado, close to the ski areas. Or, you'll find a minimill that is opening in the far outskirts of Charlotte, North Carolina, near the mountains and ski resorts there.

The point is, don't confine yourself to a narrow picture of what you can do or where you can live in a time of such unprecedented change. If companies are re-engineering or reinventing themselves, so can you!

CLARIFYING YOUR PERSONAL NEEDS AND PRIORITIES

Now that your interest has been stimulated in the new boom-towns and you have a feeling for the kind of town you would like, it's time for more practical considerations. If you are buying primarily for investment, then profit is your number-one priority. You can follow all of the guidelines for appreciation given in this chapter and throughout the book and not have to worry as much about your personal preferences.

However, if you are buying a principal residence or a vacation home, use the next set of questions to help you clarify the type of town or city you'd be happy to live in. The key is to match your lifestyle needs with the areas that are most likely to appreciate and build your net worth. Ask yourself the following questions:

What Most Appeals to You in a Living Environment?

Different small towns and growth cities offer very different living environments. Consider carefully what you need and value in a community. No detail is too small if it's important to you. For example, do you want an area that offers natural beauty, such as beaches, lakefront property, mountains, greenery, clean air, and plenty of sunshine? Do you need good schools, a low crime rate, specific recreational activities or sports, cultural activities, and community involvement? Are you looking for lower housing costs and a simpler life? Are you looking for a homogenous or exclusive community that shares your interests, or do you prefer diversity? Are you nostalgic for an old-fashioned small town that is populated by families and offers ample family activities? Do you need a particular religious emphasis in your community?

For many of us, truly reflecting on what we value is not an easy task because we take so much for granted. Things we don't like get our attention far more than things we do! This will be time very well spent, either before you begin looking at new areas or while you are looking.

What Type of Professional Infrastructure and Services Do You Need?

Another important consideration is what services you require to run your business in the new area or to continue doing business in your current location by telecommuting. For example, does the town have the basics, such as full-service copy shops, reliable overnight mail delivery, and convenient dry cleaners? Does it offer more sophisticated facilities such as video conferencing? Can the phone system handle your needs for Internet access? If it can't, are there technologies you can purchase for your home or business that will meet your needs, like a satellite dish? Do they have an airport with frequent service to major cities or airport hubs suitable for your business travel? Will the weather lock you in, preventing you from traveling to your business associates or clients? How easy is it to drive to a larger airport, if that's necessary?

What Are the Opportunities for Starting or Buying a Business?

If you want to start a new business or transfer your existing one, you will need to assess the market potential, the competition, and the startup costs. Ask yourself these questions: Does this town have a sufficient and growing number of customers for your business? Does the demographic and psychographic profile of the town match your present or intended customer base? Are there businesses like the one you want to run available for sale at a reasonable price? Has the business you intend to start already been tried, effectively limiting your potential? Or is there a successful concept that you have seen in other similar towns that hasn't been tried in this town yet?

Are There Employment Opportunities that Match My Skills and Income Needs?

If you are not going to start or buy a business in the new town, and you need employment, don't just assume that a growing town will provide the right opportunities. Many towns only employ service workers with relatively low skills, and pay them a low wage, or are dominated by narrowly focused industries such as agriculture or mining, or new businesses moving in are highly targeted and require specific skills, such as software development. Ask yourself if the town is attracting businesses for which you would like to work and that need the skills that you have. Or, consider whether you could acquire the skills that would be most needed in the town, and how long that might take. Are there educational programs available in the town at vocational schools or offered by employers? Or would you have to acquire such skills before you make the move?

Are There the Educational and Cultural Activities for You and Your Children?

If you have children, don't automatically assume that small towns have superior school systems. The schools are likely to be safer, but they may not offer the range of challenging subjects that will satisfy your kids. You may need to consider private or boarding schools, or look for a town that does have challenging programs and teachers. Other questions to consider are: Will your children mix well with the locals? Does the town have sufficient sports, recreational and cultural activities? If not, are there summer camps or weekend activities nearby? And what about your own adult-education needs? Can you meet those in the town, in a nearby city, or via the Internet?

Are You Sure This Idyllic Environment Won't Eventually Bore You?

Many people love vacationing on a remote island or in a tiny mountain town, but would soon grow bored without the entertainment, shopping, restaurants, educational opportunities, conveniences, and business services we take for granted in larger cities and suburbs. The information revolution will change this equation substantially, making many more services easily available to us—but not completely.

To make the transition to small-town life, you must value an easier, simpler lifestyle or you must have the ability to travel frequently to the city. Consider taking an extended vacation or sabbatical from your work before you make the move. Spend at least a month or more in the town that interests you. This will give you a real feel for the pace of life, the people, and the services available.

Will Growth Destroy My Idyllic New Home?

Finally, even if you find the perfect town or neighborhood for your lifestyle and business needs, it might be vulnerable to the very growth that is attracting people like you to the area. Consider whether the community has a clear plan for growth and zoning that will preserve its attractive qualities. What type of people are moving in? Are they compatible with your lifestyle? Will they be able to coexist with the locals, or will they cause strong friction and political battles? Are there businesses moving in that will cause environmental problems or traffic congestion, or unacceptable levels of noise and activity? Are there plans for large developments that aren't obvious today? Are there toxic waste dumps or pesticide hazards, or other problems from the past that aren't common knowledge? These are important considerations in choosing a new area. You don't want your idyll to become just like the suburb you've left.

SUMMARY

The most important step you can take is to clarify what you value in life and what is required for your business or employment needs. Once you have done so, you can use a number of criteria to assess which towns will meet your needs and also offer the greatest potential for business and the appreciation of your real-estate investment.

Ultimately, there is no substitute for a personal visit, perhaps an extended stay, to get a direct feel for the town. Relocating is an important decision that requires an investment of your time, even if it means a sabbatical from work, and the money it will cost to travel and stay there. Before visiting, however, you can quickly narrow your choices to the few areas that look really good on paper. There is a huge quantity of good data available to you for a relatively low cost. Read on to find out where and how to get it.

CHAPTER **10**

The Nine Shades of Penturbia:
The New-Growth Areas
in Real Estate

THE NEXT POPULATION SHIFT isn't just a small-town trend, it's also a return to community. Investment opportunities include new-growth cities, the exurbs, or any number of the revitalized urban and suburban villages. Even the small towns that are booming come in more shapes and styles than you might envision!

The point is that you have a wide variety of investment or relocation options. You might even say that the distinguishing characteristic of this population shift *is* choice. You're not choosing between home and work. For the first time, you can choose a home that supports your work and supports the kind of life you want to live every day — not just on weekends.

I have designed a summary classification of nine different types of boomtowns to help you locate the best investment. Whether you're a businessperson seeking a new retail location, an investor shopping for a hot real-estate buy, or a home buyer investigating a lifestyle change, there is a boomtown for you.

I begin this summary with the booming small towns that offer the highest potential for a quality lifestyle, business growth, and investment appreciation.

230

CATEGORY 1
RESORT TOWNS

The powerful confluence of two trends — the next major population migration to small towns and a rise in vacation home buying by aging baby boomers — will make small resort towns and recreational areas the premier real-estate buy. These high-profile smaller towns are usually found in remote geographical locations, simply because that's where the greatest natural attractions tend to be. It's natural beauty that makes these towns so special. Along with that come the opportunities for recreation, the quaint atmosphere, and, in some cases, the exclusivity.

Since there is a relatively limited supply of truly beautiful recreational meccas, these towns naturally attract the most affluent retirees and baby boomers. Their high incomes drive real-estate prices to extreme levels, making these towns unaffordable for most. Aspen, Colorado is a perfect example. Other towns include Vail, Hilton Head, St. Bart's, St. Martin's, Maui, Martha's Vineyard, South Hampton, Palm Beach, Sun Valley, Lake Tahoe, Palm Springs, Scottsdale, Jackson Hole, Santa Fe, Stowe, Bar Harbor, Carmel, Santa Barbara, Napa Valley, Lake Tahoe, Taos, Park City, and, in Canada, Whistler, Banff, and Mont Tremblant.

Aspen is perhaps the classic example of a high-profile resort town that was a brilliant investment for savvy buyers in the 1950s. Back then, you could have spent thousands on a lot that today costs millions! Aspen started its boom as a haven for an eclectic mix of wealthier people who liked the skiing and the culture. It has expanded steadily into a haven for the rich and famous and for the affluent tourist. Aspen now boasts a Hard Rock Cafe and a Planet Hollywood — hardly the vision of those who bought real estate when Aspen was just another Colorado mountain town.

What began happening in Aspen in the 1950s occurred in Santa Fe in the 1960s, Telluride in the 1970s, and in McCall, Idaho in the 1980s. As you can imagine, investing in the next booming resort town before everybody else does will be hugely profitable.

A Demographic and Lifestyle Profile of Aspen

Let's look at the basic demographic and lifestyle characteristics of Aspen, a mature boomtown. Aspen is a classic, high-end town for vacationers and telecommuters. Here we see the highest real-estate prices and back-to-the-land living at its most exclusive. Growth continues to be fairly strong in Aspen despite very high housing prices and population saturation. In fact, surrounding towns as far as 40 miles away are booming.

The Prizm lifestyle model from Claritas, which subdivides our society into over sixty lifestyle segments, shows that Aspen contains a high percentage of trend-setting groups like the "New Ecotobia" and the "God's Country" segments. The profile of Aspen looks like this:

LIFESTYLE PROFILE	PERCENT OF POPULATION
"Big Sky Families"	45.0
"God's Country"	19.5
"Big Fish, Small Pond"	13.8
"New Ecotobia"	11.8
"New Homesteaders"	9.7

Household growth in Aspen was an astonishing 32.1% between 1980 and 1990, then dropped in the next decade as the following figures for household growth show. Though Aspen clearly went through its explosive growth phase in the 1980s, growth is still very strong for such a mature town, and it will continue.

YEARS	HOUSEHOLD GROWTH PERCENTAGE
1980 to 1990	32.1
1990 to 1995	7.0
1995 to 2000 (estimate)	9.0

The real story in Aspen is that the average family income of $133,176 in 1995 is predicted to grow to $187,217 by 2000. Talk about big-city incomes, small-town living! This figure is even more astonishing when we consider that the wealthiest homeowners have vacation homes in Aspen, not primary residences, and aren't typically counted in this census data. The age distribution is skewed heavily toward baby-boomer and baby-buster families, from ages 21 to 44, not toward youngsters or retirees. This telling detail means that the inhabitants of Aspen make their living in town or telecommute. This is a true trend-setting town that we can use as a benchmark for evaluating others.

Telluride: The Ideal Investment a Decade Ago, a Lesson for Today

Let's take a quick look at Telluride, Colorado, a great example of a town that combined a high-quality lifestyle with stellar real-estate appreciation just in the last decade. In the late 1970s, Telluride was a lot like Aspen before it exploded in popularity—a charming small town that offered great skiing. It was less accessible by car than Aspen —a seven-hour drive from Denver. In fact, the best way to get to Telluride was by small plane. Then, the right people moved in, very affluent people who could afford to fly in and out frequently, or who owned private planes. In fact, many of those who began coming to Telluride were tired of the celebrity scene in places like Aspen or Jackson Hole.

Here are the tell-tale signs that, over the years, would have told you to buy property in Telluride:

- The affluent population Telluride was attracting, easily tracked in demographic and census statistics, or by watching the growth of certain segments in the Claritas lifestyle model such as "New Ecotobia."
- The blossoming of trendy downtown businesses like cappuccino cafes and gourmet ethnic restaurants, like the renowned 221 South Oak where you can get farm pheasant with quinoa risotto in a port-wine reduction.
- A booming ski business and the construction of a world-class spa and resort, The Peaks.
- Increasingly frequent airline flights, making Telluride more accessible to greater numbers of people.
- And most recently, the expansion of the communications infrastructure to support convenient and low-cost access to the Internet.

In other words, Telluride is a classic high-profile resort town with strong appreciation potential. If you had bought property there just 10 to 15 years ago, the value would have increased astronomically in that short period of time. It's still a great investment.

The two characteristics that make Telluride unique are the town's investment in sophisticated telephony, which supports the telecommuting trend, and the limited amount of land available for development, which adds upward pressure to real-estate prices. In 1992, the telephone infrastructures were upgraded for local Internet access, a key step for the town's development. Now, an astounding 40 percent of the population has Internet access, compared with about 10 percent nationwide. Telluride clearly offers a very high-tech, entrepreneurial culture that will continue to attract upwardly mobile professionals.

Telluride, population 1500, has become a boomtown long before the minimum "safe" population for investment of 5,000 that I mention in Chapter 11. The population has remained small partly because of the scarce amount of land suitable for development. In fact, the scarcity of such land is the biggest factor in Telluride's favor. It is surrounded by mountain walls that enhance its physical beauty and exclusivity. Furthermore, there are few nearby towns that can absorb the growing population. Therefore, Telluride will only see continued price pressures on real estate. Although the highest-percentage gains are probably past, it should still be a good place for investment or relocation in the 1990s.

The demographic and lifestyle profile of Telluride, using the Claritas Prizm model, is very straightforward: One hundred percent of the town is comprised of the "New Ecotobia" segment, the trendiest rural lifestyle category. These are true professional, environmentally conscious telecommuters, the epitome of the small-town living, big-city incomes megatrend.

LIFESTYLE PROFILE	PERCENTAGE OF POPULATION
"New Ecotobia"	100.0

Telluride is a classic boomtown that's still in the middle of its growth curve. Household growth has been and will continue to be extremely strong. In fact, with the kind of numbers you can see below, this town would seem to be in its earlier growth phase.

YEARS	HOUSEHOLD GROWTH PERCENTAGE
1980 to 1990	38.2
1990 to 1995	57.0
1995 to 2000 (estimate)	35.7

However, the limited amount of space available for expansion probably means that Telluride is in the middle of its growth phase. Future expansion may ultimately occur in towns nearby that could become early-stage boomtowns in the next decade. Look up the road at Ouray, which is equally scenic and starting to attract more tourism. Or for a very early-stage town, try Creed. It's bound to take off one of these days.

The average family income in Telluride is also very high: $87,586 in 1995 and projected to reach $117,818 in 2000. The age distribution is much like Aspen, weighted toward ages 21 to 44, baby-boom and baby-bust families — exactly what we want to see, especially if we are baby boomers looking to move into a community with people like us. There is a lower percentage of retirees in Telluride than in Aspen, but a higher percentage of children. This tells us that the town is populated by professional families that are living and working here and raising kids.

The biggest drawback to Telluride is its inaccessibility. Getting to Telluride by car is difficult. Getting in and out by plane is much easier, since the tourist industry supports a reasonably frequent flight schedule, especially during ski season. Flights are not as accessible in the off-season and a heavy snowfall can wreak havoc with your travel plans. Locals, who have learned this lesson, allow an extra travel day for weather delays. As a result, Telluride is an ideal place for professions that can work and communicate primarily by computers, video-conferencing, and phones, and require only occasional travel for face-to-face meetings with colleagues or customers. If your business requires frequent travel on a tight schedule, Telluride may not be the place for you.

Clearly, the ideal time to have invested in Telluride was during the 1970s and early 1980s. Properties that sold for thousands of dollars an acre then soared to millions of dollars per acre in a matter of a few years. Are there still towns like these? Yes there are. The risk is higher, but there are clear indicators that identify a town ahead of, or just at, its takeoff point on the S-curve. This is where you can reap the greatest profits in the shortest period of time.

Ashland: A More Conservative, Idyllic Lifestyle

One of the most all-around attractive towns that I have seen, a town that offers both plenty of recreational activities and world-class cultural attractions, is Ashland, Oregon. It is both clean and safe. It has room to grow, yet promises substantial real-estate appreciation. Further, since it is well into its growth phase, it offers much lower downside risk for those investing in or relocating to this area, especially when compared to the risk of a pioneering area.

Ashland offers a superlative quality of life without the congestion, excessive tourism, celebrity cachet, and astronomical property prices of an Aspen, Jackson Hole, or Hilton Head. The most unique attraction Ashland boasts is its year-round Shakespeare festival, with three different theaters, including a replica of the Globe theater, right in the middle of town. The downtown area is about as charming as any you will find. Old-fashioned specialty stores and shops offer everything from crafts to jewelry to innovative home decorations to eclectic clothing to books—even a collector's comic-book store. You can walk to any number of very good restaurants, and funky bistros and cafes. Right on Main Street, there is a health-food store, an old-fashioned ice cream shop, and even a fresh-squeezed-juice stand.

The local college in Ashland specializes in the arts, which helps sustain the town's cultural interest. There's a nice 9-hole golf course in Ashland, with a very good 18-hole golf course 20 minutes away, in the nearby town of Medford. Ashland is surrounded by mountains with plenty of trails for hiking and biking, a good ski resort just south of town, and a series of Alpine lakes just a half-hour's drive to the West. There are a number of rivers in all directions where you can enjoy kayaking and whitewater rafting. Needless to say, Ashland scores a solid ten for its rich array of recreational and cultural offerings.

Ashland is ideal for living at a slower pace, where you can walk to the market or browse in a book store. The weather is almost always cooperative. Summer days are near perfect: warm and dry during the day, cooler but still comfortable at night. And the winter weather, although cold, is much sunnier and dryer than in many other parts of Oregon. With all of its attractions and the temperate climate, Ashland has everything that most affluent baby boomers and retirees want—without the multimillion-dollar home prices, or the glitz and noise of a Planet Hollywood. You couldn't go wrong buying in or near this town!

The only disadvantage I noticed in Ashland is its inaccessibility. It is a long drive from any major city; about four hours from Portland and six hours from San Francisco, so it's not easy to get to. However, it has a small airport of its own, and there is a larger one twenty minutes north in Medford. If you don't need to travel frequently, you certainly could telecommute from Ashland.

The lifestyle and demographic profile of Ashland shows how different it is from Aspen or Telluride:

Lifestyle Prolife	Percentage of Population
"Golden Ponds"	38.7
"New Homesteaders"	25.2
"Towns and Gowns"	20.4
"Big Fish, Small Ponds"	9.0
"Gray Power"	6.6

We see a definite skew towards more traditional and older lifestyle groups, not the trendsetting "God's Country" and "Ecotobia" segments that predominate in Aspen and Telluride. However, Ashland offers a very high-quality lifestyle and higher-than-average income, though not as high as Telluride and certainly nowhere near as high as Aspen's.

Years	Household Growth by Percentage: Moderate
1980 to 1990	15.7
1990 to 1995	7.0
1995 to 2000 (estimate)	7.6

Ashland is definitely growing, but not at the same rate as Telluride, probably because it isn't a trendsetting place. This makes it more pleasant for the residents, especially for retirees and young families.

Ashland is just beginning to hit its growth phase now, and will probably attract a moderately affluent population in the future. The average family income is $47,927, a bit higher than average. It is forecast to rise to $56,158 by the year 2000. The age distribution is skewed towards retirees and baby-boom families, with fairly high percentages of children. Ashland has a more even age distribution across all ranges than Aspen or Telluride have, which demonstrates its broad appeal. Ashland is likely to be most attractive to a more traditional family or retiree looking for a solid and cultured small town.

Bisbee: A Classic Example of a Very Early Stage Boomtown

Let's take a brief look at the most classic, very early stage boomtown I've noticed lately. Bisbee, Arizona is a high desert town, 90 minutes southeast of Tucson by car. It's nearly as pretty as Tucson but much smaller, and enjoys better weather due to its five thousand-foot elevation. The local hills have azurite mineral deposits, which makes them a pretty dark turquoise color, adding an artistic twist to this charming town.

Bisbee has been growing modestly for years and appears just ripe to take off. Why? Take a look at who the town attracts: creative people including artists, New Agers, and small-scale entrepreneurs. Notice the crafts and artisan shops and galleries, such as the store downtown that sells handmade Panama hats. Pay attention to the feel of the place: the locals still get together at the saloon in the main hotel and whoop it up well into the night. The fact is that artists often migrate to very low-cost areas that have natural scenic beauty and create inter- esting communities. In the process, they begin to attract people with money. Then, a cappuccino cafe opens up in addition to Sally's Diner and the local saloon. Eventually a salad bar or an ethnic restaurant opens, then another cafe, a few boutiques, and a bookstore. Pretty soon, you've got all the makings of a boomtown. Is it any surprise that *Rolling Stone* magazine recently described Bisbee as the next Santa Fe? That's exactly the kind of tip you should be aware of in your search. It's a strong indicator that others are noticing the town, too.

Now this isn't Aspen or Telluride or Ashland. It's an early-stage town with the potential of becoming an upscale mecca, or maybe just an attractive midscale boomtown. If you go to check out Bisbee you will see it in its raw charm. Don't stay at a motel. Try the Shady Dell RV Park and Campground. You don't need an RV. They have vintage trailers from the 1930s and 1950s that have been restored and include an old *Life* magazine, a teaset and an antique radio, all for $25 to $51 a night. And for eating? Go next door to Dot's Diner, a restored eatery where you can get the workman's special for $1.99.

Houses in Bisbee are modestly priced, and there is plenty of land to develop. Costs for an acre run about $5,000 in good areas, and the cost of the average house is around $50,000. That's what Aspen was like in the 1950s, but Aspen was much more remote then. Is Bisbee going to be the next Aspen? Probably not. But if it becomes the next Telluride or Sedona, that $5,000 lot is going to be worth $50,000, $100,000, or even $250,000 in a decade or so, while good houses go for $200,000 to $400,000.

Let's review the demographic and lifestyle profile of Bisbee. We'll see how dramatically different this town looks compared to Aspen or

Telluride, and why it is a riskier investment. Bisbee is clearly still a real frontier mining town. It has many of the characteristics of a very early stage town about to break out into a new-growth resort area. It has a growing artist community, interesting and eclectic shops, and a very attractive climate and desert scenery. It has also just moved into the ideal minimum population target (5,000 plus) for a new growth town: In 1995, the population of Bisbee hit 6,771. But the Claritas Prizm model tells us that Bisbee is still largely populated by lower income, rural people:

LIFESTYLE PROFILE	PERCENTAGE OF POPULATION
"Mines & Mills"	32.0
"Rustic Elders"	28.9
"Hard Scrabble"	17.9
"Golden Ponds"	14.4
"Grain Belt"	6.8

These are hardly upper-income trendsetters, and until you actually begin to see this segment of the population move in, the investment risk is higher. On the other hand, the trendsetters are beginning to visit and vacation in Bisbee. Since the Claritas lifestyle model only rates the people that live in a town full time, not the people that have vacation homes there, these figures don't give us a full view of the total population.

Household growth in Bisbee is moderately strong, as you can see below, which is another reason seriously to consider it as a potential new boomtown.

YEARS	HOUSEHOLD GROWTH BY PERCENTAGE: STRONG
1980 to 1995	32.1
1990 to 1995	9.0
1995 to 2000 (estimate)	11.0

Investing in or moving to Bisbee is certainly a riskier proposition than investing in other, more developed towns such as Telluride, but the upside potential is enormous. It depends on how much risk you can tolerate, what you can afford, and what kind of lifestyle you're looking for. Bisbee might just be the place for you. Or, for the investor, a place to lock up hundreds of acres of raw land and just sit on it for a decade or two.

Dewees Island: The Look of a New Resort Boomtown

Have you ever heard of Dewees Island, South Carolina? It is one of the last islands off of the South Carolina coast being developed. This is being done with an eye toward preserving its natural beauty, quality of life, and charm. You can only get to the island via ferry. The lots average two acres, and are substantially cheaper than nearby developments like Isle of Palms, but they are almost sure to appreciate substantially. If you haven't heard of Dewees Island, that's good!

Identifying an Up-and-Coming Resort Town

Everyone has heard of towns like Aspen or Martha's Vineyard or Hilton Head or Scottsdale. A substantial minority of people have heard about towns in their growth stages like Telluride, Colorado; or Sedona, Arizona; or Naples, Florida; or McCall, Idaho; or Ashland, Oregon; or Branson, Missouri. But who has heard of Dewees Island, South Carolina; or Bisbee, Arizona; or Ruidiuso, New Mexico; or Moab, Utah; or Redstone, Colorado; or Pagosa Springs, Colorado; or Seaside, Florida; or Culebra, Puerto Rico; or Hilo, Hawaii? These are the type of towns that are still in their early, innovative stages and offer the highest long-term real-estate appreciation potential, and the most authentic pioneering resort-town culture for the brave, eclectic and artistic.

How do you identify these new resort towns? Chapter 12 will answer this question in more detail, but here are a few basics. The place to begin is with travel and specialty magazines. Read *Islands, Conde Nast Traveler, Travel and Leisure,* and *Outdoors,* or try more focused magazines like *The Affordable Caribbean,* or *Caribbean Life and Travel.* These publications thrive on identifying the next trendy resort or tourist area. It's also a good idea to listen to the most innovative and affluent people you know to find out where they're buying vacation homes or relocating their businesses. When you're ready to investigate an area, begin with this simple checklist:

• First, look for these towns to be at, or maybe slightly below, the minimum population targets of 3,000 to 5,000.

- Look for eclectic populations that range from artists to affluent entrepreneurs.
- Look for natural beauty or recreation attractions that haven't really been discovered yet.

So, it's up to you. Can you see moving to your ideal resort area in the coming years, well before you retire? Would you prefer living in a very small, pioneering resort town, or do you prefer the amenities and cultural attractions of an Aspen, or do you want something in between? There are many choices and many climates. The sooner you consider these questions, the sooner you can build your net worth and have the lifestyle you really want.

Some Resort Towns to Watch

Here are examples of resort towns across North America that are in different stages of development. Investing in one of these towns in the earlier stage, such as Bisbee, AZ, Pagosa Springs, CO, or Dewees Island, SC, can be the most profitable. Such towns also involve the most risk and, possibly, the longest wait for a significant return on your investment. McCall, ID is an example of an up-and-coming town where the trend is now clearer and the investment less risky.

The following lists arrange the towns from the earliest to the most mature stage. It is not exhaustive; there are many towns not mentioned here. Also, you must personally investigate any of these towns to determine if you think the growth is likely to continue, and whether it fits your lifestyle or investment preferences.

Towns in the Innovation Phase

Bisbee, AZ; Jerome, AZ; Page, AZ; Moab, UT; Silver City, NM; Pagosa Springs, CO; Redstone, CO; Marble, CO; Basalt, CO; Littleton, NH; Dewees Island, SC; Lincoln City, OR; Culebra, Puerto Rico; Vieques, Puerto Rico; Turks and Caicos Islands, Caribbean; Saba Island, Caribbean; Belize in Central America; Waterbury, VT; Whitefish, MT; Angel Fire, NM; Red River, NM; Red Lodge, MT; Pescadero, CA; Boulder, UT; Escalante, UT.

Towns in the Early-Growth Phase

Ruidoso, NM; Las Cruces, NM; Durango, CO; McCall, ID; Kiawah Island, SC; Bend/Sun River, OR; Lewisburg/Hot Springs, Sulphur Springs, VA; Banner Elk, NC; Bluffton, SC; Windemere Valley, Alberta; Rossland, British Columbia; Oakhurst/North Fork, CA; Healdsburg, CA; Yreka, CA; Cannon Beach, WA; Anacortes, WA; Cheyenne, WY; Elko, NV; Jackpot, NV; Laughlin, NV; Gardnerville/ Minden, NV; Yuma, AZ; Minturn/Red Cliff, CO; Bozeman, MT; Montserrat, Caribbean; Grenada, Caribbean; Nevis, Caribbean; Costa Rica, Central America; St. Vincent and the Grenadines, Caribbean; Hilo, The Big Island, HI.

Towns in the Midgrowth Phase

Naples, FL; Ft. Myers, FL; Sea Island, GA; Everett, GA; St. Mary's, GA; Amelia Island, FL; Ashland, OR; Telluride, CO; Sedona, AZ; Asheville, NC; Charlottesville, VA; Jackson, MS; Traverse City, MI; Steamboat Springs, CO; Glenwood Springs, CO; Beaver Creek, CO; Crested Butte, CO; Taos, NM; Sylvan Lake, Alberta; Shuswap Lake, British Columbia; Sonoma, CA; Mendocino, CA; Morrow Bay, CA; Gatlinburg, TN; Niagara Falls, NY; Coeur d'Alene, ID; Carson City, NV; St. Kitts, Caribbean; St. Lucia, Caribbean; Anguilla, Caribbean; Kona, The Big Island, HI.

Towns in the Late-Growth Phase

Jackson Hole, WY; Park City, UT; Deer Valley, UT; Reno, NV; Copper Mountain, CO; Sarasota, FL; Canmore, Alberta; Kelowna, British Columbia; Qualicum Beach, British Columbia; Key West, FL; Myrtle Beach, SC; Del Mar, CA; Branton, MO; Biloxi, MS; Jasper, Alberta; Lake of the Ozarks, MS; Maui, HI; Kuaui, HI; Martinique, Caribbean; Virgin Gorda, Caribbean; Tortola, Caribbean.

Towns in the Early-Maturity Phase

Lake Tahoe, NV; Whistler, British Columbia; Mont Tremblant, Quebec; Banff, Alberta; Sun Valley, ID; Breckenridge, CO; Keystone, Colorado; Boulder, CO; St. Helena, CA; Calistoga, California; Morrow Bay, CA; Stowe, VT; Killington, VT; Bolton Landing, NY; Bar Harbor, ME; Snowmass, CO; Santa Fe, NM; Jamaica, Caribbean; St. John's, Caribbean; Cayman Islands, Caribbean; Barbados, Caribbean; Mustique, Caribbean.

Towns in the Late-Maturity Phase

Aspen; Hilton Head; Palm Beach; Martha's Vineyard/Nantucket/ Cape Cod; South Hampton; The Poconos; St. Thomas; St. Croix; St.

Barts; Barbados; St. Maaerten/St. Martins; Nassau; Bermuda; Vail; Carmel/Monterey; Santa Barbara; Palm Springs; Napa; Lake Tahoe; Oahu.

CATEGORY 2
SMALL COLLEGE AND UNIVERSITY TOWNS —
THE LIBERAL HAVENS

Small college and university towns are typically small, serene, and offer beautiful campuses. They attract highly educated faculty and research people. Moreover, the high percentage of students tends to encourage a youthful, innovative culture. Sound inviting? They usually are. What's even better is that college towns don't get all the press and tourism that resort towns do!

The research facilities and a young, highly skilled pool of talent in college towns often attract knowledge-based business such as biotechnology, environmental sciences, and computer-software companies. These firms augment the populace with even more highly educated professionals who earn strong incomes, thereby contributing to the health of the economy.

Many colleges have theater, art, and music departments that offer an assortment of cultural events, as well as sports teams and sporting events, and other forms of live entertainment that are simply not available in even the best resort towns. Most of all, these towns can be havens for progressive, liberal-minded and academic people — including baby boomers and retirees — who want the idyllic setting of a small town.

As a result, it's more likely that you will see everything from health-food stores and organic groceries to arts and crafts shops, eclectic bookstores and comic-book shops. You can enjoy a meal at ethnic and specialty restaurants ranging from down-home cooking to haute cuisine. This stimulating but relaxed culture will attract more and more people in the coming decades. Certainly it will draw many of the baby boomers moving towards voluntary simplicity and an easier, more humane lifestyle.

Examples of such towns include Madison, WI; Bloomington, IN; Yellow Springs, OH; Rolla, MO; New Haven, CT; Plymouth, NH; Williamstown, MA; Marquette, MI; Charlottesville, VA; Oxford, MS; Tucson, AZ (which is also a new-growth city); San Luis Obispo, CA;

Eureka, CA; Eugene, OR; Ashland, OR (also a resort town); Cedar City, UT; Flagstaff, AZ; Boone, NC; Charlottesville, NC; Chapel Hill, NC; Athens, GA; Clemson, SC; and Gainesville, FL.

CATEGORY 3
CLASSIC TOWNS — HAVENS FOR
THE TRADITIONAL AND CONSERVATIVE

Classic towns have no particular attractions, no resorts or recreation, no universities or colleges, not necessarily even new businesses and factories creating a lot of jobs. They are attractive simply for their old-fashioned, all-American charm. These towns have the greatest appeal for the more conservative segments of our society, who are principally concerned with preserving family values, and for retirees who want the simple life.

Classic towns may or may not be growing and therefore offer less for the real-estate investor than some of the other boomtowns. They will, however, provide the perfect lifestyle for buyers interested in relocating to a town that is small, simple, intimate, and quiet, one which offers many of the qualities that characterize our notion of the good old days. As a result, these towns appeal to individuals who are seeking to move to a small community where they can influence their political system and promote conservative values. Many of these classic towns would be included in Norman Crampton's book *The 100 Best Small Towns in America*.

Some examples of these very small, old-fashioned towns include: Ukiah, CA; Pierre, SD; Hendersonville, NC; Hartselle, AL; Bardstown, KY; Danville, KY; Crossville, TN; Brattleboro, VT; Essex, CT; Beaufort, SC; Baraboo, WI; Nelson, British Columbia; Chemainus, British Columbia; and Bragg Creek, Alberta.

CATEGORY 4
REVITALIZED FACTORY TOWNS —
BLUE-COLLAR HEAVEN

In the 1970s and early 1980s many American factory towns felt the harsh effects of the economic recession and the increasing competition from overseas manufacturers. Economic growth slowed down or stopped. In some factory towns, the economy worsened.

Now, however, many of these factory towns are booming again. Manufacturers, distributors, high-technology companies, and even the military are once again investing in these towns. The reasons? One, the cost of real estate is within their means and they can get the necessary permits. Many manufacturers can't afford Aspen and can't build in Berkeley. Second, blue-collar ethics appeal to such companies. Many workers, having had the experience of losing a once-secure job, are eager to help new companies succeed. Third, businesses often need the basic facilities, such as power plants and waste disposal systems, that factory towns offer.

Examples of such booming factory towns: Farmington, NM; Midland/Odessa, TX; Lubbock, TX; Yakima, WA; Pasco, WA; East Wenatchee, WA; South Whidbey, WA; North Whidbey, WA; Medford, OR; Chico, CA; Paso Robles, CA; Billings, MT; Yuma, AZ; Fallon, NV; Winnemucca, NV; Elko, NV; Visalia, CA; Roseville, CA; Stockton, CA; Casper, WY; Sheridan, WY; Gillette, WY; Kalispell, MT; Green Bay/Appleton, WI; Elkhorn, WI; Ft. Atkinson, WI; Winfield, KS; McPherson, KS; Wayne, IN; Jasper, IN; Wilmington, OH; Ocala, FL; Winterville, NC; Roanoke, VA; Manassus, VA; West Creek, VA; Culpeper, VA; Pikeville, KY; Lebanon, NH; Franklin, NH; Smyma, DE; Klamath Falls, OR; Eugene, OR; Twin Falls, ID; Chandler, AZ; Prescott, AZ; Lehi, UT; Provo, UT; Roswell, NM; Stephenville, TX; Moncks Corner, SC; Jefferson, VA; Stony Creek, NC; Manchester, NH; OshKosh, WI; Hutchinson, MN; Red Wing, MN; Marshall, MN; Pleasant, IN; Macon, GA; Flowery Branch, GA; Blue Ridge, VA; and, Lewisburg, PA.

CATEGORY 5
EXURBS — THE NEW SUBURBIA

In the next decade, most families will simply move further out of the urban area, beyond the suburbs. There are many new towns and communities sprouting up outside the present ring of high-density suburban development that surrounds larger cities. These *exurbs,* as they're called, typically offer more affordable housing, less congestion, lower taxes, lower crime rates, and better schools and neighborhoods. In fact, the attractions of the exurbs are remarkably like the attraction of the suburbs 60 years ago. The most important distinction between an exurb and a suburb, however, is that most exurban dwellers work at home, in their community, or commute to nearby suburban areas. Few make the long trek into the city for work.

The disadvantage of such exurbs is that they can develop much like present-day suburbs, with the same congested traffic and ubiquitous, unattractive strip malls. For example, consider Orange County, California. It is called Orange County because 40 years ago it was a rural area that largely consisted of orange groves. It developed as an edge city or exurban community, about an hour's drive from downtown Los Angeles. Orange County once attracted high numbers of new businesses and affluent workers with its great beaches, low cost of living, minimal pollution, and a slower, easier lifestyle. Now, Orange County comprises the cities of Irvine, Newport Beach, and Laguna Beach. It is a giant sprawling suburblike area that is increasingly expensive, congested, polluted and crime-ridden, but still popular and upscale.

In fact, the greater Los Angeles area is one giant suburban sprawl that resulted from the development of many edge cities within about a 60-mile radius of downtown: Ventura, Malibu, Santa Monica, Hollywood, Pasadena, Pomona, San Bernardino, Anaheim, and Orange County. Soon, the sprawl will extend all the way south to the Mexico border.

Plotting the Suburban Radius

The key to identifying the next range of exurban boomtowns is simply to plot a circle or radius around a city's present high-density suburban development.

Plotting the Exurban Radius

To calculate the potential exurban radius, draw a circle that extends approximately sixty percent beyond the present suburban radius. While doing this, keep in mind that the area will not be a perfect circle, and that the best exurbs will tend to develop outside the best suburbs, which can accentuate the unevenness of development.

Using these calculations, the prime area for investment outside of Los Angeles would fall within a 35-mile radius beyond the present 60-mile radius of development. It would extend toward Bakersfield to the north, between Ventura and Santa Barbara to the northeast, between Pomona and Palm Springs to the west, between Pomona and

Escondido to the southeast and between San Clemente and Oceanside to the south.

If we were looking at a medium-sized metropolitan area like Phoenix, the suburban radius is more like 20 to 25 miles, which would include Paradise Valley, Scottsdale, Sun City, Tempe, Mesa, and so on. Then, the exurban radius for development in the coming decade would extend approximately 15 miles. The most promising area seems to be north of Scottsdale and Paradise Valley, because they are the most affluent suburbs, in the emerging towns of Carefree and Cave Creek. Another promising area is to the east of Scottsdale, in Fountain Hills, which has grown approximately 50 percent in the last 5 years.

Other examples of booming exurban towns would be Reston, Gaithersburg, Battlefield, Shawnee, and Opequon, Virginia, outside Washington, D.C.; Lancaster, outside Philadelphia; Colorado Springs, outside Denver; Escondido, outside San Diego; Provo and Tooele/Grantsville, outside Salt Lake City; Annapolis, outside Baltimore; Weston/Wayland, outside Boston; Cobb, outside Atlanta; Arlington and Carrollton, outside Dallas; Prairie Crossing and Barrington Hills, outside Chicago; Bellingham, Anacortes, and Mt. Vernon, outside Seattle; St. Helens, outside Portland, Oregon; Franklin, outside Nashville; Westchester County, outside New York; Chilliwack, outside Vancouver; Okotoks and High River, outside Calgary. Then, there are exurbs outside of smaller cities like Salem and Stonewall outside Richmond, Virginia; or Elgin outside of Columbia, South Carolina; or St. Mary's, Georgia outside Jacksonville; or Clayton and Dutchville, outside Raleigh; or Cranberry, outside Pittsburgh; or Divide, outside Colorado Springs.

CATEGORY 6
SUBURBAN VILLAGES — CONVENIENCE AND
A QUAINT ATMOSPHERE FOR A PRICE

You often can find small townships or communities within the suburban circles that look and feel like small resorts or recreational towns. I call these *suburban villages,* a term I borrowed from Alan Jacques, a penturbia expert in British Columbia and co-founder of The Real Estate Investment Network (R.E.I.N.).

The key characteristic of most suburban villages is scenic topography that allows an area close to a major city to offer many of the advantages of a resort or recreational area. For example, many suburban villages are adjacent to mountains, hills, or beaches. Although you feel like you are in the middle of nowhere, in fact, you're just miles from a major downtown area. This kind of geography tends to attract more affluent professionals and executives. It also tends to foster communities that offer the intimacy and charm of a small town.

I used to live in a small beach town just 30 minutes from downtown San Francisco and 20 minutes from the airport. It's called Moss Beach, and you've probably never heard of it. It's right on the beach, and offers some of the prettiest cliffs on the California coast. Postal workers know you by face and name. Often, if someone puts the wrong address on your letter you are likely to get it anyway. That's one of the things that makes it like a remote little resort town.

Other such suburban villages surrounding us include Montara to the north and El Granada, and Miramar to the south. Each has its own coffee shop, dry cleaners, post office, video store, and a few small restaurants. Ten miles to the south of Moss Beach is the "big town" of Half Moon Bay. It has a substantial shopping center — with not one but *two* major grocery stores — and a number of cafes including La Di Da, the most radical hangout for miles around. But Half Moon Bay, a quaint town in comparison with San Francisco, looks almost like a suburb when compared to Moss Beach.

This area, called the *Coastside,* is separated from the populous San Francisco Bay area by a large range of hills and narrow, winding, and windy highways. When you walk on the beach at the Fitzgerald Marine Reserve near our home, you would never guess that there is a huge metropolitan area just over the hills — perhaps that's because there are other things to tend to. For example, if you ask Tim the Ranger, he'll show you the fossils of whale vertebrae centuries old. Driving along that stretch of coast, all you see is ocean, cliffs, mom-and-pop businesses, down-home restaurants and coffee houses. This is small-town America, and scenic to boot. Yet it is within a half hour's drive of the fourth largest city in the United States and, according to many travel polls, one of the premier tourist destinations in the world.

Other examples of suburban villages include LaJolla, outside San Diego; White Rock, Port Moody, Belcarra, and Deep Cove, outside Vancouver; Sausalito and Mill Valley in Marin County, outside San Francisco; MontClair Village, in Oakland; Moraga, east of Oakland;

Paradise Valley, outside Phoenix; Boulder, outside Denver; Marblehead, outside Boston; Lake Murray, outside Columbia, SC; Fairfield and New Canaan, CT, outside New York; Annapolis, outside Baltimore; and South Beach, in Miami Beach.

CATEGORY 7
EMERGING NEW CITIES — BRIGHT, NEW HAVENS FOR HOME AND BUSINESS

There is another way to escape the high-cost suburbs while retaining access to most of the modern consumer and business services people are accustomed to: move to an emerging, affordable, growth city. These cities offer economical residential and commercial real estate, and rapidly increasing job opportunities. Most of these new cities are springing up in the southern parts of North America, places that offer a more temperate, livable climate. Most are very probusiness because they know that attracting new business is the key to their growth. Rarely do emerging cities have the scenic beauty and natural recreational attractions of the resort towns, though.

Examples of such emerging new cities include Boise, ID; Austin, TX; Madison, WI; Albuquerque, NM; Tucson, AZ; Eugene, OR; Salem, OR; Provo, UT; Colorado Springs, CO; Tallahassee, FL; Hamilton, OH; Green Bay/Appleton, WI; Brownsville, TX; El Paso, TX; Spokane, WA; Augusta, GA; Modesto, CA; Huntsville, AL; Melbourne, FL; and Kelowna, British Columbia.

CATEGORY 8
LARGE-GROWTH CITIES — THE HUB OF THE NETWORK ECONOMY

Large cities with thriving economies are going to play a new role in the emerging network economy and society. It is this trend—the proliferation of Internet communication and the organizational change it produces—that will enable more people to join the next great population shift. In the large-growth cities, busy downtown areas are no longer primarily a place to live and work. They are centers for business conventions; live entertainment such as theater, symphony, and fine dining; and family recreation and education including parks, museums, and historical monuments.

As more and more people move to smaller towns, communities, and exurbs, one of the things they sacrifice is the experience of live entertainment and learning. Sure, you can pipe in all types of television, movies, and interactive educational programs via the Internet. You can even view art this way. But such virtual entertainment is no substitute for a genuine experience of the arts. Large cities that offer the real thing will increasingly become weekend meccas for people who have moved to the exurbs or smaller towns. We can already see that this is true: The most successful large-growth cities either offer interesting consumer entertainment or do a thriving business hosting professional conventions, or both. These cities include Las Vegas, San Francisco, Orlando, Myrtle Beach, San Antonio, Phoenix, Tuscon, Nashville, Branson (Missouri), San Diego, and Vancouver.

There is another group of large cities that is enjoying a social and economic boom due to a relatively low cost of living and a favorable business climate. These cities include Atlanta, Raleigh-Durham, Greensboro, Jacksonville, Tampa/St. Petersburg, Memphis, Louisville, Houston, Dallas, Greenville/Spartanburg, Portland, Seattle, Salt Lake City, Columbus, Cincinnati, St. Louis, Milwaukee, Kansas City, Denver, Charlotte, and Calgary.

Between 1992 and 1996, only twenty cities with metropolitan-area populations exceeding one million had average annual housing-appreciation rates higher than the rate of inflation; that is, appreciation over 3 percent. These cities are considered the hottest markets by *U.S. News & World Report* (April 1, 1996).

HOTTEST MARKETS IN THE U.S., 1992–1996

CITY	AVERAGE HOUSING APPRECIATION (PERCENTAGE)
Salt Lake City	12.8
Denver	8.5
Portland	8.0
Nashville	6.4
Detroit	6.0

Greensboro	5.8
Cleveland	5.2
Kansas City	4.9
Milwaukee	4.4
San Antonio	4.1
Norfolk	3.9
Atlanta	3.9
Phoenix	3.8
Cincinnati	3.7
Tampa	3.7
Oklahoma City	3.6
Minneapolis/St. Paul	3.6
Indianapolis	3.3
Las Vegas	3.2
Miami	3.0

CATEGORY 9
URBAN VILLAGES — FASHIONABLE ENCLAVES IN THE BIG CITY

The last kind of "boomtown" in which we will see growth and appreciation is the revitalized urban neighborhood. These are especially attractive to the echo baby boomers, who will soon be moving into their household-formation years. Many of these young people will choose to move into the cities at first, especially singles and couples who don't have children.

The highest rate of appreciation occurs in the downtown neighborhoods that are regenerated by artists, entrepreneurs, and creative people who move into declining neighborhoods because they need lower rents. As they do, the new life infused into these neighborhoods results in the opening of trendy cafes, interesting restaurants and shops, art studios, and offices. These areas then become fashionable for individuals and families with higher incomes, who start to move in and inevitably raise the prices of real estate.

Examples of this kind of boomtown include South Beach in Miami (also a suburban village); Chelsea in New York City, now that SoHo and Greenwich Village have become too expensive for artists;

The Mission and SOMA districts in San Francisco; Granville Island and Yaletown in Vancouver; and Eau Claire in Calgary.

SUMMARY

This is a great time, regardless of your age, to reconsider where you would be happiest living, or where you might want to consider having a second home. In North America, there is clearly a town or city for every lifestyle, and lifestyle is what the new customized economy is ultimately all about.

CHAPTER 11

How to Spot Real-Estate Trends and Boomtowns

LONG-TERM REAL-ESTATE TRENDS are strongly influenced by demographics and the buying cycle. It's a documented fact that new generations buy certain kinds of real estate as they age. Therefore, knowing *when* the majority of a specific generation is going to reach a certain age and invest in specific kinds of property can tell us *what* and *where* the hottest real-estate buys will be.

As a new generation enters the workforce at around age 19, commercial real estate is the first sector to boom. It stimulates demand for offices and factories. It also stimulates demand for new stores and shopping malls, since these new workers are also consumers. Commercial real estate has already been making a comeback, as the echo baby boomers are entering the workforce. Next, there is increased demand for residential housing, which can be segmented into five age-specific buying cycles. For example, a person who is 62 doesn't buy the same kind of real estate that someone who is 33 buys. The five cycles, in order of age, are:

- The apartment-rental cycle, between 16 and 25.
- The starter-home-buying cycle, between 26 and 33.
- The trade-up-home-buying cycle, between 34 and 43.
- The vacation-home-buying cycle, between 44 and 52.
- The retirement-home-buying cycle, between 61 and 70.

253

There are two key real-estate sectors that will be hot through the next decade. One, vacation-home buying is strong, as aging baby boomers begin to invest in their leisure. Two, commercial real-estate and apartment rentals are making a comeback because echo baby boomers are moving away from home, entering the workforce, and forming families. The other strong sector will be trade-up-home buying by upscale baby boomers.

THE VACATION-HOME-BUYING CYCLE

The sector of the population that will most influence real-estate values in the next decade are affluent baby boomers, who are moving into their vacation-home-buying years at the fastest growth rate. This,

---

Figure 11.1: 52-Year Birth Lag, Vacation-Home Buying.

Figure 11.1 shows the vacation-home-buying cycle for baby boomers who will typically buy these properties increasingly between the ages of 44 and 52. This cycle is calculated by lagging the birth rate by 52 years.

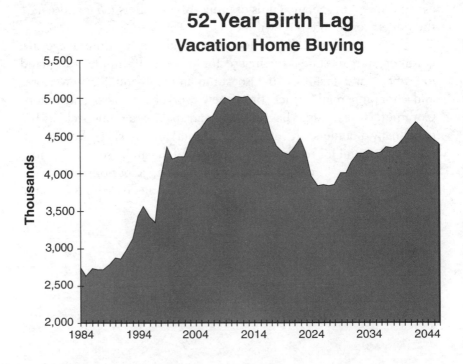

in combination with the migration to smaller towns, will make resort areas the hottest property for investors. As you can see in Figure 11.1, this buying cycle began in 1986 and will reach a peak by around 2013.

THE APARTMENT-RENTAL CYCLE

The leading edge of the echo baby-boom generation, born from 1976 to 2001, will be moving into apartments and stimulating the demand for rental properties, especially after 2002. This will create appreciation and good rental income in all areas, but it will be particularly marked in booming small towns and in urban areas. As you can see in Figure 11.2, this cycle begins in 1998, but doesn't take off until

Figure 11.2: 25.5-Year Birth Lag, Apartment Rental.

Figure 11.2 shows the apartment rental cycle for baby boomers and echo baby boomers just ahead who will typically need these properties between the ages of 16 and 25½. This cycle is calculated by lagging the birth rate by 25.5 years.

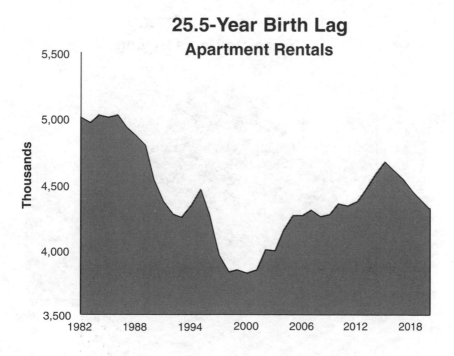

2002. It will peak at around 2015, at the earliest. The echo baby-boom generation is likely to see rising birth rates continue into approximately 2002, which would extend the booming demand for apartments until 2027. Shopping centers will also boom again.

THE TRADE-UP-HOME-BUYING CYCLE

The more typical baby-boomer family will be moving into the trade-up-home-buying cycle from age 34 to 43, a trend that will peak between 2000 and 2004. This should give upper-middle-class homes in most areas the potential for modest appreciation. *Trophy homes,* for the most affluent, have been booming more dramatically. In boom-

---

Figure 11.3: 43-Year Birth Lag, Trade-Up-Home Buying.

Figure 11.3 shows the trade-up-home-buying cycle for baby boomers, who will typically buy these properties between the ages of 34 and 43. This cycle is calculated by lagging the birth rate by 43 years.

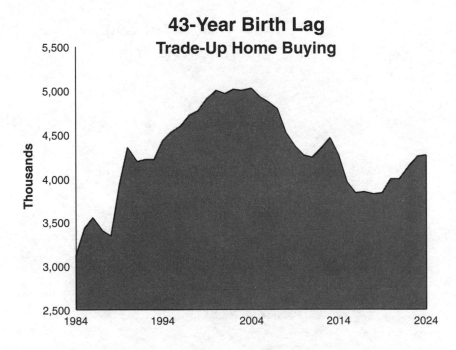

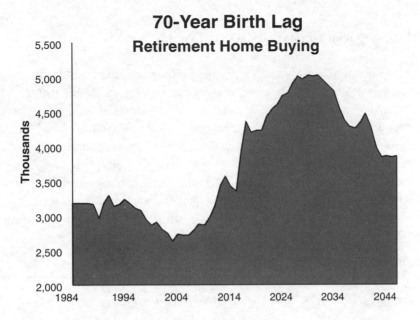

Figure 11.4: 70-Year Birth Lag, Retirement-Home Buying

Figure 11.4 shows the retirement-home-buying cycle for the Bob Hope generation and the baby-boom generation ahead, who will typically buy these properties between the ages of 61 and 70. This cycle is calculated by lagging the birth rate by 70 years.

---

ing towns and cities, this should produce very strong appreciation. As in the early 1990s, however, these most upscale suburban homes will decline in value the fastest when the boom peaks after 2009.

The Retirement-Home-Buying Cycle

The very high rate of retirement-housing growth in the past decades should slow due to the peaking demand of the Bob Hope generation between 1991 and 1995. However, there will be some modest growth in this real-estate sector due to our longer lifespans. This will in turn generate a higher percentage of the total population that falls within this age category, and push the value of retirement real estate up modestly.

THE STARTER-HOME-BUYING CYCLE

The demand for starter homes by baby boomers made this one of the hottest real-estate categories in the 1970s and 1980s. But, as we see in Figure 11.5, the demand for starter homes should slow down after 1995, now that the massive baby boom generation has bought most of their starter homes, and the baby-bust generation follows them. There may be some buoyancy in this market, however, if a booming economy and more affordable housing tempt some first-time buyers, particularly those shopping at the low end of the price range, who couldn't afford to buy property in the 1980s. High rates of immi-

---

Figure 11.5: 33-Year Birth Lag, Starter-Home Buying.

Figure 11.5 shows the starter-home-buying cycle for baby boomers and baby busters ahead. Those who will typically buy these properties range between the ages of 26 and 33. This cycle is calculated by lagging the birth rate by 33 years.

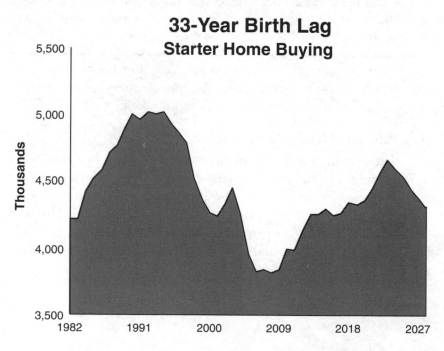

gration in the late 1980s and early 1990s have also added new buyers for starter homes. Overall, this should be the slowest growing area of residential real estate and will only appreciate in growth cities and boomtowns.

GEOGRAPHICAL MIGRATIONS AND REAL-ESTATE APPRECIATION

Broad geographical migration patterns have a noticeable impact on long-term real-estate trends. Certain areas of the country, clearly and consistently, have been growing more than others. The northeast and the upper-midwest plains states have generally been losing population, the midwest has been flat or growing modestly, and the southeast, southwest, and northwest have been growing substantially. There are three simple trends driving this phenomenon that should continue well into the future:

- People are moving south for warmer weather.
- People are moving west for a social and economic climate that is more open, innovative, and entrepreneurial.
- People are moving from the coasts to the interior of the country to escape congestion amd to lower their cost of living and doing business.

South for Warmer Weather

People in the United States are generally moving south to live in a more hospitable climate. In Canada, they are moving west to the milder coastal areas of British Columbia. For decades, there has been strong growth in almost all states south of the Mason-Dixon line, from Florida to Southern California. And, as you can see from the data in Figure 11.6, this growth is projected to continue. The exceptions tend to be states in the deep south such as Alabama, Mississippi, and Louisiana, which are experiencing more modest growth.

Only two states shown in Figure 11-6 are above the Mason-Dixon line: Pennsylvania, which is the biggest bright spot in the Northeast (along with Vermont and New Hampshire), and Washington, which has a mild climate. Five out of the twelve states are in the Southwest

Top States in Population Added
1995 to 2015

State	Projected Population Gain 1995 to 2015
California	9,911,000
Florida	6,828,000
Texas	6,495,000
Arizona	2,535,000
Georgia	2,255,000
Washington	2,147,000
North Carolina	2,001,000
Colorado	1,514,000
Virginia	1,496,000
Pennsylvania	1,215,000
Utah	1,089,000
Tennessee	1,065,000

Figure 11.6: Top States in Population Added, 1995 to 2015.

Figure 11.6 lists the states in the U.S. that will add the most in total population projected over the next 20 years. *(Source: NPA Data Services)*

and five are in the Southeast. Figure 11.6 clearly demonstrates that the southward migration we've seen in recent decades will continue and that the southwestern states will grow at the fastest rate.

West for an Open, Innovative, and Entrepreneurial Culture

Much of the social and technological innovation since the 1960s occurred in California. It then spread to surrounding states, as California grew increasingly crowded and expensive. California will continue to grow modestly, because it is the mecca for individuals and businesses seeking an open, innovative, social and professional environment. Other areas in the West will tend to grow much faster since they offer a similar lifestyle without the high price tag. From Hollywood to Silicon Valley, and now upward along the coasts into Portland, Seattle, and Vancouver, and inland to Utah, Colorado, Arizona, New Mexico, and Texas, we see the most innovative cities in America spawning most of the growth companies. These businesses, primarily in the fields of high technology and entertainment, are the backbone of the new information economy. They comprise the vast majority of the companies that will spearhead the next economic boom, The Roaring 2000s.

Many people who live in the West will tell you that there is a clear difference in culture between the western states, the East Coast, and the central areas of North America. This is partly due to the innovative business environment which spawns an array of creative high technology companies and interesting new ventures. More fundamentally, it is due to a more open, tolerant, and diverse social structure that many people prefer to the more traditional culture of the East. The preference that we have seen in recent decades for a more individualistic lifestyle will ensure that a growing number of people, especially younger people and baby boomers, will migrate westward, as we can see in Figure 11.7.

Figure 11.7 shows clearly that the real population growth is projected for the West and, especially, the Southwest! Florida is the only eastern state in this top-ten list. California is the one western state not on this list, despite the fact that it has the largest projected total population growth. This is partly due to the cost of living and the strict environmental standards which discourage many businesses from locating there. As a result, all the states around California are experiencing explosive population growth.

Great weather, abundant recreational opportunities, and an innovative social and technological environment all contribute to the fact that the Southwest, Rocky Mountains, and Northwest, in that order, will have the highest population growth and the greatest potential real-estate appreciation in the nation.

From the Coasts Back Inland for Lower Costs

We tend to prefer to live on or near the coasts for their beauty and, traditionally, we have settled there because businesses can benefit from access to shipping ports. This also means that coastal areas were the first to become congested and expensive. The Northeast, for exam-

Projected Growth Rates of the Top Ten States, 1995 to 2015

State	Projected 20-Year Growth Rate (Expressed as a percentage)
Arizona	63%
Alaska	58%
Utah	56%
Nevada	51%
Florida	49%
Colorado	42%
New Mexico	41%
Washington	41%
Idaho	35%
Texas	35%

Figure 11.7: Projected Growth Rates of the Top Ten States, 1995 to 2015.

Figure 11.7 shows the rate of population growth for the top-ten states as a percentage of their current population. By contrast with the previous chart, which lists the total numbers of population growth (and, therefore, gives undue weight to the densely populated Eastern states), figure 11.7 tells you the real story. (Source: *NPA Data Services)*

ple, is now one sprawling suburb from southern New Hampshire to Washington, D.C. The southeastern coastal states from Virginia to Florida, which have seen very high growth rates in the last few decades, are becoming increasingly saturated.

Santa Barbara, Los Angeles, and San Diego are close to merging into one metropolis; as are Monterey, Santa Cruz, San Francisco, and Santa Rosa in northern California. Fortunately, the coastal area between Santa Barbara and Carmel is not suitable for metropolitan development. In fact, those coastal areas that still had undeveloped land suitable for building have grown the fastest. These areas include

Vancouver, Seattle, and Portland in the northwest. Vancouver and Seattle are quickly approaching population saturation and are becoming increasingly expensive, which leaves only Portland to develop strongly in the coming decade.

As a result of the congestion and expense along the coastal areas, it is inevitable that people and businesses will begin looking at inland areas to find attractive towns and cities. That's why we're seeing such remarkable growth in the southerly portions of the Rocky Mountain area and in desert states including Arizona, New Mexico, Utah, and Nevada. These states are growing the fastest. Following them is the southeast area from Texas to western Florida — the Gulf Coast and Orlando; Georgia; northern Alabama; Kentucky; Richmond and Norfolk/Williamsburg/Newport News in Virginia; Charlotte and Raleigh-Durham in North Carolina; Spartanburg/Greenville, Columbia, and Charleston in South Carolina. Three of the northeastern states — Pennsylvania, Vermont, and New Hampshire — also have attractive inland areas that are appreciating in value.

There are many states in the Midwest that will attract families and businesses, especially in Minnesota, Wisconsin, Missouri, southern Ohio, southern Illinois, Kansas, and Missouri. These areas are all experiencing a revitalization that, though it does not rival growth in the Southeast and West, will nonetheless enjoy a healthy level of growth and real-estate appreciation.

If you add up all three trends of population migration — west, south and inland — you would expect the highest rates of growth in the Southwest areas of Arizona, Nevada, southern Utah, southern Colorado, and New Mexico. And guess what? That's where the biggest boom has been and will continue to be.

How to Identify the Boomtown Suitable for You

Up to this point, we've identified the four key trends that will drive the next real-estate boom. Let's summarize them before we go on to the next key issue — how to pick the perfect boomtown for you!

- Basic innovation in communication technologies is allowing more people to relocate their homes to small towns and exurbs, and telecommute to business.

- The baby boomers are moving into their vacation-home-buying years, which, in combination with the first trend, will stimulate demand for property in attractive resort towns.
- The echo baby-boom generation is now moving into its household formation years, which will stimulate demand for apartments and rental property in the cities, and has already caused commercial property in these areas to appreciate.
- There is a broad geographic migration towards areas of the country with warmer climates. You can expect the first three trends to be accentuated in the southwestern United States.

Now, it's time to clarify your own priorities. What kind of boom-town do you want to relocate to or invest in? There are two parts to doing this research, and I've outlined both of them for you. First, you can use quantitative data to come up with a selected list of towns that interest you. Next, you'll need to invest time to personally visit and evaluate each one because there are many qualitative factors affecting your final decision that can't be wrapped up in neat columns of data or expressed in a written description.

QUANTITATIVE INDICATORS

Begin by considering the broad region for its climate, lifestyle and general growth potential. You know from this report that the highest growth area in the country are states south of the Mason-Dixon line, particularly those in the southwest. After you have chosen a region, there are a number of simple statistical trends that you will want to track to determine if the area has high growth and appreciation potential. These include:

- Critical mass of population
- The rate of population growth
- The rate of job and income growth
- Real-estate appreciation
- Vacancy rates
- Quantity of land available for development
- *Psychographics,* quantitative lifestyle data

Critical Mass in Population

A critical mass in population is necessary before a small town offers the number and variety of services that will attract urban dwellers to the area. As a general rule, you will want to invest in a small town only when it has a minimum population of three thousand; an even safer bet is five thousand people. If the town has between three thousand and five thousand people, make sure that there are solid plans for growth, and that it offers some qualitative advantages over other areas before investing in it.

Many small towns that have experienced some growth already take off after reaching a population of 20,000. The critical mass for many new growth cities, or formerly small towns making the transition to a growth city, is often around 50,000.

Population Growth

Besides a minimum population, you will also want to check that the town has a steady or accelerating growth in population. This is a strong indicator that real estate is appreciating, not depreciating, and confirms that you have selected a town that other investors find attractive as well.

The best measure is not absolute population growth, or even population growth as a percentage. Instead, check the figures for growth *relative* to the county, state, or region in which the town is located. To calculate the relative growth, simply divide the town's population for one year by the population of the county, region, or state for that same year, and then plot the figure on a graph. (You can get these statistics from the U.S. Census Bureau, from state and local agencies, and from demographic marketing companies.) Do this for at least the previous ten years and farther back, if possible. If projected population data is available, plot future years as well. If a town, especially if it's small, is not growing faster than the surrounding state or regional area, then it is not a genuine growth town.

Growth in Job Opportunities and Income

In all categories of boomtowns you're considering, with the exception of areas that appeal to affluent retirees, look for growth in job markets and a rising level of income. This will indicate that there is enough money circulating in the area to boost real estate prices. Even in a growing resort area with a large percentage of retired homeowners, you would expect to see job and income growth for the people who provide goods and services to the town.

The best source for job and income statistics is demographic marketing firms. If you want information on cities and at the county level up to the year 2020, contact Woods and Poole (800-786-1915). In addition to providing past data, they can give you good estimates for 25 years into the future, based on demographic factors and business and employment trends. Data for an entire county is a reliable way to evaluate a single town only when that town comprises most of the county's population. Or, such data also can help you easily identify high-growth counties in which to look further for high-growth towns.

Rising Real-Estate Prices

Another simple statistic that you should track is the growth in the town's real-estate prices. Strong appreciation indicates that other people think this town is a good investment, too. On the other hand, if real-estate prices have been growing for a long period of time, there is a risk that prices could peak and consolidate for a period of time. You want to catch an area that is just taking off, or one that is accelerating again after a consolidation or drop in prices.

Property-price statistics are typically available from real-estate brokerage firms in an area. In Canada, you can use the very convenient *Royal Lepage Survey of Canadian House Prices,* which is available in any Canadian real estate brokerage office.

Falling Vacancy Rates

Another statistic to look for is the vacancy rate for residential properties in the town. If vacancy rates are falling, that's an indication that the demand for property is rising faster than supply. Over time, a falling vacancy rate will sustain strong price appreciation.

You can usually get vacancy rate statistics from local, regional, or national real estate brokerage firms.

Scarcity of Land Available for Development

Another quantitative variable to check is factors that limit the amount of land available for development. These would include environmental constraints, water shortages, and adjacent hills and lakes that count toward the acreage totals but cannot be developed, zoning laws, and so on.

While you're collecting this data, remember that a limited supply of suitable land plus growth equals appreciation! This is why, for example, Las Vegas is growing at an astounding rate of 8 percent per year but homeowners are enjoying only modest appreciation. There is so much cheap land available for new-housing development that the supply can nearly keep pace with the demand. Las Vegas is approaching the limits set by the surrounding mountain ranges, thus, as a result, it may see more substantial price appreciation in the future.

The story is similar in Florida. Despite very high population-growth rates, lots of flat land suitable for development *and* plenty of water have kept the price appreciation in most areas relatively modest. Contrast that with many areas in California that have geographical and ecological limitations, or Telluride, Colorado, which is surrounded by mountain walls. The appreciation in such areas due to a growing population has been phenomenal.

Psychographics: Quantitative Lifestyle Data

The final piece of quantitative data that can give us insight into a potential boomtown tells us about the local lifestyles, as we did in Chapter 10, which looked at attractive resort towns. You wouldn't expect this kind of data to appear in a report. You'd expect to have to visit a town to see what's going on, get a feel for the place. Thanks to incredible advances in census data and statistical marketing techniques, we can correlate numerous measurable demographic factors with specific lifestyle preferences. You can purchase a lifestyle analysis of any city, town, zip code, or neighborhood through a number of marketing firms, such as Claritas, CACI, or Donnelly, that cater to businesses.

Michael J. Weiss covers this topic thoroughly in his book *The Clustering of America,* using the Claritas model. Claritas is my favorite clustering and lifestyle model simply because it seems to best characterize the specific lifestyles that we can easily recognize and compare with our own preferences. Donnelly has the capacity to bring such analysis down to individual households, not just neighborhoods, which is a distinct advantage for businesses and marketers, and CACI's model revolves more around the housing dimension of lifestyle preferences, which can be more useful for developers.

These models group data into anywhere from forty to seventy distinct lifestyle choices, plenty to help you determine whether or not a new town or area suits you. These lifestyle models can help you identify a new town that is attracting people like you, whom you'd enjoy as neighbors. It is also important to use such data to identify which towns are attracting the trendsetting lifestyles of the more affluent sectors of the population. An influx of these people into an area will create the highest appreciation in real estate.

Here are some examples of the more affluent, trendsetting lifestyle segments of the Claritas model:

- "Blue Blood Estates," comprised of baby-boom homeowners with very high incomes, who live in more traditional suburbs and high-profile exurbs and growth cities.
- "Money and Brains," comprised of highly educated homeowners who often live in the trendy areas of larger cities or in college and university towns.
- "God's Country," comprised of affluent baby boomers who concentrate in professional and technical fields but prefer to live in beautiful, natural environments and smaller towns.
- "New Ecotobia," comprised of affluent, ecosensitive telecommuters who also prefer to live in the most attractive rural and resort areas.
- "Gray Power," comprised of affluent retirees who migrate to the more attractive resort and recreation areas.
- "Young Influentials," comprised of young trendsetters in fashionable urban areas.

If a Claritas report on the town you are researching shows a significant or growing influx of any of these lifestyle segments, then it confirms that you have selected a boomtown. The more affluent people always seek the best areas, and the number of these areas is limited. Therefore, such areas will see the most money chasing the fewest properties. In the simple math of supply and demand, that adds up to the best real-estate appreciation and, for some people, the highest quality of life. It is most important to study the different lifestyle categories and get a feel for which ones are closest to your preferences. That way you can quickly research towns you haven't visited to get an idea whether there are people there like you — then you can visit the towns that are most likely to excite you.

QUALITATIVE INDICATORS

Once you have narrowed your choice of towns to those that meet your criteria for lifestyles and real-estate appreciation potential, a personal visit is necessary. Only in this way will you be able to evaluate the qualitative factors that affect your choice. When you do, pay attention to the following list of considerations:

- Recreational, educational, and cultural attractions
- Renovations and improvements to the infrastructure
- Franchise investment and trendsetting businesses
- Diversified economic base
- People living *and* working in the area

Recreational, Educational and Cultural Attractions

The first thing to note when you visit the boomtown is what it offers in the way of recreation, educational facilities, and cultural attractions. Do they match your individual lifestyle preferences now? Will the town suit the interests you dream about for your future?

For example, if you like theater, then Ashland, Oregon may be the place for you. Or, if you want easy access to skiing, you might prefer Park City, Utah. Or, if you want to take college courses or get an advanced degree while living in a small town, Bloomington, Indiana might be at the top of your list. Or, for example, Durango, Colorado attracts a huge number of mountain bikers and recreational-product companies — which, as you might guess, includes mountain-bike manufacturers. Durango might be a great choice for cyclists who want to live a lifestyle oriented towards riding and recreation, and who also want to work for a company that values their specific interests and knowledge.

Renovations and Improvements to the Infrastructure

The second thing to note when you are visiting a town is whether it is making substantial investments in its public facilities. Is it expanding the airport, improving public transportation, building sports complexes, schools, cultural facilities, convention halls, and meeting centers? What kinds of tourist attractions and family entertainment facilities is the city building or improving, and what do you think of them? In short, try to evaluate whether the town has an eye towards the influx of new people and what their response is. If it is creating an environment to attract more people, this is another sure sign that the town is expanding and planning for more expansion.

Franchise and Business Entry

Another sign of a boomtown is that franchises such as Starbuck's Coffee, McDonald's and Wal-Mart are moving in. These companies do extensive demographic and lifestyle analysis before moving to an area, and they don't make such an investment unless they are convinced that there is strong growth potential.

Growth by itself, however, is not the only factor to evaluate. Consider what types of businesses are moving in, what kinds are already present, and determine whether they reflect and support the kind of lifestyle you're seeking. Such an evaluation will also give you a feel for what types of people you can expect to move into the area. For example, coffee bars and trendy cafes give a different signal than a Wal-Mart or McDonald's. The high-end businesses suggest you may be walking down Main Street of the next Aspen, whereas a Wal-Mart probably indicates that this is another low-cost business town or an exurb that eventually will look more like an extended suburb. Most boomtowns will attract both: They draw affluent people who like the quality of life, and everyday workers to provide the services.

Diversified Business Base

Although most smaller boomtowns will exhibit a clear tendency to attract the kinds of businesses that support a specific lifestyle, you will also want to look for business diversity. If the area is sustained by one key business, such as a major copper mine or a large distribution company, its decline can create a devastating effect on the local economy and adversely affect the value of your property. If there are different kinds of businesses in the area, the decline of one is likely to have a more limited effect on property values. Consider both the short- and the long-term value of your real-estate investment when evaluating the local businesses.

People Living and Working Locally

An authentic boomtown also thrives largely on its local business base, not primarily on commuters. This gives the town stability in growth, but also shows that it represents the lifestyle it is catering to, not simply making it available to people who earn their incomes elsewhere. It also indicates that this boomtown supports the ideal of a quality lifestyle that offers enough leisure time to enjoy your family, your friends, and your new community.

Talk to people in the town to find out where they live and work. Look at the traffic patterns during rush hour to determine if most people are commuting into a nearby city or suburban area. If they are, think twice about investing in this boomtown!

SUMMARY

This boom should open up your opportunities not just for lucrative jobs or entrepreneurial ventures, but for a real change in lifestyle. This is a great time to sit down with your spouse, family, or friends and really consider where you would want to live. What are the alternatives? How will technology allow us to live in a place we might not have considered? The business, career, and, especially, the real-estate opportunities are also likely to be much stronger in the best boomtowns and cities. This could be one of the most important decisions you make in your life, whether you are a baby boomer in your mid-forties, or have a new family and are in your early twenties, or about to retire. Spend the time to find the best place to live and invest. It will be worth your while.

In Part V, I will close this book by looking at the secrets of building wealth. It's not enough to just understand the key trends driving change in our economy. You have to know how to invest. Most people don't practice the simplest principles for investing. You can.

PART 5

Investment Strategies for the Roaring 2000s

CHAPTER **12**

The Seven Principles
of Successful Investing

IN THIS CHAPTER, we'll look at the process of investing: How do we achieve our goals for building wealth and a secure future in an increasingly complex world? With all the conflicting "expert" forecasts, the daily gyration of stock prices, and more than 8,000 mutual funds to choose from, does the market confuse you? Do you have any idea which investment approach — from momentum to contrarian to index strategies — to follow?

How can anyone make good investment decisions in today's burgeoning world of finance? And doesn't it seem more important than ever, with our social-security system and health care benefits in question, with less long-term job stability, with rising college costs, with lower rates of savings in our country, and with longer life expectancies? In this book, we've already looked at the secrets for understanding the powerful trends that are reshaping our economy. Now, it's time to look at the proven principles of investing and the secrets of building wealth. As simple as investing can be, only a small minority of people invest enough money to secure their future. Even fewer do it right.

We must start with a good reason to invest, because we simply don't do something unless it's important to us. Investing is not just a matter of sacrificing today so that you can have a comfortable future. 275

It's a matter of being able to shape your own life as you age, to enjoy the freedom you've earned after the kids leave the nest, and to have the resources to finance this potentially very creative time of your life. When else do you have the time, the skills, the emotional maturity and clarity, and the resources to really do what you want?

Saving and sacrificing came naturally to the Bob Hope generation. They grew up during the Depression and World War II, with an ethic of duty and sacrifice. It isn't difficult for generation Xers who have grown up in uncertain times to plan for their future. They are already saving earlier than the baby boomers ever did. The generation that has the most trouble saving and sacrificing is the huge baby boom generation. Baby boomers grew up during the most prosperous time in our country's history and, until the 1990s, never assumed that we would need to worry about the future.

Those of us who are baby boomers are worrying now. Many of us realize that we haven't saved enough to finance our long lives. Most are uncertain about whether we'll get any support from the social-security system, as well as pensions and health-care subsidies upon retirement. So what's our answer? Sure, we'll start to save a little, but we'll just work more in retirement. We're workaholics anyway—not working would be boring—so why not continue to work part-time or full-time into retirement? Why worry as much about saving for retirement as our parents did?

Baby boomers have always been driven by dreams, by pushing the limits of life rather than acquiescing to the authoritative systems that our parents accepted without question. Sure, we've bumped our heads and learned some tough lessons, but many of us haven't given up that dream. So, here's a question for you baby boomers: How are you going to really live your dreams if you have to keep working for someone else into retirement? Wouldn't you rather have financial independence? Wouldn't you rather move to the resort town of your choice when you are 50, when you're still highly active, instead of waiting until 65 or 70? Wouldn't you like to be able to start your own business? Or set up a nonprofit foundation to educate kids or save the whales? Doesn't that sound better than slugging it out in the same old stressful, perhaps increasingly boring, career as you age? Aren't most of us coming up against very strong tradeoffs between our demanding careers and our family lives? Now, there will be a younger generation coming after us, willing to work harder to compete for our positions.

Are you sure you want to just keep slugging it out in your same career or job?

The point is, if you start systematically investing now, you should be able to develop enough capital in the continuing economic boom to give you an assortment of attractive options. You could either retire comfortably when you're ready, or do what you enjoy most in your work. In fact, many people will find that they can increase their income and net worth in the so-called retirement years if they build their strongest passions into profit or nonprofit businesses. The key is to develop an avocation you can master, one that will let you stay fresh and vital and interested for years to come, one in which you could easily vacation in Costa Rica for a month, or take a sabbatical for self-study to nourish your excitement about new developments in your profession. Financial independence will become the ultimate achievement for baby boomers in the coming decades. Cultivate your own dreams first, and be clear about what you really want to do in your post-family years — then you will have the motivation to build your own level of wealth and choice.

GETTING REAL ABOUT INVESTMENT AND RETURNS

Once we clarify our purpose in saving and investing, then we come to the realities of the investment process. Have you read all of the stellar track records of the popular funds like Fidelity's Magellan, Vanguard, AIM, or Putnam? Many of them have averaged more than 20 percent growth, sustained over a period of 10 years or more. Or did you know that average stock indices have returned 10 to 11 percent, compounded annually over history, significantly beating bonds and precious metals? At even that conservative rate, you could double your money every 7 years.

Look realistically at your experience as an investor. Have you achieved such returns in your own investments over time, and consistently? Or are you just remembering the one or two good years, and forgetting the mediocre ones? Is your portfolio, like most, barely beating inflation? Have you avoided investing entirely, waiting until you have the time to master the markets, or waiting until you have the extra income to invest?

The sustained, outstanding growth achieved by many mutual

funds and indexes are real! In fact, the return on stocks since this incredible bull market began in late 1982 has been more like 16 percent, compounded annually. At that rate, your money and investments will double every 4.5 years!

The sad truth is that the great, great majority of investors don't achieve such returns, and they don't meet their long-term goals for building wealth for one simple reason: Most of them tend to buy and sell mutual funds, stocks, and other investments at the wrong time. For example, Peter Lynch pointed out that during his record-breaking tenure as portfolio manager of the Fidelity Magellan fund, the great majority of investors sold at a loss. How could this happen in such a top-performing fund? Such funds are naturally more volatile than others. Most people buy when a fund is performing well, and sell when it is declining in a correction, down far more than the market is generally. Why? We are only human! Fear and greed get the best of us as Figure 12-1 painfully illustrates.

The vast majority of us don't get the great returns on our investments that are possible for one simple reason: We let our emotions rule our decision about when to buy and sell, rather than forming an investment plan and sticking to it.

The stark reality of investment results was revealed even more clearly in a recent Dalbar study shown in Figure 12-1. They studied a large sample of investors and their actual returns from 1/1/84 to 12/31/95, which was a very good period for the stock market. Here's the sad truth. The typical do-it-yourself investor made only a 98 percent cumulative return over that 12-year period, or less than a 6 percent annual compounded rate of return. Investors who used a broker or financial advisor did better, but only marginally. They made 114 percent cumulatively. But that doesn't count commissions, fees, or loads which would have reduced that net return. Investors who bought bonds did better, earning 132 percent, despite the fact that stocks performed much better than bonds did over that time period. Investors who bought bonds with the aid of an advisor did the best, at 162 percent return. But here's the real kicker: In that same time period the S&P 500 gained 461 percent including dividends.

Most investors, with or without an advisor, made less than one-fourth of the returns that they could have simply by buying and holding an average basket of stocks on the New York Stock Exchange.

This is astounding! No wonder that wealth is concentrated in the hands of so few in our society. It is far more concentrated than income.

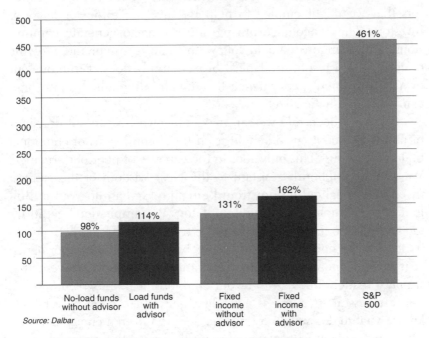

Figure 12.1 illustrates the results of the Dalbar study, which charts the actual returns of a large group of investors from 1984 to 1995, compared with various common stock indices. It is sad but true: Most investors greatly under-performed the markets in a time when we are told that we are better off making our own decisions.

The richest 1 percent of the population controls 40 percent of the financial securities and wealth, if we exclude home equity from the equation. The richest 20 percent controls over 98 percent of the same wealth, yet earns less than half that amount, only 40 percent, of the income. Investment wealth is clearly concentrated in the hands of the very few. The great majority of the gains in wealth over the last two decades has gone to the top one-half of one percent of our society — the entrepreneurs and savvy long-term investors.

Why? Most people don't have sufficient income to save enough to accumulate massive wealth, although we would be surprised at how

much we could accumulate if we systematically invested just 10 percent of our incomes. But most important, we don't understand the
simplest principles of investing. Furthermore, many brokers or advisors that we might employ to help us have the same tendency as
investors. They encourage buying and selling to generate commissions, and therefore tend to follow the natural inclinations of the
customer. As a result, the typical broker simply doesn't improve our
overall investment performance that much, although the best ones
can have a dramatic effect.

We have been told we can make our own investment decisions
primarily by people who benefit from the commissions of emotional
trading decisions. This only adds to the expense of poor performance.
We remain stubbornly resistant to the clear wisdom of the greatest
investors throughout history, from Benjamin Graham to Warren Buffet to Peter Lynch to Sir John Templeton. We simply don't get it! It's
too tempting to try to beat the odds, to try to time the markets, and to
try to pick the hottest stocks and funds by studying their performance
year to year, month to month. We want to gamble, not invest. It is
simply a matter of being run by our emotions: fear and greed.

Successful investing is a lot like diet and exercise. Everybody
knows what to do, but almost no one does it. Given a choice between
eating broccoli or chocolate cake, we'll choose the chocolate cake
every time, even though we know the broccoli is better for us. Broccoli
is boring. Well, investing for the long term is equally boring. But are
gambling and the excitement of beating the odds worth it? Is it wise
when your future, your retirement, your kids' education, and your
ability to do what you really want with your life is at stake? If the
answer is yes, maybe you should set aside some money every year and
spend it at the crap tables in Las Vegas. The odds are better and at
least you'll know you are gambling, and keep it within limits!

The recent book *The Millionaire Next Door* by Thomas J. Stanley and William D. Danko (Longstreet Press, 1996) makes a similar
point. The people who actually build wealth in our country are the
3.5 percent with a net worth in excess of $1 million. They are typically
frugal people, 80 percent self-made in wealth, who often live simple
lives in everyday neighborhoods, systematically save 10 to 15 percent
of their income before they pay their bills, and make long-term investments in companies and real estate they understand. They don't check
the markets every day, they don't trade or buy and sell often. They have

a boring, systematic approach, something like what Warren Buffet recommends. If you want to build wealth, boring works. If you want to have fun, Las Vegas is the place.

As investors, we simply don't do the obvious. We don't buy and hold solid investments we understand, or professionally managed mutual funds that have superior long-term track records. Instead, we chase the hottest stocks or funds in the short term and buy and sell them at the wrong time.

We don't have clear goals. We don't follow a clear system. We don't all have the time and expertise to make sense out of thousands and thousands of stocks, bonds, and mutual funds, all the confusing ratings, and all the various and conflicting investment approaches we read about — from momentum investing to contrarian investing to index investing. It takes an unbiased, professional advisor or an uncommon level of self-discipline to take the emotions out and to sort through this array of choices. Ask yourself this: If only 20 percent of professional money managers beat the stock averages over time, are you likely to? These people have more training, better access to information, much lower trading and transaction costs, staffs to support their research, and sophisticated computer software.

If you needed a serious heart operation, would you go to a discount surgeon? If you are an accomplished surgeon, would you trust your life to someone whose training consisted of reading *How to Be a Successful Surgeon in Three Minutes a Day?* Do you have the time in your busy schedule to become an expert investor? Or would you be better off focusing on what you do best, and letting a professional build wealth for you as effectively and systematically as you serve your clients in your own profession?

If you aren't one of those naturally gifted, experienced, or contrarian investors like Warren Buffet or Peter Lynch, and you aren't a full-time investment professional, your chance of achieving strong, consistent returns is very low — even if you are highly intelligent and extremely skilled in your own profession. Successful investing begins when you accept one simple truth: Most investors never achieve the returns of the best mutual funds or even the stock averages.

There is a rapidly growing group of independent financial planners and financial consultants within brokerage firms and financial-services institutions (who no longer call themselves brokers) that take a long-term perspective, design balanced portfolios around your goals and risk tolerance, and focus on keeping you on the system just like a personal trainer keeps you on an exercise program. They start by getting to know your goals and your investment style, and help educate you about the process of investment. They don't offer you the latest hot tips on what to buy this week. That's a sure danger signal.

Getting objective advice and being guided by reason and not emotion is the way to invest successfully. It is very difficult for most of us to transcend our fear and greed without an objective advisor or mentor. However, we should understand that the financial services industry is changing rapidly. We now have new options for investing and building wealth. There are a wide variety of ways you can get objective advice, ranging from financial advisors that will spend time with you face to face, and deal with complex tax, estate, and insurance issues, to firms like 1-800-MUTUALS that handle simple portfolio building over the phone or Internet. Financial planners typically charge from 1 percent to 2 percent of assets, while 1-800-MUTUALS and other firms charge as little as .5 to 1 percent. It all depends on the complexity of your financial situation and your need for service. But isn't paying a fee and upping your chance to earn the 461 percent shown in Figure 12.1 better than paying no fees and settling for 98 percent? The key is not the fees, but finding the right advisor. And what about the price of your time? Is it really worth doing your own investment research and dealing with the uncertainty of making the wrong decisions?

THE SEVEN PRINCIPLES FOR BUILDING WEALTH

Here are the secrets to building wealth that I have found in the many years of my research and from observing the top experts in the field:

- Principle 1. Save at least 10 percent of your pretax income.
- Principle 2. Use buy-and-hold strategies to stay invested in fundamental bull markets.
- Principle 3. Mutual funds are the best vehicle for most.
- Principle 4. Use asset allocation for the best risk versus return.
- Principle 5. Take the emotions out by investing systematically.

- Principle 6. Find an objective financial advisor.
- Principle 7. Align your personal real-estate investments with growth trends.

Principle 1
Save At Least 10 Percent of Your Pretax Income

Building wealth is a matter of how much you save and invest, not how much you earn. Many high-income people have almost no wealth, while others who are paid a modest amount are steadily increasing their personal wealth. The simple truth is this: If you deal with your current life needs, your expenses, and budget first, you will almost certainly come up with no money to save and invest no matter what your income is. That's because there are always things you think you need right now more than you need wealth later: new clothes for the kids, a better car, a vacation, a dinner at that great new restaurant.

For baby boomers who grew up in an affluent era, and always assumed times would be good, placing a priority on saving is especially difficult. Most of us think that real wealth is beyond our means. Yet the millionaires studied in *The Millionaire Next Door* were self-made, either by owning everyday businesses or by consistently saving 10 to 15 percent or more of their incomes. If you save this much, you can become relatively rich at almost any income level. If you can average a 15 percent return in a balanced mutual-fund portfolio in the next decade, and put aside 10 percent of your pretax income every year, you would have a portfolio worth more than two times your income in 10 years, five times your income in 20 years and over ten times in 30 years (enough to sustain your income for the rest of your life).

Plain and simple, that's how you build wealth: the old-fashioned way. Very few people do this, because they don't have the discipline to save for investment and you can't invest money if you don't have it to invest. Start by automatically putting 10 percent or more of your income after taxes into an investment account, and work your household expenses around what's left. It's usually a good idea to sit down with a financial counselor to make sure you do this accurately and objectively. Professional advisors know to include things like periodic payments and emergency funds in a budget, so that you don't end up dipping into your savings to pay for infrequent but predictable expenses like car maintenance or dental work.

Principle 2
Use Buy and Hold Strategies to Stay Invested in
Fundamental Bull Markets

In this book I have shown the incredible predictability of a variety
of long-term trends — from economic growth to inflation to the consumption of Coca-Cola in the third world. The simple fact is that, in
the long term, our economy is highly predictable. As a result, the key
to building wealth is to systematically invest in long-term fundamental
trends instead of trying to time the markets or pick the hottest stocks
or funds.

A financial planner did a simple study. If you had bought the top
mutual funds recommended in February of every year by *Money*
magazine you would have made only 10 percent annually versus 16
percent in the S&P 500 if you had held those funds. But, more
typically, if you had bought those funds every year, then sold them the
next to buy the latest hot funds, you would have made only a 2 percent
annual return. Trying to pick the hottest funds year to year and trading
in and out of funds doesn't work.

Let's look at market timing. Elaine Garzarelli had been the most
widely respected market timer from the late 1980s into the 1990s,
until she stumbled in 1996. She warned investors of the 1987 crash
and the 1990 correction. Understand that even when such an analyst
makes those calls, she doesn't get you out right at the top and right
back in at the next bottom. But her then-famous model got people out
around 5200 to 5400 in July of 1996 and back in at 7000! There is no
way that even the few people who listened to her in 1987 and 1990
made enough gains to offset missing that bull market rise. And of
course, most investors started listening to her just in time for the big
miss! Even the most talented market timers have lived by the sword
and died by the sword over time. Do you think you can outgun
Elaine? Do you know anyone who has consistenty timed the market
over time? Let me give you one piece of advice: Never buy a timing
service. A small minority of unscrupulous financial planners have
been pushing this high-profit item for them that only loses you money
at a price.

The risk in highly predictable markets is not being in the market,
but being out. The markets closely follow the spending directions of
new generations over the long term. In the short term, they make
sudden leaps, like the two incredible bull markets from June 1984 to

August 1987, and from December 1994 into 1997! If you missed those half-dozen years of gains, you missed about 80 percent of the 15-year bull market from 1982 until 1997!

Similarly, although the S&P 500 averaged 17.5 percent annual gains in the decade of the 1980s, your gains would have been just 3.9 percent if you missed the best 40 days. The market is very effective at making major moves when least expected. You simply have to be patiently invested in bull markets to see the benefits. The upward momentum in bull markets is much stronger than the average statistics show: The market is up more of the time and average gains are higher, in the 15 to 20 percent range. Corrections are brief and often sharp, which provide even the best market timers with few buying opportunities.

Trading in and out to try and time the market corrections is almost always fatal. The corrections are generally sudden, and sometimes severe, but the emotional reaction to them is almost always overblown. For example, since this bull market started in late 1982, no correction has lasted top to bottom more than 6 months. 1984 saw the longest correction, a 20 percent decline in 6 months. Then, the bond and stock markets assumed erroneously that the rapid growth in the economy would bring back accelerating inflation rates. Instead, inflation continued to fall and the market rallied. The correction in 1987 lasted only a few days in the crash and 2 months from top to bottom. Even after the worst correction since 1974, stocks regained upward momentum within 3 months and hit new highs within 2 years. The last substantial correction of 20 percent in the Dow in 1990 lasted only 3½ months before driving rapidly to new highs.

The lesson: Never try to pick the perfect bottom for selling or trading out, especially during a market correction. Timing is enormously difficult, especially in strong markets that rebound rapidly. Buy-and-hold strategies work best for the overwhelming majority of investors. And we should buy aggressively in corrections when we have the funds available.

Principle 3
Mutual Funds Are the Best Vehicle for Most

The best mutual funds offer their investors diversification, far lower research and trading costs, a disciplined approach to investing, and clear performance records. In fact, the best managers are the people who most closely track the 3 percent of the companies that are creating this new economy.

A small minority of funds achieve consistently solid returns, adjusted for risk and volatility. A handful of such managers at the best growth funds such as AIM, Putnam, PBHG, T.Rowe Price, Fidelity, Federated, Van Kampen/American, Kaufmann, and Twentieth Century, and lesser-known funds like Acorn, Oakmark, and Brandywine, have proven their ability to produce solid returns over an extended period of time. Note that I am just giving a few examples. There are many good funds to consider and many new ones emerging. Chasing the many funds that are hot this year and cold next year is precisely the way not to build wealth. Buying and holding the funds managed by the best long-term money managers is the way to build wealth. The key decision then becomes picking the right funds for your risk tolerance and putting them in a portfolio that gives you the best returns for the risk taken.

Principle 4
Use Asset Allocation for the Biggest Risk versus Return

The biggest returns over time come primarily from the appropriate asset allocation, as opposed to picking the best funds or from market timing. This allows you to diversify while staying invested in good funds. By combining funds that perform over time in different patterns, like international, small cap, large cap stocks, and fixed income or bonds, you can increase your rate of return at a lower risk level or decrease your risk and volatility at a similar rate of return. You can also add categories like real estate, including R.E.I.T. funds, or even precious metals.

For example, most people would assume that the safest portfolio would contain government-backed bonds. However, history clearly shows that a portfolio that replaces 30 percent of the bonds with much riskier high-growth, small-cap stocks would actually achieve higher returns at the same or lower risk level. That's because the gyrations in these two categories often offset each other, reducing overall volatility and risk. It gets better only as you add more sectors of funds that perform differently up to an optimum range of four to seven sectors.

Investors literally are paid for their ability to tolerate performance volatility over time. You must first realistically determine the risk you can tolerate. You must choose funds allocated in a portfolio that suit your risk tolerance, so that you can live with the actual performance and not be tempted to sell in a panic at the wrong time. The highest performing funds are typically not appropriate for most people since, in a correction, they tend to decline up to twice as much as the market. That means that a 20 percent correction in the stock averages will typically produce a 40 percent loss in a high-performing fund. If experts then forecast more losses, which they almost always do, most people will panic and sell at a loss.

You will often only get a clear view of the implications of risk and your real tolerance when you consult an objective financial advisor or investment mentor. It is not enough to pose the question "If my investments declined 10 percent, would I sell or hold?" That's because when the markets go down 10 percent, they always look like they are going to go down 20 or 30 percent! As a result, you won't tend to react like you think you will. An advisor can remind you of the error of selling in corrections and instead encourage you to buy. He or she can also help you adjust your portfolio's asset allocation strategy over time after getting a better idea of how risk tolerant you are in real-life situations.

Principle 5
Take the Emotions Out by Investing Systematically

Markets change over time, even in a long-term bull market. Also, different sectors perform better or worse as these changes occur. Therefore, you need a systematic method of managing your portfolio over time, buying in the most advantageous sectors without trying to time the markets.

The best and simplest model that I have found is the Markowitz model, which won a Nobel prize in 1990. For effective diversification, you divide your portfolio into four different sectors: large company, small company, international, and fixed income. You can weigh the percentages and the aggressiveness of the funds in each sector and match them to your risk tolerance. This means deciding between growth or value in large- and small-cap stock sectors, between emerging countries or developed countries in international sectors, and between long term or short term, and high-credit rating or lower-credit rating, in fixed-income sectors.

Then, regularly rotate your portfolio with a predetermined system to keep this asset allocation balanced over time in a way that builds in a slight bias towards buying in the lowest-performing sectors. Do this without attempting to time specific markets of funds. You simply automatically buy a bit more toward the lower-performing segments as you regularly add money while maintaining the overall direction of your original asset allocation targets. For example, you could have a system of investing 30 percent of new moneys (60 percent of the total) each into the two lowest-performing sectors of your portfolio over the last two years and 20 percent (or 40 percent of the total) into the two highest-performing sectors. Then every two years you could balance back to the original 25 percent weighting in each sector.

In a stable portfolio with little or no additional funds, you would rebalance the portfolio, returning it to your original targets for each of the four sectors, once every year or two. This would naturally push the gains from the stronger sectors into the lower-performing sectors. This tends to generate better returns at a lower level of risk and volatility by systematically buying sectors at better long term valuations. It also suppresses the very-human tendency to sell in corrections and buy near-short-term tops in each of the sectors.

Here's a quick example. Assume you decided on a 25 percent portfolio allocation among the four basic sectors: fixed income, large cap, small cap, and international. Let's say you just sat fully invested through the incredible overall bull market in 1995 and early 1996 — lucky you! Now it's April 30, 1996, time for your rational rebalancing time. To make this simple, let's say that your $100,000 portfolio, which you rebalanced as of April 30, 1995 into 25 percent, or $25,000 in each sector, now had the following worth. The fixed income had appreciated by 35 percent to $33,750. The large cap had performed the best and had appreciated 50 percent to $37,500. The small cap had appreciated 30 percent to $32,500. And the international had performed the most poorly at only an 11 percent gain to $27,750. Your portfolio would now total $131,500 and you would have had a 31.5 percent return over the past 12 months.

Now, that's a great return. Chances are now lower of repeating such returns in the high-performing sectors next year, even in a relatively good economy. So, what does the system do? It reallocates each sector back to 25 percent, or $32,812.50, which would result in your selling $937.50 of fixed income, $4,687.50 of large cap, and buying $312.50 of small cap and $5,312.50 of international.

Principle 6
Find an Objective Financial Advisor

An objective advisor can help you evaluate your financial goals, your tolerance for risk, and can keep you on a system of investment. More and more of the financial advisors in the established firms and independent financial planners are moving towards the systematic approach to asset allocation and investing I have outlined as the industry is learning from the myriad new studies supporting this approach. You should simply find an advisor that does understand and operate in this manner.

It's not easy to realistically determine your own risk tolerance or your real goals in life. It's even harder to resist the temptation to buy near the tops of strong surges, and to sell near the bottoms of strong corrections. An objective advisor, like a coach, can educate you on the proven principles of investing and keep you on the system. For 1 percent or a little more of your assets annually, this is a bargain. You can pay even less on larger portfolios, as low as one-half percent. It not only insures results over time, but allows you to spend your valuable time on what you love most, your career, your family and friends, and leisure activities. If you aren't willing to pay for a professional advisor, at least get an experienced friend to be your mentor or join an investment club. Meet with a number of financial advisors through word-of-mouth references, and take the time to choose the one that you trust and that best understands investors like you.

Principle 7
Align Your Personal Real Estate with Growth Trends

You shouldn't view your home primarily as an investment. After all, most people choose where to live based on their lifestyle, what kind of environment they like, proximity to work or leisure activities, the quality of the school district, and so on. For most of us, our homes *are* a large part of our net worth, so it makes sense to at least consider the appreciation potential of different choices that fit our lifestyle needs.

That's why it's a good idea, when you purchase your home or vacation house, to consider long-term real-estate trends as we did in Part IV. Buying personal real estate in areas that promise long-term growth and appreciation, perhaps buying the type of home that will be most in demand when you are likely to move or retire, can substantially enhance your long-term wealth. I'll discuss real estate in more detail at the end of this chapter, examining some creative strategies for private-property investment and other strategies for people who prefer to invest in real estate other than their residence.

Investing really is simple if you are wise enough to follow these simple principles. To summarize them in two sentences: Buy quality funds or investments that you understand in fundamental bull markets, and take the emotions out of the process by consulting an unbiased advisor who can help you determine your tolerance for risk and keep you on a system that is directed towards your goals. Above all, never sell in corrections — that is the biggest single investment mistake you can make. Only sell if the long-term fundamentals that originally caused you to buy the stock or fund have changed.

Warren Buffet is perhaps the most boring and most successful investor of our times. He simply invests systematically in long-term trends. He buys major holdings in companies like Coca-Cola. Is there any question that billions of people around the world, especially in emerging third-world countries, will be drinking more soft drinks as they industrialize and reach middle-class living standards? Don't you think that, in this age of global TV, the brand names that dominate our market will have a clear edge in the third world?

Is Coca-Cola a well-managed company? *Fortune* rated it number one in its most admired large companies poll of other CEOs. Are you aware that Coke dominates foreign markets much more than it does in the United States? How much more fundamental can you get than that? Buffet buys Coca-Cola, buys more Coca-Cola, and then buys even more if it corrects and goes down. Buffet would change his strategy only if the fundamentals changed; for example, if Pepsi made an all-out assault on foreign markets. In 1997, he started buying McDonald's when the stock started underperforming due to shorter-term problems. He doesn't think that will have much to do with how many people will eat McDonald's hamburgers 10 to 20 years from now. The only caveat is that Warren Buffet is a professional, full-time investor who tracks the performance and valuations of such companies. Most of us don't have the time or expertise, which is why mutual funds are a better choice.

Unless you are one of these disciplined investors that has proven to yourself that you can generate healthy returns over time, it's time to get serious about investments and talk with a qualified financial planner or advisor. Find an advisor that spends time educating you, rather than selling you. Someone who has a system for investing that makes sense rather than hot tips for the latest funds or stocks, and doesn't play on your fear and greed. If you systematically invest in the customized economies of the developed world and in the multinational companies that are doing a booming business in the developing world, you should prosper beyond your dreams. You'll have the financial independence to do what you truly want to in life, even well before retirement. Financial independence can be a critical step in moving from the self-esteem to the self-actualization stage discussed in chapter 8.

POLITICS AND PROFIT: WHY MID- TO LATE 1998 MAY BE A GREAT TIME TO INVEST

The greatest buying opportunities since 1994 and late 1997 may occur in 1998, due to a very predictable cycle of corrections that dates back to the founding of the Federal Reserve. You should make sure you are strongly invested in equities and mutual funds by mid- to late 1998. Why? I am obviously not an advocate of short-term timing. No one has proven capable of calling market swings consistently over time. And, in an incredible bull market like this one, the biggest risk is being out of the market, as I have already stated. But there is one short-term cycle that has been very reliable and should not be ignored, even if it doesn't continue as consistently as it has in the past.

Figure 12.2 shows graphically and empirically how the stock market has tended to take a substantial correction into the midterm elections, between the presidential elections. The Federal Reserve tends to tighten the economy at the midterm elections to give itself the leeway to loosen interest rates for the presidential election 2 years later. In other words, fiscal and monetary policies tend to be more unfavorable into the midterm elections and more favorable into the presidential elections.

The track record of this cycle is nothing short of remarkable. The gains in the stock market from the low in the correction year to the high in the year following in such 4-year cycles has averaged 50 percent! I mentioned this cycle in my newsletter in late 1994, and even to my surprise, we saw a 45 percent gain in stocks in 1995, a rally which continued into the election year of 1996 and beyond into late 1997.

This cycle suggests that the next strong overall stock market surge

4-Year Cycle — S&P 500

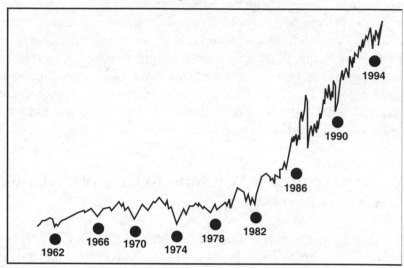

Figure 12.2: 4-Year Political Cycle in Stocks — S&P 500.

Figure 12.2 shows the effect of the 4-year political cycle on the stock market
from 1960 to 1994.

---

is likely to occur from early to mid-1998 into 1999, and continuing
into 2001. So, don't miss this next surge. I recommend investing
heavily on any substantial corrections in 1998. Furthermore, I recommend investing fully on any correction in which the Dow drops to the
7200 to 7600 range, which would represent the lower side of the Dow
channel shown in Figure 12.3. Or, if the Nasdaq takes another 20
percent or so correction as it did between 1996 and early 1997 and in
late 1997, especially if it happens to fall to 1465 or lower. The most
likely time for this to occur will be between May and August of 1998
or at the latest between October and November.

Figures 12.3 and 12.4 give us the most likely paths of the Dow
and stocks over the rest of this unprecedented boom. Since 1994,
stocks appear to have broken up into the acceleration or growth phase
of an S-curve path as Figure 12.3 shows. This is not just due to investor
psychology, but due to the fundamentals changing in a predictable
manner, as I pointed out in Chapter 1. We are seeing the baby boomers moving into their peak years of earning, while savings and invest-

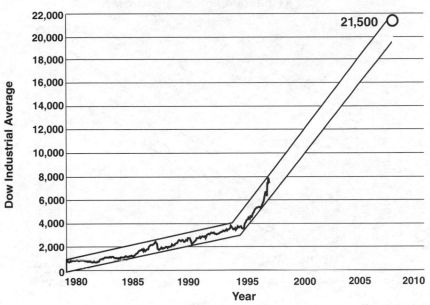

Figure 12.3: Dow Channel Projection 1997–2008.

---

ment accelerate, debt ratios plateau or fall, and inflation remains low and likely to continue in that path. A large wave of immigrants is adding to these trends. Most important, we are seeing the productivity revolution from network technologies, causing earnings of stocks to grow much faster than sales. Figure 12.4 shows a broader channel using a ratio scale instead of a normal arithmetic scale. This channel would assume that stocks continue to grow at the same average 16% rate over the next decade.

If the Dow can keep from breaking below 7400 on a monthly closing basis in the next 4-year-cycle low, which I predict will occur in early to mid-1998, then the first channel of growth (Figure 12.3) for stocks is likely to be the minimum growth trajectory for the next decade. This should create a peak Dow of around 21,500. If the Dow breaks above this channel in future years, then the more aggressive ratio trajectory (Figure 12.4) is more likely to be the trend. That trajectory would allow for a Dow as high as 35,000. Paradoxically, a break in 1998 below 7400 down to as low as 6200 to 6300 on a

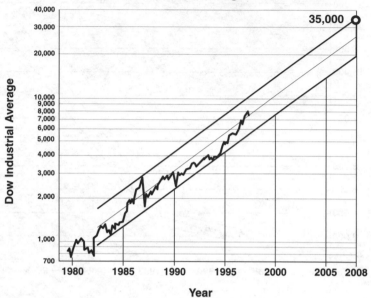

Figure 12.4: Dow Channel Projection 1997–2008.

monthly closing basis would favor the more aggressive channel. Given the higher rates of global growth that the larger, multinational companies are experiencing, the more aggressive channel is more likely. It would also allow for more volatility in stock price swings and more advantageous buying opportunities. The best buying opportunities in 1998 will come first near the lows in January 1998 between 7200 to 7600. If the correction is deeper, buy aggressively around 6200 to 6500. Even if we don't see the markets correct into these ranges, be sure to be fully invested between July and November of 1998.

The next 4-year-cycle buying opportunity will come in mid- to late 2002. That cycle is likely to be milder than that of 1998. There has been a tendency for stronger corrections to come every 8 years, for example, 1974, 1982, and 1990. Don't miss 1998 as a buying opportunity if we see a substantial correction. These channels of potential stock growth can be a good guide to when stocks are highly valued or undervalued. Obviously, you can profit more from buying in the lower ranges of the channel that proves to be most accurate in the coming years.

Long-Term Portfolio Strategies

Due to the predictable generation cycles and the economic response to these cycles discussed in Part I, there will be distinct periods where it is advantageous to adjust your investment strategies. I am not advocating short-term timing of the market. Rather, I recommend considering the balance and composition of your portfolio in light of some highly predictable changes in long-term trends.

Phase 1
Late 1998 to Late 2008: The Roaring 2000s

For the 10 years from late 1998 to 2008, stocks should clearly outperform bonds. Real estate should do well in general and the best sectors of real estate — such as exurban, small-town, and resort-town properties — should also appreciate strongly. The economy will start to grow at moderately strong rates from late 1997 into 2002. Then, economic growth and productivity should accelerate even more than expected, due to the impact of the network revolution and the household-formation cycle of the next generation. Niche-market products and technologies will move more strongly into the mainstream consumer markets by then. Inflation will remain low to moderate, but may rise a bit in 1998 and 1999. Bonds may react to the strong growth of the economy and rising inflation temporarily in 1998, stimulating a 4-year correction cycle. At times, the underperforming bond markets could well weigh on the stock advances, but it is likely that the stock market will increasingly diverge from the bond markets, responding more sensitively to economic growth and corporate earnings, which should be very strong into at least 2008.

Therefore, the best investment strategy for Phase 1 is to convert your portfolio primarily into stocks and mutual funds, and to invest in growth real estate. That means investing in the companies that are positioned to dominate the race for leadership in the new network economy. It also means investing in the companies and funds that will profit from the industrialization boom in the developing world. Exurban and small-town real-estate investment will be the big winner in this era.

Large-cap stocks have largely outperformed small-cap from 1984 to 1997 with the exception of 1991 to 1994. They do best when the economy is expanding broadly and inflation is low. In such environments, many bondholders and foreign investors switch to larger stocks, preferring the steady growth and international diversification that makes the best large-cap multinational stocks perform more predictably, like a bond. Small-cap stocks tend to outperform in the off periods, like 1932 to 1946 and 1968 to 1983, in higher-growth, higher-innovation, and/or rising inflation or deflationary eras.

I think that 1998 to 1999 or 2000 is likely to slightly favor smaller-cap stocks. Then, the increasing race for leadership as we move towards the top of this boom will favor larger and larger companies, many of which will be former small-cap companies that have grown at very high rates and become large-cap stocks as Microsoft, Intel, and Starbucks Coffee did in the past. This also occurred in the Roaring Twenties. Large-cap stocks averaged 19 percent annual growth, while small caps lost 4.5 percent annually, on average, in that decade. Therefore, leaning a bit toward buying small caps may be advantageous in the coming 4-year cycle, from 1998 into late 2001 or early 2002, while buying more large-cap stocks and funds from late 2002 into 2006 to 2008 will be a better strategy. International stocks and funds have lagged in performance over the past years and should continue playing catchup in the coming years, as has already been occurring in the past few years. The Asian meltdown in late 1997 created great value there and to a lesser extent around the world. Therefore, I expect global stocks to perform very well from 1998 into 2008.

To summarize an asset allocation strategy for late 1998 into late 2008:

- Buy growth stocks, both small and large cap, leaning a bit more toward large caps; and invest more heavily in the emerging countries in the international sector.
- Add real estate or R.E.I.T. funds, which are catching up from underperforming in the early 1990s and are likely to rebound from a 1998 correction from rising interest rates if it occurs.
- Since the bond play will be largely over by early 1998, convert bond holdings to stocks and real estate, except where you need bonds for income or portfolio diversification. Move toward shorter-term maturities in bonds to decrease the risk of short-term inflationary scares.
- Use international diversification in your stocks and mutual funds to achieve portfolio diversification rather than bonds, where possible. Remember, 2002 could see a substantial correction for adding to stock positions with the next 4-year cycle.

Here is a sample portfolio. Note that you could lean toward 30 percent large cap and 20 percent small cap from 1998 into 2008.

15 percent small cap

35 percent large cap

10 percent R.E.I.T. funds

20 percent international (emerging country — Asia [except Japan], Latin America, Russia and eastern Europe, etc.)

10 percent international (developed country — Europe, Hong Kong, Canada, Australia, etc.)

10 percent High-Yield Bond Funds (Seligman High-Yield Bond Fund is the best example)

Phase 2
Late 2008 to 2020 or 2023: The Next Depression

As we approach 2009, it will be time to start harvesting stock and most real-estate investments. Somewhere around late 2006 to late 2008, or when the Dow reaches toward 21,500 or above 30,000, according to which channel proves out over the coming year, it will be time to begin making major shifts in your long-term portfolio and asset allocation. You should be increasingly cautious and conservative as our economy enters a deflationary period of decline.

Many small-town real-estate investments could weather the depression well. I anticipate continued migration to small towns well into the 2020s, because of the more attractive real estate values there and the S-curve pattern of accelerated growth. But this next depression will be the final death toll for suburban and large-city real estate. The baby-boom residential buying spree will be long over, and business expansion in commercial real estate will come to a halt and decline with the end of the long boom. Some may want to hold part of their better real-estate investments in smaller towns where growth has not nearly saturated and prices are still very attractive, especially compared to metropolitan areas and to more saturated smaller towns nearby. Many may want to keep your homes or most cherished vacation getaways, but my advice is to sell whatever you can and look for better buying opportunities after the first crisis fully hits, and we see bargains in values in stocks and real estate.

Bonds will be the biggest beneficiary of a long, deflationary spiral, as will T-bills; certain international equity markets should perform well, especially Japan, which will finally be in an upward spending wave. Europe which will see its boom extend modestly, at best until about 2014 to 2017, before declining. Australia and New Zealand should also see buoyancy in their economies due to more favorable demographic trends. Emerging countries are likely to suffer from increasing volatility and a decline in exports in the worldwide slump, even if their own demographic trends support economic growth. But then they are likely to surge again after the first big correction. Also, remember that small-cap stocks do well in off periods, but only after the first serious stock decline of, say, 40 percent or more.

To summarize an asset-allocation strategy for late 2006 or late 2008 into 2020 to 2023:

- Phase 1. From late 2006 to late 2008, shift increasingly from stocks into long-term treasury or very high quality corporate bonds.
- Phase 2. From 2009 to 2010, or after the first serious U.S. and global stock correction, shift 20 to 40 percent of your bond portfolio into Japanese stocks and perhaps some European.
- Phase 3. From 2015 to 2023 look for great long-term buying opportunities in stocks and real estate. Focus on exurban real estate, emerging countries globally, and small caps in the U.S.
- Phase 4. From 2020 to 2023 on, start moving back into a classic portfolio of, say, 30 percent large caps, 20 percent small caps, 10 percent real estate, 30 percent international, and 10 percent bonds for the next long-term bull market.

Now let's take the wisdom of the simple but effective Markowitz portfolio-allocation system and combine it with mutual funds and packaged, professionally managed, investments. Here's the ultimate strategy for simple, elegant investing: Pick the top two to four long-term mutual funds in each of the recommended sectors of your portfolio.

Simply follow the strategy described above but with mutual funds instead of individual stocks. This is the best way to simplify the investment process! If we rebalance according to the Markowitz method or another system this would also benefit mutual-fund families, because it would tend to supply them with investment funds when they could best employ them to achieve the highest gains. Instead, most mutual funds are received at the top of a market cycle when they have the least chance of reinvesting for the highest gains.

Financial advisors and investors interested in learning more about the services I offer for investing can refer to the "For More Information" page at the back of this book.

Let's go one step further. Tax deferral is the other powerful principle behind building long-term wealth. Investors should shelter whatever they legally can in 401K plans, IRAs, SEPs, or KEOGH plans. Only allocate moneys you can commit over the very long term, because there are severe penalties for withdrawal ahead of retirement.

That also brings up the other powerful area of packaged investments for the new era. Variable annuities and variable universal life-insurance products allow investors to meet basic insurance needs to protect their income for their families, while investing the cash value of such policies in mutual funds with high long-term gains that can be tax-deferred. The investor simply borrows against the cash value of the policy when needed at market rates of interest, and allows the equity to accumulate without being taxed. Then, the policy benefits for universal life pass to your heirs, tax-free, so that your family avoids paying estate taxes.

PROFITING FROM REAL ESTATE

Real estate is typically the largest portion of personal wealth. You could significantly increase your prospects for future wealth by considering a real-estate investment in any of the boomtown areas I've identified in Part IV. You can either relocate or, if you have the extra capital, remain where you are and simply buy a vacation home or other property in one of these areas.

When you are evaluating your next real-estate investment, consider these different options:

- When it comes time to move into a trade-up home, consider moving a little farther out, to a booming exurb, instead of buying in the same low-growth suburban area.
- If you are considering the purchase of a vacation home, why not do it now and beat the massive baby-boom rush? Waiting is likely to cost you more, and the appreciation will be higher from buying early. You can also rent out the property when not using it, to help

cover the mortgage and insurance costs. Remember, the interest on property loans of up to $1,000,000 is tax deductible, which can include a combination of your primary residence and your vacation home. Another strategy is to buy one or even several time-shares in attractive areas. This gives you multiple vacation options, and the ability to trade with other owners in the time-share program.

- Consider buying a retirement home in an attractive resort area now or in the near future. You can either use it as a vacation home now and/or rent it out until you retire.

- If you are a younger family, planning to have children, and evaluating where to work and live, seriously consider a booming new city or a booming small town. Companies in these areas are likely to be growing faster, your cost of living will be lower, and your property will appreciate more than if you stay in the same old suburb. If you and your spouse aren't planning to have children or don't mind having kids in the city, consider moving into a revitalized section of a large city where professional opportunities are strong and housing is appreciating.

- If you are a baby boomer in midlife, consider what kind of life you want when the kids are on their own. Why not take a good look at moving to a great resort or college town? Check out the prospects for relocating your business, or for telecommuting, or think about starting a new business. Your residence will almost surely appreciate rapidly if you pick a genuine boomtown, and your stress level is likely to decline.

- The ultimate real-estate strategy — the way to achieve both a high-quality lifestyle and build even more personal wealth — will be popular with the most affluent baby boomers. Go for the best of both worlds. Buy your main residence in a high-quality resort area, preferably in a state or country that has low income taxes. Then buy or rent a condo or home in a trendy urban area. The tax savings from relocating from a high tax state, where income taxes can run from 7 to 11 percent, to a lower one can often more than pay for the rental or mortgage costs on the downtown flat. You simply have to spend a majority of your time in the lower-cost-tax state.

Strategies for Real Estate Investors

There are many people who get into the business of investing in real estate. This is not my area of expertise, but it is obvious that the people who do the best invest in properties they know and understand. Randomly investing in real estate and hot development schemes is for movie stars who often seem to love to make money and then lose it. Real-estate developments and partnerships are risky and require knowledge of the business and trends — just like investing in the stock market. The one difference is that real estate isn't as liquid as stocks, so if you've made a mistake it will be harder to get out.

There are two options that I think make the most sense for an amateur investor: low down payment and break-even cash-flow rental properties, and buying and holding low-cost raw land. These options definitely require some homework. You need to learn what you need to know, and what to watch for, from someone with real-estate investing experience.

Low Down Payment and Break-Even Cash-Flow Rental Properties

Alan Jacques and Tim Johnson with The Real Estate Network have helped a lot of individual investors profit from low down payment and break-even cash-flow rental properties in British Columbia and Alberta, where the penturbia trend is very much alive. The strategy is to look for attractive growth towns and areas with the indicators discussed in Chapter 11. Then look for condominiums and rental units, including business and office properties, that can be purchased for a low down payment, preferably 5 or 10 percent maximum, and rented out to create a break-even or positive cash flow after your mortgage, taxes, and maintenance costs. It's important, however, to closely examine the properties and fully understand the management and maintenance requirements. Don't be naive and think that renting is an easy business.

Another thing to consider when shopping for condominium rental properties: Condos typically don't appreciate as well as detached single-family homes. Larger condos with more bedrooms, and the flexibility to create home offices, appreciate better than smaller one- or two-bedroom apartments. Buying rental housing in a booming area is a better strategy than buying a condo, especially if you have the skills to fix it up and maintain it.

This strategy of buying break-even cash-flow rental properties greatly minimizes the risks of real-estate investment. It allows you to buy more properties and build more equity as your cash flow increases. Alan Jacques claims that the ability to find such break-even rental properties is a sign that you are in an early-stage boomtown area. You simply can't find such properties in high-cost suburban and urban areas.

Buying and Holding Low-Cost Raw Land

Another real-estate investment strategy that is riskier, but can be very rewarding, is buying large plots of raw land well outside of booming small towns and exurban areas. The attraction to this strategy is that it can be highly profitable, and you don't have to get involved in building or renting or maintenance. You just buy cheap raw land and let it sit for years or even decades — until the development comes your way. It is also fun finding places that you think are hot prospects and watching other people reach the same conclusion. In fact, for many people just owning land is a thrill.

A friend of mine bought several acres of land outside of McCall, Idaho, with the intention of building a vacation and retirement home there. The property tripled in value in three years. I saw a real-estate company buy raw land outside of Palmdale and Lancaster, two booming exurban towns in the high desert just outside of Los Angeles, and the last sparsely populated area within 60 miles of downtown. Their strategy was simple: They just bought in a circle outside of the developed areas of these booming towns, whenever property would come up at an attractive price. They made a fortune in less than a decade. As we discussed in Chapter 10, if you had had the prescience to buy raw land anywhere in or near Aspen in the 1950s or 1960s, Santa Fe in the 1960s or 1970s, or Telluride in the 1970s or 1980s, you would have made your fortune, too. Now, towns 30 to 45 minutes from Aspen are booming.

The disadvantages of this investment strategy are obvious: You may have to wait a long time for development to grow out your way, development may move in another direction, zoning problems may develop that you didn't anticipate, or you may even find out that there is toxic waste buried nearby that wasn't disclosed by the seller. Furthermore, you can't deduct the interest on a raw-land investment as you can on residential or rental properties.

SUMMARY

When the world explodes in a boom like this, the greatest opportunities for building personal wealth come from the inevitable growth in company equity and the rising value of select real estate. If you will systematically save 10 percent or more of your net income before you pay your bills, and begin systematically investing in mutual funds and real estate now, you can become wealthy long before you thought possible. Perhaps you'll even be able to retire when we reach the peak of the greatest economic boom in history — regardless of your age today.

Best of success to you!

Products and Services
from the H. S. Dent Foundation

For Corporations and Executives

Keynote Presentations
In-house Training Seminars
Intranet and CD-ROM Training Systems
Business Consulting
Executive Strategy Sessions
H. S. Dent Forecast Newsletter
Quantity Discounts on Books and Materials

For Financial Advisors and Institutional Investors

Investment Funds for Client Portfolios
Marketing and Seminar Systems
Audiotapes fpr Prospecting
Interactive CD-ROM Training and Education Systems
H. S. Dent Forecast Newsletter
Desk and Wall Charts of the "Spending Wave" and Key Charts
Special Reports on the Markets and the Financial Services Industry

For Individuals and Investors

H. S. Dent Forecast Newsletter
H. S. Dent Internet Site . . . www.hsdent.com
Investment Strategies and Services
Books
Videotapes
Audiotapes
CD-ROMS
Special Reports

Call Toll-Free Today: 1-800-371-9119

Or visit our Website: www.hsdent.com

Index

Page numbers in *italics* refer to figures.

About the Author

HARRY S. DENT, JR., is president of the H. S. Dent Foundation. His mission is simple: "helping people understand change." He graduated from Harvard Business School as a Baker Scholar. He has consulted at the highest levels of business strategy for Fortune 100 companies and has managed several small growth businesses. He is the author of *The Great Boom Ahead.* He and his wife, Cee, currently reside in Oakland, California. They plan in the near future to live and work from a small island in the Caribbean.